We work at knowing the truth about our lifetime even if its images, derived from various people, are not consistent with each other. We exist as separate beings, but at the same time each of us acts as a medium propelled by a power we do not know well, a current of the great river, as it were, through which we resemble each other in our common style or form. The truth about us will remind us of a mosaic composed of little stones of different value and colors.

Czeslaw Milosz

STAR-CROSSED

A Hollywood Love Story in Three Acts

Ron Austin

William B. Eerdmans Publishing Company

Grand Rapids, Michigan / Cambridge, U.K.

Published 2013 by
Wm. B. Eerdmans Publishing Co.
2140 Oak Industrial Drive N.E., Grand Rapids, Michigan 49505 /
P.O. Box 163, Cambridge CB3 9PU U.K.

Printed in the United States of America

19 18 17 16 15 14 13   7 6 5 4 3 2 1

Library of Congress Cataloging-in-Publication Data

Austin, Ron.
Star-crossed: a Hollywood love story in three acts / Ron Austin.
pages   cm
Includes bibliographical references and index.
ISBN 978-0-8028-6919-7 (pbk.: alk. paper)
1. Austin, Ron. 2. Christian biography. 3. Television producers and directors
— California — Los Angeles — Biography. 4. Christianity and other religions
— Judaism. 5. Judaism — Relations — Christianity.   I. Title.

BR1725.A864A3   2013

277.3′082092 — dc23
[B]

2013008084

www.eerdmans.com

As always, for Ruth

Contents

CONTENTS

Acknowledgments

My first acknowledgment is an author's admission. The people and events in this book have been recounted with as much accuracy as my memory allows; however, looking back over seventy-five years, I may have inadvertently "misremembered" some details. I have also undoubtedly conflated the time and space of some events, but I believe that they are all accurate in essence.

Many of the people whose love, friendship, and encouragement shaped my life are not mentioned in this book. There are two reasons for this. First, I've been blessed with too many such people, including family members, teachers, and fellow workers, to cite them all. Second, this book is not meant as a full account of my own life but is an attempt to describe how two lives, Ruth's and mine, came together. I pray that no friend or friendship will ever slip from my grateful memory, and I hope that this is understood. I know that my daughters and the members of our extended families expect no thanks, but they have it anyway.

In the years following Ruth's death, my "spiritual brother," Paul Wolff, an ordained *magid*, a storyteller in the Hasidic tradition, and I deepened our friendship. In time, our conversation included others, Catholic and Jewish, and has lasted now for twenty years. Psychologist Jim Carolla, a Catholic, added his years of experience as a therapist. Still later, Rabbi Scott Shapiro joined us. Our friendships enabled us to have extraordinarily open discussions. We all agree that the understanding we gained from each other deepened our own faith perspectives. This book would not have been possible without these spiritual brothers.

I've acknowledged the unfailing support of my lifelong friend and writing partner, Jim Buchanan, but I should also mention some writers of the previous generation who became friends and mentors, including Walter Newman, Bill Bowers, and Ed North. I could also cite many other Hollywood writer-friends who contributed their wit and sophistication to our regular gatherings. Many are now waiting for us on that celestial picket line, undoubtedly still protesting sin, greed, and bad writing, but probably not in that order.

While I cannot acknowledge all of my many Writers Guild colleagues, I must single out the "Friday the Thirteenth Club" group originally assembled by Frank "Ace" Thompson. This fellowship, originally formed out of a love for movies and baseball, has lasted for more than a quarter-century, and over time has included a bevy of Writers Guild award-winners. My knowledge of Hollywood, and myself, was greatly enhanced by these good friends, some now departed and sorely missed. My thanks, then, to Bob Collins, George Eckstein, Phil Fehrle, John Furia, Mike Hoey, Millard Kaufman, Chris Knopf, Peter Lefcourt, Rick Mittleman, Cliff Osmond, Parke Perine, Brad Radnitz, Del Reisman, Gene Reynolds, Gaby Wilson, Norton Wright, and, gracing these mugs, Marge Bowers and Noreen Stone.

I have on several occasions thanked my confessors and spiritual directors in print as well as in person, and, as I can't thank them enough, I want to again acknowledge my indebtedness to Fathers Charles Cummins, Denis Meehan, Anthony Scannell, Mark Vilano, Ralph Weishaar, Father Michael Sweeney of the Dominican School of Philosophy and Theology at Berkeley, the Dominican friars at the Priory of St. Albert the Great in Oakland, and Father Patrick Boyle and the Cistercians of the Abbey of the Holy Trinity in Huntsville, Utah.

My colleagues at the Windhover Forum — Sister Margaret Devlin, Michael Feeley, Lino Lauro, Leah Buturain Schneider, Father Alexei Smith, and Jim Hanink and Lew Oleson of the original group — have my gratitude for their decades of love and prayers. My many friends in the Focolare movement also have my admiration for being models of compassion and reconciliation. Every one of you is part of this story — perhaps more than you know.

"Old friends" implies patience and shared maturity even more than age and endurance. Three such friends of a half-century or more deserve particular thanks: Ed Eisenstein, Marv Mattis, and Ed Schuman, whose Jewish sensibilities were clearly evident in their integrity and compassion.

I greatly appreciate my long association with Eerdmans Publishing, and want to thank Sandra DeGroot, Bill Eerdmans, Jim Chiampas, Mary Hietbrink, and their colleagues for their support and contributions.

Gabriel Meyer, my trusted friend and editor, always gets last place on my thanks list because of his ultimate and invaluable help, and I trust that he recognizes that "the last shall be first." George Moore is also "first and last" in my gratitude because more than any other friend he has lived the whole of this long story with me. Both Gabriel and George created this book as they shaped my life.

*   *   *

During my last years, I lost most of my ambitions, certainly all of the early Hollywood aspirations, but I still retained one ego-driven goal. I wanted to become the poster boy for gerontology. This was due to my conceit that I had accomplished all of my best work, if I had any best work, after the age of sixty-five. Depending upon one's understanding of "best," or if you will settle for "relevant," it's largely true. What's more, after losing part of my eyesight, I've traveled widely, lectured and taught at universities, and have written books and numerous articles despite my limitations.

I offer this not as a boast but as an encouragement to anyone similarly impaired or feeling that they have nothing more to contribute past the age of sixty or seventy or older. It is also my final expression of thanks to the many people — family, friends, and kind strangers — who made and continue to make my work possible.

Introduction

I've never written a love story before. I find that it is all the more difficult when the love was, and is, my own. I'm convinced that it is, moreover, one of God's love stories, and so the cast of characters extends back and forth in time and space. If I'm at the heart of the story, it is only because that's where I am and can't hide.

The story can't be easily circumscribed because the love that I entered into began before time — but my share in it began in 1934, when I was born in Hollywood, California. The story's inspiration comes from the love I shared with Ruth, a Jewish girl from Brooklyn. I don't think that this can or should be turned into a movie, but the setting was primarily Hollywood, then as now a state of mind as well as a location for movies and other greater and lesser events.

My world was primarily Jewish then, and as I am a Christian, a Roman Catholic, the telling of this story is an obligation I owe not just to my Jewish children and grandchildren, but to others as well, as a form of witnessing, as we Christians say, to the transformative power of love between Christians and Jews.

As with most of human history, the framework of the story is tragic. It began during what is now aptly referred to as the "Thirty Years' War," that is, the bloody period from 1914 to 1945, history's most self-destructive era. Ruth and I were shaped by this long siege of war, the Great Depression, revolution, genocide, and then by the psychic necessity of surviving it. Holocaust survivors aren't all Jewish.

Our romance began early, in our teens, spurred on by irresistible desires. Neither of us knew intact families. My mother and Ruth's father had both died before we knew them. Our desire for each other was, understandably, deeply psychological but equally physical. The great unending biological instincts of our species are at least as strong as those of birds, but God turns them into love. I can't say that I ever really understood this process, but that isn't what the story is about. If this were a movie, there would be no sex scenes.

"A sidelong glance" is what makes a good movie, not the clarification of character motivations or even the ending. What lasts is the brief glimpse of what is true and good and, thus, beautiful. The form of this love story is not, therefore, a three-act play leading to a happy or an unhappy ending. It is, unapologetically, what the French call a *bricolage* — a collection of remembered glances more than a form of analysis. Given my age, there is an additional obligation, however, to provide the kind of perspective that "living the times" rather than just studying them imposes. Some self-justifying slips of memory are unavoidable, but I'll try to place the glances in the context of what else was happening, and, to the best of my ability, even what came before.

While I have had a lifelong interest in and respect for philosophy, theology, and historiography, this is not an intellectual history, and certainly not the history of an intellectual. My reflections are on the society in which I lived, particularly the Jewish ambiance and how it formed my attitudes and even my grasp of reality. The Jewish legacy of liberation and liberalism shaped much of modern American culture, and my view of this development was unique for a Gentile — "from the inside," so to speak, within the Jewish world of Ruth's family, my lifelong friends, and my colleagues in Hollywood. I was exposed to far more than ideas. In my own way, I shared their hopes and fears.

This is not a political story, but politics played an important part in it. As with my acting career, my years as a young communist were brief, but they led to my being disillusioned and blacklisted, and in that order. In retrospect, both were important personal turning points. My Hollywood of the forties and fifties was formed, even battered to a high degree, by political strife — less by Marxism or radicalism per se than by an impulse that created what I believe was a form of Jewish romanticism. I'm going to try to sort out some of these themes largely by avoiding old categories of "left" and "right," which will probably offend the nostalgists and the last of the ideologues.

This is a "Hollywood" story in many respects, but one told, I hope, without the obscuring veil of glamour. I began as a young actor and in time became a writer and producer. Hollywood was my hometown and my workplace — sometimes as prosaic as any other. Though I am what was called "a Hollywood brat," my ambition to be an actor grew less out of artistic inspiration than my need as a child to escape from reality — and, as with most media artists, the narcissistic impulse was never far away. With Ruth's help, I was able to turn this neurosis into a profession. I was more or less functional as a human being until I was blindsided by the crisis of "success" and began to forget who I was. I'll relate this part of the story without regret, blame, or self-reproach. I'm grateful for the experience and even more for having survived it.

Somewhere along the way I became a Christian. If my story was a drama with a structure, this would occur somewhere in the second act.

This story twist will probably deprive me of some readers, ones either weary or leery of inspirational conversion stories, or perhaps antagonistic to religion itself. I'm not unsympathetic to this aversion. I have no desire to convert or persuade anyone who is not already in the process of change. This is a futile effort, in any case, and my personal story is too particular for emulation. I was transformed before I came to any religious belief, not the other way around. It began with the gradual loss of my fantasy world. My habitual escape from reality since childhood meant either staying down in that well or eventually facing the truth, or at least as much as I could take at any given time. This first occurred when I recognized my limitations as an actor, and then when I had to accept the loss of my utopian political beliefs. I spent most of the blacklist years as a social worker in the poorest *barrio* in East Los Angeles, where I faced the reality of poverty and its consequences. My family had known the shared communal poverty of the Depression years, but I had been spared not all but most of the destructive effects of broken families, crime, and addiction. I returned eventually to Hollywood, but never lost the sense that a larger, somehow "more real" world existed.

In time, I faced the reality of death. This began with the muted memory of the death of my mother and with exploring the depth of that deprivation through therapy. It was Ruth's love, however, that restored a feminine presence in my life, the equilibrium that came from recovering the ever-present, dependable love that I had lost. Somehow remembered, it had constantly re-emerged as an unspoken longing.

Finally, at some point, the discovery of beauty in life as well as in the arts sustained me. Ruth first worked as a painter in the animation studios and then became an accomplished watercolorist, and her work on the walls of our home refreshed me daily.

The truth is that I have been rescued by many people, more than I can recount. If I still stayed in a dark room at times, that was my own fault and choosing. It was not for lack of family and friends who endured my pride and other worse and lesser weaknesses. I would have to "rise and fall" again and again. It was the height of what I sensed was a ridiculous success that left me empty and disillusioned. It was only then, in the midst of that disillusionment, that I received the gift of God's grace and forgiveness. This happened with a remarkable rapidity and with no effort on my part. My only task was to accept what was being given.

In subsequent years, I would be "graced" again — that is, receive the gift of healing and affirmation that I could not have induced myself. This happened in the intensive care unit of a hospital; in a cemetery after Ruth's death; at a retreat house; in a deep forest. They were only "glances," but they were also unforgettable. At times, I have simply been over-whelmed with an inexplicable joy and reassurance. I received these gifts in utter silence and have no further words to offer about them.

*   *   *

Reaching a certain age obliges one to remember and to recall as much as one can. One needs to seek a truth beyond mere accuracy. I've tried to do this for several reasons. Clearly, my life has been spent "building bridges" or at least looking for bridge-building material, and this is perhaps my final effort at drawing Jews and Christians together. I would hope that a glimpse into my life with Ruth might help Jews and Christians to better understand each other's needs, fears, and hopes, and to accept their differences as well.

I'm also writing out of a more immediate concern. The dialogue between Jews and Catholics during my lifetime, following the Holocaust and the Second Vatican Council, has been miraculously healing and fruitful, the first such reconciliation in centuries. But even as we enter a new and promising era with a newly consecrated pope, there may be troubled times ahead, and they should be anticipated with a determination not to let what has been accomplished be lost or damaged.

The reason for my disquiet is twofold. The first is that anxiety about the security of Israel, already so high as to create bitter divisions among Jews themselves, will undoubtedly remain acute and possibly worsen. The implications of Jewish demographics — a declining Jewish population due to low birthrates and assimilation, especially in the United

States — must also be a concern. Both of these are concerns about the future, if not the literal survival of Jewish life and culture. Add to this the persistence of anti-Semitism even in Europe as well as a relentless criticism of Israel by left-wing "progressives" once perceived as reliable Jewish allies, and a high level of anxiety can be expected for the indefinite future. Jewish fears and insecurity are woven into the collective memory and reside far deeper than politics or even rationality. Any conflict perceived as threatening to Jews, even simple misunderstandings, can be potentially destructive of relationships.

The younger generation of Christians may be better informed, on the one hand, but, on the other, less responsive to Jewish sensibilities than the generations most directly affected by the Holocaust and its aftermath. Younger Catholics, in my experience, perceive Jews not primarily as victims of history but as intelligent, hard-working people whose attainments are worthy of admiration and emulation. They also tend to view Jews not as a persecuted minority but as one possessing wealth and influence beyond their numbers. There is genuine admiration in this, but also some envy and occasional resentment. There may be vestiges of anti-Semitism in these attitudes, but the church has worked hard through education and preaching for half a century to eradicate this prejudice. It would be a mistake to perceive instances of insensitivity as hostility.

Misunderstandings, however, are likely to occur, and Jews cannot expect a new generation of Catholics and other Christians to respond to them with a solicitude formed by a historical tragedy now no longer a matter of direct experience.

As a Catholic convert married to a Jewish woman for four decades and with Jewish children and grandchildren, this is not a theoretical concern for me. I write in the hope that some potential future conflicts as well as lingering misperceptions can be addressed now, and not when pain and anger may put us at risk of rupture and withdrawal.

I write also as a Catholic committed to my church and its teachings. It would be presumptuous of me, despite my lifelong relationship with the Jewish people, to try to offer a Jewish perspective on the thorny questions I'm posing. My interpretation of Jewish concepts and history will clearly reflect my Christian understanding. I would hope, therefore, that this effort might provide a brief primer for my fellow Catholics regarding Jewish hopes and fears, and, in turn, give our Jewish friends some sense of our own.

I'm not a scholar. My purpose is to provide an overview that is accessible, not original. If I have any unique perspective, it has come from personal experience. My purpose is not to amend or even add to the scholarly exchanges or the formal dialogues, but to relate both to what I perceive to be the present attitudes of Jews and Catholics who are not directly involved in this dialogue, except perhaps through circumstance or friendship.

One final caveat: This is the personal story of two people, a Catholic and a Jew, who loved each other. It isn't a full or adequate account of the vitally important interfaith and ecumenical explorations of our time. However, I would hope that my fellow Christians — Protestants, evangelicals, and Eastern Orthodox — as well as Muslims, members of our Abrahamic family, and Buddhists, Hindus, and others who share so many of our spiritual and ethical beliefs will welcome a story that affirms our universal human nature, our ideals, and, undoubtedly, our future.

*   *   *

About the Title

My being "star-crossed" refers only in part to the "stars" of Hollywood, those luminaries whose iconic presences shaped the imagination of American popular culture. I had the opportunity to work with or know many of them, perhaps the most illustrious, at least in terms of international recognition — Charlie Chaplin, Buster Keaton, Fred Astaire, Gene Kelly, and Ronald Reagan — as well as some of Hollywood's "Golden Age" personalities such as Loretta Young, Melvyn Douglas, and Walter Pidgeon. The TV stars — Andy Griffith, Sam Waterston, and the lovely young actresses in *Charlie's Angels* — are part of the last chapters in my Hollywood life. Many of these people are woven into this story, and I'm lucky to have had such fascinating company; but this isn't the story of a career, only some reflections on a life.

The most prominent star that guided my life was Ruth's Star of David, the symbol of the Jewish people and faith. It is an ancient hexagram originally called the *Magen David*, which means literally the "Shield of David." It can serve as a form of blessing, as I believe it has for me.

In my lifetime and Ruth's, it was used by the Nazis as the notorious "yellow star" — a badge that Jews were required to wear to identify themselves during the terror of the Third Reich. It survived those tragic years and is now emblazoned on the flag of Israel. The scholar Gershom

Scholem believed that the Star of David has grown in force as a symbol by triumphantly overcoming the "shame of persecution."

Its origins are unclear. It was used as an amulet in the Middle Ages, but the Jewish menorah is a much older religious symbol. In any case, the Star of David has decorated many Jewish prayer books, synagogues, and graves for centuries. It is a symbol that has had many interpretations. It has, for instance, been related to the six Hebrew words that compose the *Shema*, the central prayer of Judaism: "Listen, O Israel: the Lord is our God, the Lord is One."

I am drawn to a traditional understanding found in the Kabbalah in which the Star's points represent the "sacred number" seven. It is composed of six "masculine" points completed by a "feminine" center. The Star is also identical to the Hindu Shatkona, a symbol of the uniting of male and female.

This symbol, then, represents the center of my life — a loving Jewish woman who remains the "star" of my story and of this book.

Long Shots and Close-ups

CHAPTER ONE

Two Roads to Hollywood

Our story together has to begin before we do.

By 1900, Ruth's grandfather, Jacob, after great hardship and sacrifice, had reached America. He was a Jewish immigrant from the Pale of Settlement, the area in then-Imperial Russia to which Jews were restricted, and from a city in what is now Ukraine. Jacob was a tailor, and he and his wife settled first in the Harlem district of New York City, where Ruth's mother, Alma, was raised. Throughout her life, Alma claimed to have been born in Harlem in 1905. She was actually born in Russia a few years earlier, but she felt more comfortable with an American birthplace as well as a slight abridgement of her age. When Ruth's father, Benjamin, died, probably from a condition related to his army service in the First World War, she was only three. Alma, now a single mother, worked as a bookkeeper in the garment industry, and she and Ruth moved in with her parents, then in the Williamsburg area of Brooklyn.

Because her grandfather spoke little English and her grandmother none at all, Ruth's first language was Yiddish. They later moved to the Flatbush neighborhood, with its heavily ethnic mix of Irish, Italians, and Jews. One of Ruth's earliest memories was of sitting on her grandmother's lap in front of the window of their upstairs flat and watching the flower-filled Catholic processions emerging from the Italian funeral parlor across the street. A less pleasant recollection was that of the hostility of the Catholic kids, particularly around Easter time, and how they threw rocks concealed in snowballs at her after school. "Christ-killer" was a common epithet aimed at Jews.

In 1900 my maternal grandfather, Ellis, was tending sheep in the foothills of the Wasatch range of Utah's Rocky Mountains. His father, a Mormon farmer and polygamist with three wives, had more than a dozen surviving children, and their acreage was adjacent to that of other family members, brothers, uncles, and cousins. These were immigrants from England, farm laborers, many displaced by the enclosure laws that deprived the poor of common land. This extended family, in time, constituted a small town in northern Utah. Many of the elders were part of the first generation of pioneers. My great-grandfather had been the "secretary" — that is, the record-keeper — of a wagon train coming West, jotting down daily in crude pencil the names of those, mostly children, who died along the way. These were my mother's people, strong survivors in what had been a wilderness. Though the Mormons considered themselves derived from a lost tribe of Israel, there were no Jews in these mountains.

My father came from a similar Mormon family, and his father had been directed by the patriarch Brigham Young to homestead in the far north and was thus one of the first settlers in what was then the remote Bear River Valley. These were sugar beet farmers, using irrigation to dig out a living from a harsh, dry land, employing skills that they had once learned from raising similar crops for generations in the green fields of East Anglia.

It was a hard life, and my father fled from it. He went "over the wall" at sixteen, lying about his age so that he could join the adventure of the Great War in 1914, the same conflict that led to Ruth's father's illness and death. My father never left America or found much military adventure, but, when discharged, his pent-up energy pointed him to California. Still very young, he dreamed of a fortune in land or oil or oranges, something like W. C. Fields' fantasy in his hilarious *It's a Gift*. Unlike the character in Fields' movie, my father never struck it rich. But he held on to his dreams, and stayed in Hollywood for the rest of his life.

Ruth's mother also followed countless others to California after the Second World War, not searching for riches but longing to escape the confines of Brooklyn and a failed second marriage. Still a bookkeeper in the "*shmata* trade," the garment industry, at first she had to share an apartment with a cousin due to the postwar housing shortage. This was also in Hollywood, and in 1949 that's where I met Ruth. I found her dark good looks very attractive despite her funny accent.

It was a long road to Hollywood for both families, and neither Jacob nor Ellis nor any other family member in Brooklyn or Utah would have imagined what was to be a surprising and certainly unwelcome crossing of ancestral bloodlines.

*   *   *

"Our Town"

Hollywood has been described in the past as a "Jewish empire," but that was more hyperbolic than accurate, expressing either Jewish pride or Gentile resentment. There has also been a perception of the Hollywood media industry as pursuing narrow Jewish interests. Historically, this is both inaccurate and unfair in its implications.

Given its origins as a once-marginal Jewish business, Hollywood has always been associated with American Jewry and, over time, became virtually synonymous with successful Jewish assimilation. The Jewish interests during the time when Hollywood was perhaps close to a "Jewish empire," as historian Neal Gabler called it, were wholly consistent with the egalitarian values of the New Deal, patriotism during the war, and the perpetuation of the "American dream" shared by countless other immigrant groups. Liberalism predominated, but wasn't exclusive. The most powerful man in Hollywood, the pioneering chief of MGM, Louis B. Mayer, was, in fact, a prominent Republican and a good friend of President Herbert Hoover.

The Hollywood of my youth was, however, certainly a "Jewish town" in that the studios had been established and were still managed by Jewish entrepreneurs. Much of the prominent talent — writers, actors, and directors, many of whom had fled from Europe — were Jewish as well, though the actors then commonly changed their names to avoid still-widespread prejudice. Even some of the earliest stars of the silent era, such as Douglas Fairbanks, Theda Bara, and Hedy Lamarr, are still not widely known as having had Jewish parentage. Even the early star "Cowboy Billy Anderson" was Jewish.

In my teens I was an aspiring actor, inspired by a remarkable acting teacher, Viola Spolin, who was also Jewish. I was often awed to be in the company of actors so highly regarded by their peers, such as Morris Carnovsky, J. Edward Bromberg, and Howard Da Silva, then playing character parts in movies, but once stellar Broadway performers. They were also among the founders of the Group Theater, the ensemble that had pioneered theatrical realism in America. I had no inclination toward prejudice, only respect.

My only sense of distinction was a feeling of inferiority at my lack of culture and education. This is not to disparage my family; in those days education came second to survival. My family had arrived in Hollywood in the depths of the Great Depression, and farmers as well as workers were struggling simply to make a living and keep the family together.

My mother had died young, and from the age of three I lived mostly with an aunt, an older sister of my mother. She was childless and had moved to Hollywood to keep my lonely young mother company, two farm girls in the wilds of the big city. Her husband, a Texan from a share-cropper's family, literally rode the rails to the Central Valley of California to pick grapefruit. He then found work digging ditches for the WPA, the government work program. Eventually, he and my aunt worked as servants in the luxurious homes of Beverly Hills.

Since the early days of the studios, Beverly Hills was the center of the movie industry's social life. Nearby, a modest residential area, virtually a "servants' quarter," sprang up on its eastern boundary. This is where we lived, first in a tiny rented bungalow and later in what was called a "railroad flat," a long, narrow space divided into rooms. I had a pull-down bed in what served as the dining room. It was a modest but pleasant place with neighbors not much higher on the social ladder than my aunt and uncle — a gardener, a chauffeur, a waiter, a bellhop, and, moving up, a mailman and even a musician. My father had found work as a milkman, in the early years still driving a horse-drawn wagon along Wilshire Boulevard. During the thirties, most people were almost as poor as we were, and while I later sensed the marked class differences, I never felt a sense of shame or even inferiority. In the years following my mother's death, one of my caretakers was a housekeeper, a full-blooded Cherokee Indian woman whom I called Granny. My father brought us vegetables he had bought from the wholesale market, and I remember pulling my little wagon from door to door as Granny and I sold those vegetables to our neighbors. I must have been about five; I'm sure the sight of a red-haired little boy must have helped sales. This is a very pleasant memory of what, for me, was a game.

The neighborhood was safe and a delight for us kids, because at that time there were great expanses of vacant, undeveloped land that, though forbidden, we would secretly explore, especially the reed-filled spots with dark pools of water that smelled of the oil deposits below. Over time, and especially during the postwar boom years, this became the fashionable district of "West Hollywood." The vacant land and pools of oily water disappeared almost overnight.

Unlike my Jewish friends, we possessed almost no books other than, as I recall, an old Bible, the Book of Mormon, and an occasional *Reader's Digest*. I saw my father, still single after my mother's death, off and on. He was solicitous, if distant, and supported me financially as best he could. This was his nature, not a sign of indifference. He would periodically give me fatherly advice about hygiene as well as "pep talks" right out of Horatio Alger about seeking success in life and "sticking up for yourself!" I was never to run from a fight. I took him quite seriously, and because I was one of the smallest of the boys in my class for many years, my defiance put me at some risk until I figured out how to crack jokes rather than throw punches, a kind of early career choice. My father, in his own way, was a rather dreamy romantic himself, and, when around, was an inspirational figure.

More specific direction about my future, however, came from another and rather unusual source. My father's good friend was a former vaudevillian, a once-successful magician known on the circuit as "The Great Muse." He was now an aging insurance agent but greatly respected by my father as a highly cultured person because he had once been a vaudeville headliner. Mr. Muse — his real name — began to use me occasionally as an assistant when he revived his act for charity events. I would be dressed in a Chinese robe and skullcap (it was a "Chinese act"), quite jarring with my red hair and freckles, and I usually got a laugh just by appearing as I clanged a gong and announced "the Great Muse!" It was the beginning, you might say, of my "career." I began and in some ways always remained an entertainer.

My Early "Career"

Entertainers have always been outsiders, not quite fully acceptable in society even when admired. The minstrels and jesters always used the servants' entrance, and I would have been content to do the same. But, in my case, I found my entry into a greater world by entertaining. It was, however, a Jewish world into which I was integrated, just as Jews, through their many accomplishments, had succeeded in assimilating into the larger Gentile world.

My next entrance was actually through the kitchen. For several years during and after the war, my aunt worked as a laundress and second maid to the noted composer Jerome Kern, one of the true pioneers of the Broadway musical. At times she was also employed by producer Arthur

Hornblow, Jr., and his wife, the actress Myrna Loy. But it was at the Kerns' luxurious home in Beverly Hills that I first peered from the kitchen door into a new and glamorous world — just a glance, mind you — that at times included lyricist Oscar Hammerstein of *Show Boat* and *Oklahoma!* fame, and the popular movie comedian Danny Kaye and his wife, Sylvia. I had no clear idea then who these people were.

The view from the servants' quarters was, of course, limited; but Mr. Kern was gracious and once gave me an autographed copy of his classic "Smoke Gets in Your Eyes" in order to encourage my trumpet-playing (an ambition that lasted little more than a year). My aunt's attitude toward the Kerns was similar to that of the rest of the servants — she was respectful and grateful for employment. I can't recall how the fact that the Kerns were Jewish as well as rich and famous affected me, if at all.

The Second World War, for us, began with the bombing of Pearl Harbor, which we kids greeted with great excitement as the dawn of a thrilling adventure. I was a newspaper boy at that time, and I remember shouting the announcement "War!" with glee as I sold my papers to the drivers of cars stopped at a signal. The newsreels of the European and Pacific battles soon followed and would provide fuel for our imaginary games for years to come.

On the other hand, the war quickly forced major changes in our lives, which undoubtedly left many scars from the fear and insecurity they caused. My father disappeared into war work in the Bay Area shipyards, and my uncle was drafted into the army (he survived the invasion of Iwo Jima in the Pacific). During the war years I became, off and on, the seventh kid on the family farm of another aunt and uncle in Utah. This gave me my first opportunity to meet my extended family, most of whom were still farming the Bear River Valley.

It was a deeply religious and loving family in a rural, close-knit Mormon community, and a whole new world to me with its horses, cows, and outhouses. It seemed a long way from any war. Eventually, there were German POWs working the fields opposite our farm. They were young men often stripped to the waist in the hot sun and watched by armed guards. We kids would creep over to the fence and mock them with shouts of "Heil Hitler!" and then run for cover as most of them laughed.

My only memory of Jews in our Hollywood neighborhood is an unpleasant one but representative of the mixed attitudes of working-class Gentiles at the time. I remember remarks about Jews as "draft dodgers" and black marketeers, a renewal of old stereotypes that meant nothing to me. There was one old Jewish woman on our block, however, who periodically would shout at us kids to keep off her lawn — a patch of grass in front of a duplex — in a heavy accent which we mocked. A "Jew" for me then meant only a mean old woman. We did at times thoughtlessly parrot the remarks of adults and speak of "Mrs Jews-a-velt," meaning Eleanor, the president's wife, in the same derogatory way. I don't know where we first heard that or what it meant to us. I never associated any of these taunts with the Jewish kids at school who were becoming my best friends.

Nor did I sense anything anti-Jewish in our attitudes when I was back with my aunt and we would occasionally enjoy a rich meal of leftovers from parties at the Kern home where she was once again employed. There was certainly a recognition that they were rich and we were poor, but that just seemed normal, the way things had always been. Mr. Kern was a Jew, but his gentle, ever-polite good humor evidenced his true nature and provided a pleasant, lasting memory for me.

The legacy of the kitchen view — my glance into another world — was as formative as perhaps anything else that happened in my childhood. Unlike other kids who might have fantasized about a career in movies, I considered it, unreasonably, a reasonable option. Mr. Kern and his illustrious guest Danny Kaye were, after all, real people, not fantasy figures. They lived very nice lives and had other people do their dishes and cut their lawns for them. Why couldn't this happen to a red-haired kid from the streets of Hollywood?

I decided to go into show business when I was twelve. Actually, I initially decided to become Danny Kaye, despite the fact that there already was such a person, and that I could neither sing nor dance. (Later I would decide to become Charlie Chaplin and then Laurence Olivier, but those positions were also filled.) My well-developed capacity for disappearing into a fantasy land fueled this ambition, and I persuaded my friend Danny Schwartz — a Jewish kid my age who, like me, had freckles and amazing *chutzpah* — to form a comedy team. We stole some ideas for our sketches from movies, including Kaye's, and then included some "blue" material, as it was then called. These were sexually suggestive jokes that I heard with my father one night when he took me, inexplicably, to an American Legion "smoker." They were relatively innocent jokes but certainly inappropriate for twelve-year-olds; in any case, neither Danny nor I understood them. Then we borrowed or stole some old dresses and mops for wigs so we could do an imitation of the "two Andrews Sisters," put all the stuff in a trunk (also an idea borrowed from movies), and declared ourselves a team — Danny Sherwood and Dizzy Lynn (that was me).

9

We lugged that trunk on the bus to central Hollywood for an audition, and, amazingly — a mystery to this day — the management of the famous and still-operating Hollywood Canteen decided to put us on stage. This was less than a year after the war, and GIs "demobbed" from the Pacific were pouring through Hollywood on their way home. I'm sure some might have contemplated returning to their bases after witnessing "Danny and Dizzy's" comedy routine. We lasted two performances, which is two more than I can imagine anyone enduring.

The reception wouldn't have mattered, though. I was in show business.

Danny and I got other auditions and later "played" a bar mitzvah, as I recall, but then, sensing how bad we were, we finally "broke up the act." My fantasy life and my real life were now remarkably intertwined. I persuaded my father, who was prone to fantasies himself, to pay for some "head shots" — professional photos of me — and then walked the Sunset Strip by myself, seeking an agent. Nothing much came of that, and I'm not sure into what ditch my narcissism was leading me when Danny called and told me about an open audition for kid actors at a theater in Hollywood.

It turned out to be at the Circle Theater, later a historic monument because the Circle Players began the Little Theatre Movement in Hollywood. The company included Charlie Chaplin's two sons, Sydney and Charlie, Jr., as well as Edward G. Robinson's son and an assortment of highly talented character actors. Many would go on to become familiar faces in movies and TV, including Bill Schallert, Kathleen Freeman, Strother Martin, and Joe Mantell. Bill became Patty Duke's TV father as well as president of the Screen Actors Guild. Bill and I would meet on picket lines more than once over the years, as he came out to support our Writers Guild strikes. Kathleen was Jerry Lewis's favorite stooge; Strother achieved movie immortality by telling Paul Newman in *Cool Hand Luke*, "What we got here is a failure to communicate!" Joe became even more famous by reminding the distraught Jack Nicholson that "it's Chinatown, Jake."

What was most fortunate for me, beyond the timing of Danny's call, was that they were looking for young boys to play "street kids," rough types such as those in the "Dead End Kids" movies. I was nothing of the sort, but, coming directly from my paper route, unlike the well-dressed lads in line with their stage mothers and agents, I was at least appropriately dressed in dirty clothes. I got one of the four parts.

The play was the premiere of one of William Saroyan's lesser works, but it ran for several months at the Circle in Hollywood and then for some charity performances in San Francisco. The Circle was small in scale but big in reputation in the postwar period, drawing numerous movie celebrities. After performances, particularly on opening nights, I had the privilege of meeting, among others, the great French director Jean Renoir, stars such as Fanny Brice, Sam Jaffe, David Niven, Edward G. Robinson, Gene Tierney, Shelley Winters, and a tall, handsome, and rather gallant Italian named Vittorio De Sica. Of course, I didn't know who he was. In later years, I would attend Renoir's master classes, and he and De Sica, the pioneer of Italian neo-realism, would become, and remain, with Chaplin, my artistic heroes.

I had not only entered the theater but, in a sense, leaped or fallen into an adult world. It was an odd way for an adolescent boy to first experience feminine allures, but for me it was in sharing dressing rooms and makeup mirrors. Syd Chaplin, Charlie's son, was courting — as I remember — Gloria de Haven at the time, but prior to that he had dated a cute blonde who had been raised in the orphanage across the street from the Circle, and who had just changed her name to Marilyn Monroe. The real beauty, however, was the petite brunette that actor Roddy McDowell brought to our performances, the very young Elizabeth Taylor. I was just a kid, too young to be jealous.

Needless to say, this was an exciting world for me, but it had its disadvantages. We played six nights a week, which precluded a lot of sleep and any homework. I had no problem with this. The world of the theater, I decided, would be my schooling. This wasn't the view of my aunt or the local authorities. However, sometime earlier, my vaudevillian mentor Mr. Muse had given me some avuncular advice about my future education.

Since he had decided that I was clearly cut out for show business (I was perhaps eleven at that time), he saw no reason for me to even consider college. It would suffice for a performer's education to emulate his own. He advised that I should simply read "all of the Bible, Shakespeare, and Shaw." The playwright Bernard Shaw, now perhaps best known for providing the source material for *My Fair Lady*, was then a model of wit and wisdom, particularly among show people. Over the years, I actually took this advice to heart and read much of all three. The Bible bored and confused me, but I loved Shakespeare and, eventually, Shaw, though at first I understood little of either.

Whatever the merits of the Great Muse's counsel, skipping school didn't conform to the laws governing minors, and it certainly didn't allow me to keep up with my precocious Jewish friends, who, by the time of high school, considered a winning debate team more prestigious than football or track. I wasn't exactly slighted, but I came to know what *goyishe kop* means — in effect, "a Gentile brain." It isn't a compliment.

In time, however, I would absorb many of the ideas of these bright kids as well as the opinions of the articulate theater people with whom I now worked. My acting career would never really take off, but I was getting some small parts in theater productions and often still playing six nights a week. My aunt, a good Mormon and a sensible woman, would never have allowed this, but my father, ever the romantic, gave his approval. This, of course, further doomed my grades but was fortunate for my future.

There was usually time backstage for long discussions about theater, art, and politics, and though my grasp was limited, I soaked up what I heard. Much of what I remember was a highly emotional amalgam of Marx, Freud, and Stanislavski. It was a heady but unreliable mix of radical politics and sexual liberation as envisioned by actors, most of whom experienced "truth" as wholly subjective. I concluded that to be a good actor, which was still my ambition, I needed to learn "motivation," to be sexually liberated (an idea I found inherently attractive), and to be politically radical.

Despite some occasional movie auditions, my acting work remained limited to the theater, and lasted for only five years. Nonetheless, this period molded my life to come. Charlie Chaplin was occasionally the director of our dress rehearsals at the Circle, particularly when his son, Syd, played the lead, and it was Chaplin who pointed me by example to the world of art. As with "Mr. Kern," to this day I still tend to speak of Chaplin as "Mr. Chaplin," while the rest of the world calls him "Charlie."

Viola Spolin, my acting teacher at her Young Actors Company, the most innovative acting school for young people in the nation, provided the technique and the discipline, or at least as much of the latter to which I would submit at that rebellious age. Vi's influence over time went beyond acting technique. Her approach was based on her early work as a social worker with poor children and was aimed at building self-confidence and self-esteem. The use of the imagination was meant to be transformative in personal terms, and her sometimes demanding discipline in teaching us to "focus" or to simply "see" and touch the other person was a lasting gift.

Vi's rigorous training also forced me to deal with my real abilities. At age seventeen, I was fortunate enough to recognize my emotional limits as an actor, and I began to imagine myself as a writer or director. From then on I would hide behind words and the camera.

My "Jewish" Education

Given my "Jewish world," it is not accidental that my first bit of writing was a sketch I composed for myself and an equally young actress from Vi's group for a school program celebrating Brotherhood Week. It was a crude but well-meaning denunciation of bigotry (I played the bigot), and it found such favor with the school administrators that it was broadcast the next week on local radio, my first and only work in that venerable medium.

I was also fortunate to be living still with my doting though increasingly exasperated aunt in West Hollywood. The area had grown more diverse during the war and, more importantly for my future, was on the edge of a growing Jewish middle-class neighborhood. The Jews of Los Angeles had been moving west for a generation, and the Fairfax district was a move up from East L.A. and, in time, became the Jewish social center, with wonderful delis, bakeries, and bookstores. It remains a partially Orthodox and Russian Jewish neighborhood to this day.

Fairfax High was in the middle of the district and was therefore virtually a Jewish school with, as I recall, a student population that was more than 80 percent Jewish. Fairfax had an intellectual atmosphere, more like a college than a high school. The campus politics were intense and only partially evolved around the customary social cliques. The full range of left-wing militants could be found in debate at lunchtime, including the Young Communist League kids, the YCL, still stubbornly defending Stalin's regime; the Trotskyites, supporters of Stalin's arch-rival Leon Trotsky, who were far more open in their radicalism and, to their chagrin, often mistaken for Party-line communists; and the Zionists, who, in their teens, were already "making *aliyah*" — that is, traveling to Israel to live on *kibbutzim,* the collective farms. Needless to say, most of the kids were like any others — far more interested in status, sports, and sex than politics.

Among the left-wing activists I befriended were two bright and highly articulate "red diaper babies" — George and Gershon. George Moore, who would remain my lifelong friend, was the son of a successful comedy writer, a former president of the Radio Writers Guild, and a prominent Party member who was among the first in Hollywood to be blacklisted.

He had returned to New York in the hope of finding work in the theater, and George lived with his mother, a woman so sophisticated that she intimidated me. George wasn't Jewish, but at Fairfax almost all the cute, smart girls were, and, like me, he later married one of them.

Gershon was Jewish, but his family members were dedicated communists who scorned all religion. His father was a functionary in the Party and a union organizer. I spent many hours at their modest, book-filled home listening to the "gospel of Marx," and it was Gershon who eventually recruited me into the Young Communist League.

By the end of high school, I had become, initially, a "Shavian," thanks to Mr. Muse, which meant I thought of myself as a devotee of Shaw, and thus a socialist who valued wit far more than morality. In truth, I had little of either. By graduation I had read Marx's *Communist Manifesto* and declared myself a Marxist.

I didn't finish high school without experiencing a few bumps in the road. I hadn't appreciated how fortunate I was to attend Fairfax until I was expelled. After several unheeded warnings, I was placed in the "Alcatraz classes" for juvenile delinquents in another school. This was for chronic truancy, not criminality, my excuse being my late nights in the theater. Already a self-advertising rebel, I had also been suspended for passing petitions in support of the "Hollywood Ten," the writers subpoenaed before the House Un-American Activities Committee. Because they refused to testify before the Committee, they all went to jail. I was just placed in "agricultural classes," a form of detention that allowed us miscreants to get class credits for weeding. I was finally given a diploma, and one of my counselors, glad to be rid of me, urged me to join the Navy.

It's difficult to know where my irregular education and even more tentative acting career might have led me, whether to Broadway or jail or, more likely, to unemployment and bohemian idleness. The first of many rescues, however, had fortunately begun. I had met Ruth in acting school.

Her mother had enrolled her for the sole purpose of finding an elocution course to eradicate her "funny" Brooklyn accent, which, I guess, embarrassed them both. Alma had no way of knowing that the classes in which Ruth was enrolled were at the pioneering Young Actors Company of Viola Spolin. The YAC would, in time, provide the foundation for improvisational theater in America. This is not an exaggeration. Vi's son, Paul Sills, went on to found Chicago's Second City, and Vi herself fostered several talented actors such as Tony Award winners Alan Arkin and Paul Sand and TV star Valerie Harper. Paul Sand, a remarkable talent who would eventually have his own TV show, was in our early years a kind of big brother to me, and the best man at our wedding.

As I recall, Vi had seen me in a production at the Circle Theater and had generously given me a scholarship for which, at that self-obsessed age, I was arrogantly ungrateful. I owe her much — and not just for the fine theater training. It was at Vi's theater school where you could say that I met my future. I met Ruth at the makeup table.

CHAPTER TWO

Interlude: Jewish Hopes and Fears

Before I can thread the strands of our story any further, I have to go back to a time long before Jacob the tailor came to America and Ellis the farm boy searched for his lost sheep in the Utah foothills.

I hope it won't be viewed as presumptuous if I explore some of the origins of the thoughts and attitudes that shaped the Jewish world that Ruth and I shared. I'm neither qualified nor inclined to write a definitive analysis. I'll settle for clues.

* * *

The social advancements of modern European Jewry were the results of the age of Enlightenment, called *Haskalah* in Hebrew. This new freedom of thought inspired Jewish thinkers to break free from their own world, confined for centuries to the ghetto. Now further liberated by social assimilation and economic success, Jews of the nineteenth century, such as the philosopher Moses Mendelssohn, confidently incorporated Jewish ideals into the liberalism of the newly developing nation-state. This was particularly true in Germany, at the time the most advanced of the European countries in education, culture, and science.

During the nineteenth century, there were intense debates among thinkers on the relative merits of Christianity and Judaism, with Jews claiming their beliefs to be more compatible with modern rationalism. This dialogue, however, led many Jews — estimated as high as a quarter of a million — to convert to the dominant Christian religion. Such was the case with Moses Mendelssohn's own family. His famous grandson, Felix, a fervent Lutheran, would even compose a "Reformation" symphony. These conversions were for the most part less about theology than social acceptance.

Nevertheless, by the end of the nineteenth century, numerous prominent and distinctly Jewish thinkers wielded significant influence in Europe. There can be no account of the influence of modern Jewish consciousness without recognizing the centrality of Karl Marx and Sigmund Freud. The ideas of these two powerful revolutionaries had an enormous impact, particularly on the Jewish world. Given the extensive literature on both, it seems superfluous to comment further on their particular theories. My purpose, in any case, is less to analyze what they said than to determine what my generation heard and absorbed. To do so, we need to probe the underlying Jewish roots of the movements they inspired.

*   *   *

It is understandable that European Jewry, still facing discrimination and insecurity, looked for ways to transform society. Many turned to socialism, a movement that had attracted Jewish support from the beginning. From the 1840s until the 1870s, Jews were an important part of the international socialist movement. Some leaders also formed the Hebrew Socialist Movement, which concentrated on Jewish workers and Jewish solutions, and in 1897 the highly influential organization called The Bund was organized. This form of Jewish socialism or collectivism would merge with Yiddish culture and by the 1920s be an important element in Yiddish literature and theater.

In Israel, then Palestine, the collective agrarian movement known as *kibbutzim,* led by the idealistic socialist A. D. Gordon, came out of this historical development. Similarly, the initial formation of the American labor movement was led by Samuel Gompers, the Jewish leader of the cigarmakers union and founder of the American Federation of Labor.

However, by the 1890s, Karl Marx's revolutionary socialism dominated Jewish intellectual circles. The adherents were secular Jews, yet the spirit of their enterprise was rooted in the messianic vision of a "new world" and the creation of not just a "new Jew," but "the new man."

*   *   *

In Hollywood, we also eagerly embraced our idea of revolution, sincerely looking for a means to reshape the world. But there was a gap, if not a chasm, between our ideals and the competitive world in which we lived. Marx's theories about alienation only added to our own, not because we were the "proletariat" of Hollywood — far from it — but because we were constantly forced to compromise our artistic standards in order to be successful.

Our drive for personal success was thus in uncomfortable contradiction to the left-wing principle of self-sacrificing struggle for the cause. Our obsession as writers, radical or not, wasn't as much about money as it was about status. We didn't need to be on the Hollywood party "A-list" as much as we wanted to be admired and accepted by the elite, the "creative community."

This was an obsession hardly limited to the Jews of Hollywood, but there was a distinctly Jewish dimension to this overwhelming need to succeed. Money was the key symbol. Money was a psychological chit, a currency that bought a kind of mental status as well as a Brentwood estate or a new Jag. There was an income level that brought the feeling, however fleeting, that you were no longer stained with the stigma of insecurity.

Alfred Kazin and Norman Podhoretz, icons of success in the world of New York Jewish intellectuals of that era, have both written with brutal candor about the "bitch goddess" of success and the extraordinary desire to "make it." The apogee of this drive was perhaps the self-invention of the intellectual as celebrity, a personal identity more significant than anything one may have written. Norman Mailer's "Advertisement for Myself" was emblematic, and Kazin admired his friend Mailer as a "genius fraud" who used his immense talent to don a disguise. Kazin lamented that by the end of the sixties, in Jewish circles, "show business" had replaced socialism, and "winners and losers" were seen as different species.

Both Kazin and Podhoretz were from relatively poor and distinctly Jewish backgrounds and, as they admitted, were rivalrous to the point of vindictiveness with other Jewish luminaries. Ironically, the upper-middle-class Jewish world in New York, for all of its culture and sophistication, became a kind of gilded ghetto. My Hollywood was a version of the same ghetto in that there were few lasting personal connections to a wider social orbit and certainly not to the working-class Gentile world, the so-called "middle America" whose inhabitants would later be dismissed by the next generation as "rednecks" and "hard hats."

The troubling effect of this sense of distance wasn't the precarious status that came with New York or Hollywood success but the lingering fear of an unknown Other perceived as envious and resentful, if not threatening.

Alfred Kazin's diaries, published posthumously, revealed, in a way both illuminating and touching, his lifelong obsession: the question of what it meant to be a Jew.

*   *   *

The Rise of Anti-Semitism

As the modern age unfolded, it became clear that the Enlightenment, far from eradicating the deep roots of anti-Semitism, had left them largely untouched. In fact, some of the most celebrated Enlightenment figures, such as Voltaire and Goethe, advocated a grudging emancipation that evidenced little respect for Jews.

I will be using the terms "anti-Semite" and "anti-Semitism" throughout, but I do so with reservations. Beside the obvious flaw of referring to a racial category — Semites — that includes Arabs and others, the problem is more than simply semantic inexactitude. The term tends to obscure the different types and sources of antipathy or hostility toward Jews by lumping them indiscriminately together.

Many times over the years people who were unaware of my Jewish ties used derogatory terms or displayed negative attitudes toward Jews in my presence. However, the difference between ignorance, inherited social prejudice, or religious bias, on the one hand, and pathological hatred on the other, is evident and significant. To categorize a person as an "anti-Semite" because of provincial bias is not only obtuse but subverts the possibility of correction. In any case, there is, as Hannah Arendt observed, an important distinction to be made between the anti-Jewish prejudices of the historical past and the virulent attitudes that emerged after the Enlightenment and emancipation. To ignore this distinction leads to despair and to the cynical view that all Gentiles are irremediably hostile to Jews.

Scholars have recognized that the phenomenon of "Jew-hatred" began in pre-history, as symbolized by King Amalek in Exodus or the despotic figure of Haman, whose desire to destroy the Jews is chronicled in the book of Esther, composed not later than the third century BCE.

It is, however, in the context of rising hopes and expectations associated with liberalism and the emergence of the nation-state that we need to examine the resurgence of anti-Jewish prejudices in their most modern forms.

The spread of liberalism in the nineteenth century had meant not just more religious tolerance for Jews but greater political freedom as well. In what might be viewed as a historical irony, in 1829 Catholics and Jews achieved political emancipation in England simultaneously. In 1869, the German Chancellor, Bismarck, eliminated legal discrimination against Jews; and later, as a sign of progress in France, the notorious anti-Semite Max Regis was actually imprisoned for libeling Jews.

By the end of the century, however, an ominous movement arose to counter these liberal and revolutionary impulses. There was an alarming rise in anti-Jewish attitudes throughout Europe. Violent pogroms erupted in Russia, tolerated if not encouraged by the Tsar; there was also increasing discrimination against Jews in Russia, Poland, Galicia, and the other eastern provinces. The Kishinev pogrom of 1903 was so bloody that it prompted worldwide protests, including a diplomatic but admonishing letter to the Russian Tsar from President Teddy Roosevelt.

In some ways, the rise of virulent anti-Jewish sentiments and political movements in France and Germany were even more dismaying, for it was in these countries that many Jews felt confident that they had found not only success but security and acceptance. However, by 1880 there were mass protests in Germany denouncing the influence of Jews "on daily life," and in 1887 the book *The Jewish Problem in Europe* was a best seller. Indicative of these conflicting trends in Europe at century's end, a new mayor of Vienna was elected in 1895 on an anti-Jewish platform, but, spurning this intolerance, the Emperor Franz Josef refused to confirm him. Adolf Hitler would later call this politician, Herr Karl Luger, the "greatest mayor in history." His anti-Semitism had its unique side in that he once proclaimed, "I'll tell you who's a Jew and who isn't!"

Much of the early optimism about assimilation had been based on the myopia of more privileged and accomplished Jews. There had, in fact, always been suspicion if not resentment toward Jews, especially as they rose in society, and particularly among the growing number of nationalists.

Napoleon himself is an ambivalent figure. In 1807 the Emperor arrogantly assembled his own Jewish "Sanhedrin" — a gathering of the most prominent Jewish representatives — to listen to his latest edicts. Despite assurances of their loyalty, Napoleon had determined that Jews would have to be compelled to be "good citizens" and that this meant rejecting their past. "Usury," he announced, would have to be abolished, though, on the other hand, Jews were expected to continue to generously fund and supply his conquering armies. In 1800, the Tsar had made a similar declaration, making a "change of the way of life" a condition for the assimilation of Russia's Jews.

Even otherwise sympathetic liberals often spoke of the "Jewish problem" as one of how to incorporate a people of questionable character into the greater society. These prejudices were not only based on ancient animosities and religious antagonisms but derived, in part, from the influx of thousands of "oriental Jews," as the immigrants from the East were called. Often an embarrassment to the assimilated German and French Jews, many of these immigrants, fleeing from poverty and pogroms, were the poor "rag-and-bone" peddlers of the ghettos of the Pale. Most were religious to the point of superstition, and suspicious of and resistant to the ways of the *goyim*. Anti-Jewish stereotypes drew upon the characteristics of these poor newcomers, alien and clannish, resentful of their low status, and toughened by centuries of deprivation into shrewd hard-bargainers. This is the "type" that Dickens rendered in his characterization of the mean-spirited Fagin in *Oliver Twist*.

During the nineteenth century, popular literature and drama primarily reflected Christian concepts and values. For instance, Lew Wallace's extraordinarily popular 1879 work *Ben-Hur* wasn't anti-Jewish as such, but presented Christian faith as the ultimate goal of Judaism. Some plays and vaudeville skits, however, portrayed Jews as "buffoons" and "knaves" — amusing but amoral. This unfortunately created the lasting stereotype of the Jew as "social misfit." While this is a common comic conceit and a theme found in Jewish humor itself, it also perpetuated a sense of estrangement that spread into the wider culture. This is a subject close to the concerns of anyone from Hollywood.

Some of the Jewish stereotypes of the time were less benign. In 1868 a self-dubbed "Sir John Retcliffe" — in truth, a German Jew named Goedsche — wrote a novel entitled *Biarritz* containing a chapter in which Jewish conspirators reveal their plans for world domination. Some historians argue that this became the basis for the notorious "Protocols of Zion," a "document" used by anti-Semites ever since as proof of a perennial worldwide Jewish conspiracy. There are other sources, equally fictitious, nominated for the dubious distinction of the inspiration for the "Protocols," but the theme of sinister Jewish influences ran deep. In the 1890s, Svengali, a character in du Maurier's novel *Trilby*, was a Jewish villain, and the story can be read as an exposure of a diabolic Jewish desire for control of others.

One cannot describe the growth of anti-Semitism in the nineteenth century without citing the baleful influence of Richard Wagner. This is unfortunate because Wagner was a genius whose supremely innovative music expresses great passion and even a sense of sanctity. Wagner, however, was one of the Europeans, particularly Germans, who became obsessed with utopian ideals based on national and racial purity.

Wagner was not a consistent or even a very clear thinker, but his toxic ideas were articulated by the English author Houston Stewart Chamberlain, who eventually married into the Wagner clan. In his highly influential book *The Origins of Nineteenth-Century Civilization*, Chamberlain offered a seemingly more rational but even more rabid ideology, incorporating Wagner's idea of religion as national "regeneration."

In this highly literate but distorted version of Christianity, Chamberlain claimed that Jesus was not a Jew and disavowed traditional church teachings to the contrary as heretical. The denial of Jesus as a Jew is the sure sign of resurgent paganism. What is missing in Wagner and Chamberlain's Christ figure is any sense of love and compassion. Wagner's operatic theme of "redemption through sacrifice" reverts to a paganism in which suffering becomes self-annihilation. The Wagnerian hero is semi-divine but more Roman than Christian in the heroic but suicidal embrace of death.

This form of pernicious anti-Jewish ideology is not only a modern phenomenon; in fact, it is a reaction against modernity itself. Modernity's deconstruction of tradition and concepts of honor and virtue were blamed on foreign elements, primarily Jews, who, according to Wagner and Chamberlain, had a racially inherited "evil conscience" that promoted corruption. The most influential philosophers of the time, such as Nietzsche and Schopenhauer, held similar views, and, incorporating the racial notions of the French writer Gobineau, this apprehension was turned into a pseudo-science that identified and condemned all racially "inferior" peoples.

Wagner, in his infamous 1869 "Jews and Music" article, condemned Jews as "imitators" of authentic culture, incapable of originality. During his last years, he continued to condemn Jews for what he found revolting in the vulgarity and commercialism of modern life. In one of his outbursts, while stopping short of proposing genocide, he advocated the expulsion of Jews from Germany. In the meantime, true to his capricious mentality, he retained the Jewish conductor Emmanuel Levy as a major figure at his Bayreuth Festival.

What Wagner was seeking in his nationalism as well as in his music was a "higher unity" — unattainable in the real world but glimpsed in his operas. As the Eastern Orthodox theologian Olivier Clement observed, "the disintegrative tendency was always stronger than the power to unify" in the highly individualistic society of the West. In time, this search for "wholeness" — increasingly diminishing in modern society — led to a denial of liberty and the persecution of all minorities. As Clement concludes, this was the real descent from Wagner to Adolf Hitler. Hitler's book *Mein Kampf* ("My Struggle") was a poor imitation of Houston Chamberlain's theories, but the cultivated scholar had provided him with his inescapable and deadly conclusions.

* * *

In 1900 the Jewish population was almost two million worldwide, with relatively few Jews in Palestine. Half a million — more than a fourth of the total — now lived in New York, and the rest remained scattered in European cities — Budapest, London, Vienna, Odessa, and Berlin. This meant that 40 percent of the worldwide Jewish population now lived in the United States, with half still in Russia and Eastern Europe. It was in Europe and in Russia, therefore, where the "Jewish problem" became acute.

* * *

The Turning Point: The Dreyfus Affair

The overt anti-Semitism that rose in France was undoubtedly exacerbated by the wounded national pride that followed the defeat of the French by the Germans in 1870. A desire for revenge, a sense of foreboding under the decadent reign of Louis Napoleon, the anxieties engendered by rapid change and loss of traditional status — all these things contributed to a xenophobic need for scapegoats.

From the Jewish perspective, it was the notorious Dreyfus affair that marked the turn of the century and forced many to look for exit signs. A French Jew, a military officer and patriot from an established family, Alfred Dreyfus was accused of spying for the Germans, and in 1896 he was dishonored and imprisoned following a frame-up by fellow officers. Anti-Semitism was at the heart of the affair, and though Dreyfus was finally exonerated and reinstated in 1906 (albeit after years of imprisonment on Devil's Island), the case had exposed the depth and persistence of the cultural animosity toward Jews. This was perhaps the low point in the modern era in relations between Catholics and Jews, as many Catholics viewed Dreyfus's presumed guilt as proof of the corruption of an anti-clerical French Republic that had disavowed the Catholic faith.

Hannah Arendt, in her important work *The Origins of Totalitarianism*, argued that modern anti-Semitism was directly related to the breakdown of liberalism and the growing appeal of totalitarianism. Furthermore, the demise of nineteenth-century liberalism was due less to its reactionary opponents than to its internal corruption and the gradual loss of belief in its ideals. The Dreyfus affair tends to confirm this viewpoint.

The "Dreyfusards" — the defenders of Dreyfus — were not a unified liberal or "progressive" force but a distinct minority within each segment of society. The political left, particularly the Parisian socialists, were split; many radicals considered Dreyfus to be their "class enemy." As a German observer of the time noted, French workers were interested solely in their economic interests, and many, such as the Parisian butchers, were ferociously anti-Semitic. Nor were Jews the leading defenders of Dreyfus. Many, in fact, wanted to ignore or suppress the controversy. In fact, the Catholic intellectual Charles Péguy was one of the most important Dreyfusards. Péguy was also one of the few who understood the issue of anti-Semitism as a spiritual problem deeper than class or political conflicts.

One can only have compassion for Dreyfus himself, who, after years of cruel and unjust imprisonment, was said to look like "a corpse." It is sadly telling that, in the end, all that this cruelly victimized man hoped to achieve from the tragedy was a restoration of his honor, name, and place in the society that had turned on him.

Dreyfus's exoneration and the rise to power of his defenders in the Third Republic have led to an oversimplified interpretation of the long-term political consequences. The Dreyfus affair resulted in no lasting victory for democracy or liberalism. The French anti-Semites, led by petit-bourgeois opportunists, bankrupt aristocrats, defensive Catholics, and outright criminals, had agitated the "masses" into frenzies of irrational violence, and one of the results was a sense of alarm about the dangers inherent in populist democracy. Anti-Semite rabble-rousers such as Max Regis proclaimed their grisly political goal as wanting to "water the tree of freedom with the blood of Jews." The ideal of the "will of the people" and the concept of freedom itself were thus badly tarnished.

In any case, easy categories of "left" and "right" are confounded in a careful reading of the Dreyfus affair in that the mob violence was directed against Jews not so much as social undesirables but as symbols of the corruption of the newly established order. The failure of revolutionary goals, the defeat of Napoleon, the bloody 1848 uprising, the even bloodier suppression of the Paris Commune, and, finally, the corruption within France's Third Republic itself led to an explosion of frustration.

In short, the Dreyfus affair, unlike the movie depiction, was less of a victory than a failure of liberal hopes. It was also an alarming sign of what was to come, and many Jews of the day saw it as such.

*   *   *

As we've noted, one of the most perceptive analysts of modern history, Hannah Arendt, believed that modern anti-Semitism was a nineteenth-century phenomenon and not the same as the "anti-Jewish" prejudices of previous times. Modern anti-Semitism had its roots in a pseudo-scientific concept of race, which meant that identity and characteristics were biologically fixed and irredeemable. This biological determinism provided the rationale for genocidal policies that claimed to "purify" a people or race.

By the end of the century, corruption had infected every political party in France, and when the state itself was viewed as hopelessly corrupt, its Jewish advisors were equally compromised. The Panama Scandal, a financial debacle in the 1890s that implicated several Jewish financiers, then provided the perfect opportunity for Jews to become, once again, the scapegoats for what was, in reality, the moral failure of the society.

*   *   *

The Path to America

With the gradual demise of the liberal consensus and the rise of nationalism and extremist ideologies, the Jewish predicament in Europe became perilous. Many Jews realized that it was time to escape, and there were several paths taken, some by choice, others simply in flight and desperation. Their diverse escape paths, from assimilation to Zionism, designated the goals and impulses that shaped my Jewish world.

The predominant path of escape became that of emigration to America, and among the hundreds of thousands who passed through the "gates of liberty" was Ruth's grandfather, Jacob.

The further path of assimilation then became the major highway for American Jews, including, in time, those in Hollywood. While many have successfully clung to and defended their Jewish heritage, others deposited it as a price of admission to the "American dream." This assimilationist path, in any case, meant a continuous interaction with Christians as well as the secular culture. Whatever the desired goal or the resulting resistance, Jewish assimilation meant a merging of beliefs and hopes, and, of course, people. Ruth and I were among the fortunate ones who merged.

In the United States, the conditions for Jewish immigrants were largely favorable due to the long tradition of religious tolerance as expressed in the Bill of Rights. As early as 1865, the House of Representatives had rejected a resolution that would have officially deemed the United States a "Christian nation." In 1897, President Grover Cleveland vetoed a literacy test for immigrants as anti-Semitic. Following the mass immigration of the 1890s, Jewish culture also began to flourish on American shores. The nineties in New York are now considered the "Golden Age of Yiddish Theater," and the resorts in the nearby Catskill Mountains were established, providing opportunities for promising young Jewish entertainers and comedians for decades to come. Among one of the earliest to succeed was my hero-to-be, Danny Kaye.

The reception given the "greenhorns," as the Jewish immigrants called themselves, was mixed. Jewish organizations, particularly the fraternal burial societies, gave considerable assistance to their landsmen from the old country; but there were also fierce debates among Jews themselves concerning the deplorable conditions in Lower East Side tenements. The Jews now trapped in this new American ghetto were portrayed by some religious Jews as "victims of assimilation," and books and articles appeared that deplored the problem, not just of poverty but of an incipient "Jewish criminality" as well. This sad aspect of the story would emerge later in Jewish involvement in organized crime, including figures such as Louis "Lepke" Buchalter, Meyer Lansky, and "Bugsy" Siegel and other founders of Las Vegas as a gambling capital.

The Jewish assimilationist path was the "modern" path, and to assess its success we need only consider the role of Jews in the development of modern American culture. The Jewish influence in the popular arts has been so considerable and is so well-chronicled that it is sufficient to merely recite names such as Gershwin, Kern, Berlin, Rodgers, and Sondheim, or those of Goldwyn, Mayer, and Steven Spielberg. It was in or at the movies, the most influential of modern arts, where we can see the most direct influence of Jewish aspirations and hopes.

We'll go to the movies again later, and more than once.

*   *   *

In this account of Jewish history, I don't pretend to have offered an adequate survey of either modern Jewish thought or its extensive influence. I wished only to catch the refracted light and shadows of what my generation inherited.

The Holocaust would later provide the lens through which we viewed the postwar world. Anti-Semitism was no longer experienced as merely painful or ugly, a prejudice or an exclusion, but as the shadow of a nightmare. The war had also ended in two atomic blasts that revealed an unprecedented destructive force, and the emotional fallout from this added to our generational anxieties. Yet in the years ahead we were also able to testify to the possibility of faith and hope.

Ruth and I were able to do this because, through our love, we did so together.

CHAPTER THREE

Life Together

The first day that Ruth and I were on stage together at the Young Actors Company, she had predicted that she and I would someday marry. Years later I learned about this from our friend Jackie Joseph. Jackie would go on to become a successful comedy actress, but she wasn't joking.

I don't know how Ruth knew this, but her prediction didn't take long to fulfill. In a youthful surge, I loved and wooed her, and during the year following her graduation and my more-or-less ejection from high school, we were married. We were both eighteen.

Based on contemporary standards, we were more prepared for adult responsibilities than one might assume. Ruth had learned to do housework and cook at age twelve and in the following years prepared the evening meals for her hard-working mother. I was wild and irresponsible, but, in addition to acting, I had worked at a number of jobs since I was a kid. Even so, we were still too young in many ways, and neither family was thrilled by what we saw as our courageous breaking of ethnic boundaries.

One of Ruth's relatives, a very old man who spoke only Yiddish, and who, like many in the family, always called her "Ruch-a-lah," wouldn't speak to me at our wedding — or later, for that matter. He may have represented an extreme wing of Ruth's Jewish family, but his objection was sound enough. Marrying a Gentile was bad enough, but committing oneself to a teenage Gentile actor went beyond good sense.

My grandparents and the aunt and uncle with whom I'd lived on the farm during the war came from Utah for the wedding. The ceremony took place by the pool of Ruth's one well-to-do relative, an uncle, and my family members, while uncomfortable in this luxurious setting, were supportive. It was, needless to say, a mixed crowd.

My father was also supportive, but strangely so. A predictable objection might have been his overt anti-Semitism. Not that he singled out Jews for special disdain; he had strong prejudices against all minorities. He was blessedly inconsistent, however, and in his later years he had two long inter-racial relationships, an inexplicable breaking of his own code. He genuinely liked Ruth. He never displayed open affection for her, but then he never had shown me that kind of affection, either. He told my aunt, I learned later, that he had no objection to my marrying Ruth even though she was Jewish. "She'll make him rich," he predicted. You might wince at the underlying bias, but, depending upon what you understand by "rich," he was right.

Ruth and I were too much in love, too young and reckless and already too independent to be stopped. The families accepted the inevitable and, over time, became not only supportive but affectionate. Many of them even liked each other.

Ruth had shown early promise as an artist and had been offered a job in the animation industry. Once we were married, she dropped out of the UCLA art school to support us. The Great Muse's advice notwithstanding, she demanded that I go to college. This was a very Jewish attitude. So, for that matter, was her initial insistence that we get married. I, of course, preferred my original plan, which was for us to run away to New York City and live in sin; but Ruth stoutly rejected both options. So I obediently entered Los Angeles City College as a drama major, and Ruth went to work at the Warner Brothers' animation department painting Bugs Bunny and Daffy Duck and the other characters in the "Looney Tunes and Merrie Melodies" cartoon series. I later claimed that Bugs Bunny had put me through college, but it was actually Ruth.

*   *   *

My Subversive Life

I considered myself some kind of a communist in my last year of high school, and upon entering City College, I maintained this radical commitment. It was clearly bad timing. The Cold War, the struggle between America and Soviet Russia, liberalism and communism, grew increasingly intense and, given the nuclear threat, frightening. The Korean War was escalating, and the mood in the country was fearful and suspicious. The Hollywood Ten, led by the head of the Communist Party in Hollywood, John Howard Lawson (later my playwriting teacher), had gone to jail, and the Rosenbergs were about to be executed as Russian spies. It was a bad time to be a young communist. Yet that is what I defiantly became.

While my militancy had something to do with a sense of class exploitation, it was driven mostly by late adolescent rebellion and the influence of some talented older actors I admired. My hero, Chaplin, was in effect banished from America as a communist sympathizer, which only inspired me to further emulation. This is ironic because Chaplin, though vaguely socialistic and in his own terms a "citizen of the world," was never a communist. He was, in fact, known as one of the most successful and tight-fisted capitalists in Hollywood.

Despite the threatening atmosphere, I continued to blindly defend Marxism as the road to the future. I joined the Young Communist League, the YCL, the venerable youth wing of the Party founded in the 1920s, but then in the process of renaming itself the "Labor Youth League" in a futile effort to disguise its affiliation. This was during my first year at L.A. City College. I was "cleared" for membership, so to speak, first by a militant young woman named "Rita" who, ahead of her time, wore a kind of Jewish "Afro" and a man's leather jacket. I was then finally approved by a senior operative named "Irv" who welcomed me by calling me "comrade" — a rare usage in those fearful times. "Irv" struck me as a mysterious but appealing figure because he had a gaunt look similar to that of John Carradine as the doomed labor organizer in John Ford's classic movie *The Grapes of Wrath*. Clearly my imagination was always more theatrical than political.

The caution that "Rita" and "Irv" displayed in recruiting me wasn't without cause. It became clear years later that the FBI had placed an informant, if not an agent, in our City College group. This may sound melodramatic, but some of us in YCL "leadership" were sometimes followed, and on one occasion a flash photo was snapped through a window when I was leading a discussion in "Beginning Marxism." This was obviously intended as intimidation rather than detection. I still remember with embarrassment how a clearly frightened college administrator risked his job by warning me that the FBI was on campus asking questions about me. What embarrasses me to this day is how ungrateful I was to this brave man, whom I disdained then as a mere "wishy-washy liberal."

I was first elected the chairman of the City College YCL and then moved up for a short while to chair the Southern California student division. My predecessor, my friend George, had been sent to the Soviet Union for a youth congress. My new position led to some meetings with prominent Party leaders, some just released from prison after the Supreme Court ruled their convictions under the Smith Act unconstitutional; but the Communist Party was in serious trouble even without legal prosecution.

Deep divisions had appeared during and after the war, and a great number of dissidents of various ideological stripes had been expelled, some clearly as the result of direct orders from Moscow. I had only glimmerings of this at the time. Once, when I unwittingly suggested that we invite a noted left-wing writer to speak at a college gathering, I found myself chastised and informed that he was a "Trotskyite," not to be trusted. I was compliant, but I was beginning to suspect that "Trotskyite" or "right-wing opportunist" were merely coded epithets for anyone who disagreed with the Party line of the moment.

Despite this uneasiness, I supported the Party line throughout most of my college years, probably more out of obstinacy than conviction. Anti-Semitic slurs often flavored the "red-baiting" of those days, and this kept me even closer to the communist cause. My belief broke down finally more through the dialectics of honest debate with good friends — again, most of them Jewish — than through the dialectics of history.

*　　*　　*

Paradoxically, while I remained a radical committed to the "proletariat," I myself was socially ascending into a more elevated world of art, literature, and culture, even if perceived through a narrow leftist lens. My education was erratic but challenging. My assumptions may have been wrong, but, despite this or perhaps in the long run because of it, I was being forced to think.

My working-class background, however, remained significant, especially for others. I was quickly moved into leadership positions, due more to who I was than any particular ability, although my acting background had prepared me to be an effective public speaker. This may seem a startling statistic, but among all the YCL kids that I met during my years of activity, there was only one genuinely working-class white Gentile to be found — me.

We had several leaders from racial minorities, particularly blacks, but the white kids were overwhelmingly Jewish and from the middle class, from families of successful professionals such as writers and academics. While these intellectuals were loyal communists, several were also highly sophisticated wits, such as Dorothy Parker of the famous Algonquin "Round Table," and my friend George's father, who had an intimidating reputation for sharp repartee. The Party leader, John Howard Lawson, was a rather humorless but brilliant man and a celebrated avant-garde playwright. The even better-known Dalton Trumbo, I remember, had a dapper moustache and used a long cigarette holder. This may have been a prop, but it impressed me. I may have been heading for trouble, but I was moving up socially.

The YCL leaders, all older Party members, nonetheless began to prepare me to be a "cadre," a specially trained organizer, and wanted me to drop out of college and enter "the shops" — meaning one of the industrial factories such as auto or steel, where I could serve the Party by working my way up in the union ranks. Several of the Jewish guys did this, including Gershon, who, encouraged by his father, became a packing-house worker. This proved, in time, a disastrous move, politically and personally. Gershon, a hypersensitive Jewish intellectual, faced overt anti-Semitism among the other workers. He found himself quickly isolated and eventually had a nervous breakdown.

Ruth would have none of this. Her hard-working mother hadn't raised a compliant or passive daughter, and she had no intention of being married to a packing-house worker, or even a UAW shop steward. It was one of the few times in our marriage when options weren't even discussed. I was going to stay in college, period. It wasn't the first or last time that Ruth would save me from my excesses.

*　　*　　*

The Death of the Old Left

In later years I would watch the "old Hollywood" die; but first I witnessed the death of the old Left in Hollywood. Given the persistent image of Hollywood as ultra-liberal, this may seem an exaggeration, but only to those who never understood the essence of what it meant to be on the "Left."

This designation didn't suggest merely a political commitment that one could discharge through activism or a financial contribution, but indicated a self-defining relationship. It provided a framework of friends, comrades, for whom, most importantly, one was willing to sacrifice oneself. The Left was, in short, a secular religion with its own saints, martyrs, and hallowed leaders — a devotion at times so irrational that it revealed a need deeper than politics. This bears no resemblance to even the most partisan American's allegiance to a president or candidate. Stalin, Mao, or Castro in our circles elicited a loyalty so deep as to sustain the denial of any evidence of corruption or malfeasance, no matter how overwhelming.

An eager student of Marxist theory, I had at times pleased my Party instructors by offering a "class analysis" of events and the Party's positions. I began, though, to examine the Left itself from this perspective. The Party and certainly the YCL were hardly representative of the American working class. In fact, the Left was quite ignorant of how most working-class Americans really thought and lived.

Ruth was also restive. Always too mature and sensible to be tempted by fanaticism, she passively resisted her "mass org assignments" — this was the term for an obligatory involvement, usually surreptitious, in noncommunist organizations such as the Young Democrats or the NAACP. Ruth eventually became an officer in the Screen Cartoonists Union, but she participated in the other YCL activities with reluctance. I don't think it's a sexist assumption on my part to say that her election to a union post was based more on her being young and cute than militant. In any case, she never ideologically influenced Bugs Bunny or anyone else.

I was in the film school at UCLA when I broke with the Left. My "last hurrah" was my first (and only) produced play. This was written under the guidance of Kenneth Macgowan in his celebrated playwriting workshop. It was my good fortune to be accepted into Macgowan's class, and he provided me with skills that I would use for the rest of my career as a writer. I was doubly fortunate because I had previously attended John Howard Lawson's workshop, sponsored by a Party front organization. Lawson's teachings were highly ideological at that time, so much so that I began, even then, to question some of his judgments. For instance, Arthur Miller, though an "unfriendly witness" himself and later lionized as such, had apparently displeased the Party and was thoroughly denounced as "bourgeois." But Lawson, a highly intelligent man and a true scholar despite his rigidity, had provided me with a solid foundation in dramatic structure and some good analytical tools. I was the beneficiary of Lawson's structuralism and Macgowan's greater emphasis on characterization, which were, in fact, complementary.

My play that Macgowan's workshop produced was an indirect but not-too-subtle denunciation of the blacklist, which, though I never imagined it at the time, would soon be part of my own story. The play was competent enough to be singled out for praise in an anthologist's review of West Coast theater that year. My thesis screenplay, on the other hand, not only was obviously communist propaganda but was based on a short story from "Masses and Mainstream," the official Party journal. It was quickly suppressed by the senior faculty, one of whom admitted to me privately that it was simply too risky for them during those years. They were very generous to me, though, and allowed me a second chance to write a thesis work, which I could direct.

The final break with the Party was, in retrospect, more farce than drama. As the chairman of the Student Division of the YCL, by then the "League," I was made responsible for distributing a new "youth magazine" that the Party had created. Unfortunately, this magazine was aimed at "working-class youth," at least in the imagination of Party leaders. This meant that it had hot-rod cars as the main theme of the first (and only) issue. It even had a hot-rod on the cover. I tried to explain that it would be difficult for us to meet our sales quota (arbitrarily determined without consultation) for a hot-rod magazine. You must understand that not only our university members but those students with whom they frequently debated were the "bright kids," with stereotypical unruly hair, glasses, and heavy briefcases. If the magazine had featured articles concerning the influence of Hegel on the young Marx or analyzing Lenin's denunciation of Kautsky, we would have had some chance at circulation. But hot-rods? No.

Not only were my concerns dismissed, but as soon as our student division delegation was seated at the League's county assembly, we were harshly denounced by some guy from New York who excoriated us, predictably, as "bourgeois." We were elitists who considered ourselves superior to "working people" and — I don't remember exactly — probably "right-wing opportunists" as well. This guy, who looked like a very short Trotsky, got really worked up, and so we "elitists" just sat and took it. But I do remember looking down at my shoes, the only safe spot to gaze, and silently concluding, abruptly but definitively, *That's it.* If the Party leaders, several of whom I truly respected, were so out of touch with reality, then how could I continue to commit my life and future into their hands? The time had come to leave.

Ruth was delighted with my conclusion.

I never resigned. I simply faded away. The following year, Khrushchev revealed the extent of Stalin's crimes at the Twentieth Congress of the Soviet Party, and though it was hardly his intention, he confirmed the criminal nature of the regime itself. The CIA or someone got hold of the text and released it to the rest of the world. Stalin's murderous deeds, and actually those of Lenin as well, were even worse than the reactionary "yellow press" had imagined. The suppression of the Hungarian revolt came in the same year, 1956, and as a political force and certainly as a source of hope, the Left was over. The "soft left" of the honest democratic socialists and others would survive, but the historic Left, the militant inheritors of Robespierre's violent dream, was, to use one of their own favorite words, moribund. It would take another three decades before we could celebrate the funeral.

I encountered some of my old comrades in the aftermath. Most had quickly followed me out; some were bitter. Jerry, a quiet kid from a genuinely Jewish working-class family, members of the radical furriers union, had gone to the Soviet Union just before the roof fell in and found such overt anti-Semitism that he didn't have to wait to hear Khrushchev's speech.

A few held out. Herb, a sweet guy protected by an invincible innocence, told me that the Hungarian uprising and the denunciations of Stalin were both the deplorable work of "fascists." Near campus, I met another couple, both loyal "red diaper babies" trying to hang on to their faith, who quizzed me cautiously about my political status. I was candid with them, and they, in turn, were trusting enough to tell me that following my unannounced departure, Party leaders had put out the word that I had been an FBI agent all along. This was a familiar pattern. Before executing the old Bolsheviks, Stalin had made them all confess that they had been "British agents." I just laughed. I don't know what they believed or didn't, and by that point, I didn't really care.

*　　*　　*

One of the most myopic deficits of the Hollywood Left in my day had been its attempt to "explain" the anti-Semitism that persisted even after the exposure of the horrors of the Holocaust. What surfaced among Hollywood radicals, fed by Marx and Freud, was the notion that anti-Semitism was either a symptom of the corrupting influence of capitalism or a sign of deep personal neurosis. In either case, the prejudice would in time be overcome by either revolution or prolonged therapy. Sadly, the first of these illusions was dispelled by the emergence of virulent anti-Semitism in the Soviet Union. Freud's bias against religion and his ambivalence about his own Jewish identity may not refute a psychoanalytical theory about anti-Jewish prejudices, but, in any case, no "cure" was forthcoming.

*   *   *

A writer friend of mine, a dedicated leftist with a strong sense of his Jewish identity, collaborated with John Howard Lawson during Lawson's later years. "Jack" Lawson was, as I've indicated, the head of the Communist Party in Hollywood, the first president of the Screen Writers Guild, and a formidable intellectual. Despite his reputation as a hard-line Party disciplinarian — Budd Schulberg spurned him as the "grand poo-bah" — Lawson was also a genuine scholar. He once gave Ruth and me a signed copy of his book, *The Hidden History*, a thoroughly Marxist reading of history, but a thoughtful one. A graduate of Williams College, Jack, who came from a prosperous Jewish family, had been socially assimilated before he was politically radicalized. My friend told me that Lawson, in a rare personal moment, once lamented, "I'd like to do it all over again, and know that I was a Jew." I have no way of verifying this story, but there is no reason for my friend to have invented it.

What had Jack Lawson in his last years intuited about his own life and Jewishness, and, even more, what had he sensed might have been the true "hidden history" that had somehow eluded him?

CHAPTER FOUR

Traveling Light

I graduated from the UCLA film school, then one of only three in the country, and faced a new challenge — finding a job. Despite the relatively few college grads in cinema at that time, Hollywood jobs were scarce unless you had either studio or union connections. I had neither.

I've had a lifelong fascination with reality. Even simply the notion that there is something "real" has always intrigued me. This was sometimes an inadequate compass, but it did lead me to initially want to make documentaries, and, more important, to seek a larger world outside of Hollywood, perhaps one where I might eventually feel at home.

I had an opportunity to make my first documentary, one of a dozen or so that I would later make, when a non-profit organization that sponsored films about what was then termed "drug addiction" gave me the opportunity to write and direct.

I also had the opportunity to spend a full day with a then-unemployed but genuine movie star. He had generously volunteered his services as our narrator. His name was Ronald Reagan. With his wife, Nancy, he graciously hosted Ruth and me and the crew at their home while we recorded the track. He displayed great skills, including being a quick read, that explained his success and would mark his even more remarkable future. Their maid was off that day, and so Nancy made us all tuna-fish sandwiches. Funny, the things you remember.

*   *   *

The first real job I secured in the media was also in documentary work. This was as a cameraman and later as the associate producer of *Nightwatch*, the first "police reality" show on TV. The filming was a formidable technological challenge because at that time, the mid-fifties, film light sensitivity was limited, and video was unknown.

Nightwatch proved a valuable experiment in technique, but it was even more valuable as an experience. Recording actual crime scenes and investigations opened my eyes to urban reality. For over a year I explored the world of violent crime, addiction, and prostitution. In time, I paid the price of becoming somewhat callous, a consequence of prolonged exposure to that dark world. Late one night I filmed an interview with a stabbing victim in the back of a car in a Venice slum, not realizing the seriousness of his wounds. He died before reaching the hospital.

I was receiving a valuable education in the highly unromantic nature of crime and its severe effects on all involved. At that time this was new to me, but it was a grim world I would often enter in the coming years, first as a social worker and decades later as a prison chaplain. I witnessed the brutality and racism of some officers as well as their genuine compassion and bravery. These experiences became the basis of much of my TV writing in subsequent years.

A couple of years followed during which I made documentaries for television, for the most part "quicky" travel films that early TV needed to fill the many unprogrammed hours. It was a great education because I traveled not only to Mexico, Brazil, and Canada but to often-remote parts of America. This provided an opportunity to meet a great variety of Americans, who, in the days before TV flattened our speech, spoke with differing and nearly indecipherable accents. We almost needed a translator when filming "hillbillies" in the then-isolated Ozarks. Some still made their own musical instruments as well as the more profitable "moonshine" whiskey.

Brazil in the fifties was poor, unstable, and exciting. Brazilians were just beginning a musical innovation that merged Latin rhythms with jazz. Called *bossa nova*, it would quickly become popular around the world, and we heard these enchanting rhythms on the streets of Rio's slums as well as in their celebrated nightclubs.

Mexico was an even more lasting and inspiring adventure. Tracing Cortés's invasion route from Vera Cruz to Mexico City, we made a documentary about Mexican history, filming ancient ruins and the-then openly exposed statuary that would later be protected in Mexico's magnificent Anthropology Museum. I spent several days in a coastal fishing village near Vera Cruz, filming the lives of the people, drifting out at dawn on long canoes with the fishermen, who cast huge nets to bring in their catch.

We once made our way up a primitive dirt road into the Sierra Madre to film sixteenth-century Franciscan missions still being used as churches. This rural poverty was stark, and it outraged me, strengthening my already strong bias against religion. I blamed the Catholic Church in particular for somehow inducing an acceptance of these appalling conditions. Yet I fell in love with Mexico and Mexicans, and fifty years later would not only make Mexico my home but, as a Catholic, attend daily mass at one of the equally venerable churches.

Adventures in the Texas panhandle, a trip down the Mississippi, and exploring the historic colonial villages of New England opened my eyes to the great variety of ways of life within America itself. Ruth often accompanied and assisted me, taking some remarkable and artful photographs of our locales. On one trip to the Big Apple, we were able to visit her family members still living in the old Flatbush neighborhood of her youth. Ruth visited her father's grave for the first time since her childhood. While moved by these experiences, she had no desire to return to New York. She was a sun-tanned Californian now, and she had too many painful memories of poverty and discrimination to want to linger in "the old neighborhood" for long.

This early work was exciting but paid poorly, and I would soon have a family to support: Ruth was pregnant with our first daughter, Teresa. I still also had ambitions to make "real movies," so I began to write, seriously and regularly, stories and screenplays, hoping to find an agent and then a job as a writer. Success came with surprising quickness — with failure following on its heels.

*   *   *

Exiled

The blacklist didn't sneak up on me. It knocked on my door repeatedly. The process began when I refused to sign a loyalty oath required for induction into the army. I had no enthusiasm for entering the armed forces, but I was willing to serve, despite my vaguely pacifist convictions. The problem was that the "oath" wasn't simply a pledge of allegiance. It was actually a sworn affidavit that one had never belonged to any of a long list of "subversive" organizations, mostly thinly disguised communist "fronts." I had not only belonged to several but had been a leader in at least a couple, including the YCL.

I was in a difficult position, similar in some ways to those in Hollywood caught up in the ideological strife of the HUAC (House Un-American Activities Committee) congressional investigations. I was estranged from the Party — though, looking back, not sufficiently enough to see the whole picture — but I was unwilling to comply with demands I considered unfair and even unconstitutional. I still considered myself "on the Left" — just not a left that quite existed at the moment. In any case, I couldn't sign the oath and most certainly wouldn't comply with the real test: I wouldn't provide names.

I was then officially declared a security risk to the government of the United States. This was scary. I don't think I'd ever taken myself quite that seriously. It was also ridiculous. For all of our youthful foolishness in YCL and other similar organizations, there was never any thought of committing a crime, even a misdemeanor, much less anything treasonous. Subsequently, in a last futile effort to avoid the blacklist, I told the FBI that I would willingly testify at any open trial or hearing under oath if criminal charges were brought against anyone I knew. This was desperation on my part. The script was being written by Kafka, not Jefferson.

After their repeated visits to my friends and employers, which unnerved all of them, I finally confronted two of the interrogators in person. They were from army intelligence and came to the studio where I was employed making TV documentaries. I was angered by what appeared to be a naked attempt at intimidation and told them so in a long speech filled with indignant anger. They were taken aback. They actually didn't know who I was.

One of my friends, an aspiring filmmaker and only vaguely a leftist and never a member of anything, had, in a moment of unimaginable stupidity, given the army my name as a character reference. He was hoping to serve his duty by making films for the Signal Corps. Appalled at the possible consequences for this dear cluck, I quickly explained to the two baffled army officers that I myself was having some trouble with security clearance, but assured them that my friend had no political history whatsoever. It was the truth, but I'm not sure what it told them about his level of intelligence. It must have worked. He spent two years making films for the Signal Corps and, clearly talented, went on to be a distinguished film editor in Hollywood.

There was one other incident that was gratifying in the midst of the enveloping disaster. My employer, the wealthy son of a notorious right-wing publisher, was an easygoing guy who had used his father's money to become a minor TV personality, mostly hosting travel films. He had given me my first professional opportunities as a director and producer — valuable credits, though in lieu of decent pay. Unbeknownst to me, the FBI had made several visits to our studio offices to inquire about my loyalty, greatly agitating the secretary, a devout Republican. My boss, when told of this, did a remarkable thing. He called me into his office and confronted me. He asked me directly if I was some kind of a communist or an otherwise disloyal or dangerous person. He was the only person during the whole of that time who ever had the guts to confront me directly.

I appreciated his directness and reciprocated. I told him that I had been involved in left-wing politics in college, that I had no such affiliation at present, and that the problem was not that I declined to affirm my loyalty but that I refused to give the names of others once similarly involved. I made it clear that this would be my position even if it cost me my job. He was satisfied. It seemed to him that not providing names to the government didn't seem wrong under the circumstances. "To hell with them!" was his conclusion, and I went back to work. I think he saw the issue as a question of individual rights versus government intrusion. He was taking a very conservative position, for which I was certainly grateful.

*   *   *

A short time later, I had even better good fortune. A professor at the UCLA film school, the one who had given me my second chance at a thesis film, recommended me for a job as a story reader. It was my first real break in mainstream Hollywood. I was hired as a part-time story reader on the Loretta Young Show, a popular dramatic anthology program hosted by and occasionally starring the still-lovely Academy-award-winning actress. Loretta was planning to film some episodes in Europe the next season, and my assignment was to find the right kind of stories, which I did diligently. This position also gave me my first chance to spend time on a sound stage watching real professionals at work.

The bigger break came when, using my newly acquired access, I "spec-ed" a script for the show, the industry term for writing without pay, a practice discouraged by the Writers Guild but frequently the only way in for new writers. To my astonished delight, Loretta read it herself, liked it, and bought it. I remember seeing her comment written on the cover page: "He writes well, doesn't he!" It was a major turning point. I joined the Writers Guild and got an agent. I was finally what I wanted to be: a professional Hollywood writer.

That same year I also became a father when Teresa was born. The birth of a child is never bad timing, but it presented a challenge. Ruth left her work in the animation industry to take care of Terry, and for the first time I was to be the main support of the family. Fortunately, I quickly got a second assignment from Loretta Young and wrote what I believe was an even better script. My friends in the story department were pleased and proud of me.

The FBI agents came calling, it seemed, in a matter of days.

I now had a great deal at stake. It was no longer a matter of youthful defiance of authority with a touch of romantic daring thrown in. I now had the beginnings of a long-sought career and a family to support. So, for the first time, when the two FBI agents came to the door, I asked them to come in.

Again, it was useless. In effect, I admitted my past affiliations. "I know that you know what I did in the past," I told them, probably more pleadingly than was becoming, "and what organizations I belonged to." They clearly knew everything. The dossier from my army security hearing was complete with details of every activity, more evidence that they had penetrated our group. The dossier even charged me with having "a close and persistent relationship" with Ruth. This was "officialese" meaning guilt by association with another member of the YCL. We certainly were guilty of association. Teresa was proof of that.

"So you must also know," I continued, "that I quit years ago and have nothing to do with anything political now." One of the agents, the talker, made the usual case for the government. I had to give them the names of everyone I knew in the past, and trust them as to what use they would make of this information. I knew that most of the YCL kids, probably almost all, were also disillusioned and disaffiliated, and that several were in the sciences and probably seeking government security clearances. In any case, I wasn't going to put anyone else at risk. Again, I offered to testify at any trial or hearing, any procedure that gave people the right to defend themselves.

"What do you think Loretta Young is going to say about this?" the agent asked. I'll never forget that question. It came like a shot to the guts. I never knew what Loretta knew or thought about any of it. Nor do I think my friends in the story department would have willingly harmed me or even cooperated in doing so. In those days, the blacklist worked primarily through the advertising agencies that controlled the shows. Names went on a list, and that was that. Loretta, who knew nothing of me personally, wouldn't have had a say in any of it. But the times had made people fearful. My phone calls were never answered, and I never spoke with her or anyone else on the show again. Neither of the scripts, though paid for, were produced.

In retrospect, the only surprise was how long it had taken for me to be blacklisted. Most of the "red scare" events, such as the HUAC hearings and the Hiss trial, took place in the late forties and early fifties. It isn't widely understood that the blacklist as an institution, so to speak, lasted until a lawsuit brought it down in 1961. I was blacklisted in the late fifties almost, I suspect, as an afterthought, or perhaps as the last gasp of a bureaucratic procedure. Again, I felt that the story credit should have gone to Kafka.

My agent, Ilse Lahn, a wily survivor herself of European political intrigues (she had driven an ambulance during the Spanish Civil War), was able to quickly confirm my blacklisted status. There were at that time two attorneys well-known in Hollywood as conduits to the House Committee and, I guess, the FBI. One arranged for the "friendly witnesses" to clear themselves, and the other helped the more reluctant — usually celebrities — to possibly "make a deal" with the Committee and then give only names of those previously identified. The latter attorney could only confirm my status.

I was blacklisted, and, maybe worse, I knew it.

*   *   *

The Myths of the Blacklist

I have seldom written about my blacklist years, primarily because I never wanted to inflict further pain on those who had suffered a similar fate. Most of those I knew were writers, many years later my fellow stalwarts in the Writers Guild. They had paid a much higher price than I had, losing established positions in the middle or even at the end of their careers. I felt real affection for some of the "old reds," many as good-hearted as they were ideologically muddled, though I could no longer respect their political judgments. We had, after all, been apologists, however naïvely, for one of the most brutal and tyrannical regimes in history.

But a myth — actually, several myths — have persisted about the blacklist and the role of the Communist Party in Hollywood, and myths invariably distort a history from which we might learn some lessons. I'll try to puncture some without too many deep thrusts.

Though frequently described as such, the investigation into "subversive activities" in Hollywood was not a "witch hunt." Witches are most often figments of a troubled imagination; in Hollywood there was, in reality, a communist agenda and a largely covert operation attempting to gain influence in, if not control of, the Hollywood guilds and unions. The hysteria, injustices, and opportunism that characterized the times shouldn't obscure this reality.

The later political mythifying of this postwar period has been extensive and not limited to Hollywood or the blacklist. HUAC had its origins in an investigation of pro-Nazi activities and was only one of over thirty committees that investigated corruption and "subversion" after the war. This was, in part, clearly a partisan onslaught aimed at the New Deal and Franklin Roosevelt's successor, Harry Truman.

HUAC, in particular, was dominated by publicity-seeking opportunists, some of whom went to jail themselves for corruption. But the exposure of communist influence in government as well as Soviet espionage led to revelations that were disturbing to everyone, and not just political grandstanding. The ex-GIs entering postwar politics were hypersensitive to any form of "appeasement," and many compared Roosevelt's power-sharing agreement with Stalin at Yalta to the Munich compromise with Hitler, a concession that led to the war and the deaths of so many of their buddies. Most of all they feared another Pearl Harbor, this time a strike by the Soviets using atomic weapons.

One of the young congressmen leading the charge against the Truman administration, blaming its "appeasement" policy for the fall of China to the communists, was also one of the first "red hunters" to receive media attention, particularly regarding communist influence in the labor unions. In fact, he claimed in his campaigns at the time to have been among the first to expose communist subversion. This was the "Cold War warrior" John F. Kennedy. His brother Robert, now equally idealized by liberals, worked as a legal investigator and interrogator for the Kennedy family friend, Senator Joe McCarthy, and passionately defended McCarthy's notorious and later censured "red hunt."

All this proves, I guess, is that myths die hard.

*   *   *

The blacklist in Hollywood was no myth, however, in the sense that it was a very real and damaging procedure that ended the careers and shattered the lives of many people. This was, as I saw it, immoral if not illegal in that only a few had the opportunity to defend themselves or to clarify their actions or beliefs. Unfortunately, many who did have the opportunity to openly declare their convictions, such as those called before the various investigating committees, did so without candor or conviction. It was understandable that the Fifth Amendment — the right to refuse to testify for fear of self-incrimination — would be employed to avoid jail sentences, but, as a result of this tactic, there was no declaration or defense of the revolutionary ideas to which all true communists subscribed. The impression was given — and meant to be given — that only liberal ideals of free speech and association were at risk. This was hardly a Marxist or revolutionary stance. While it was never debated publicly, many in the Party were dismayed by this defense strategy. My friend George's father, a loyal communist and among the first to be blacklisted, wrote a scathing letter to Party leaders and resigned his membership. Not a few felt that either the First Amendment should be the sole basis of defense, or a bold and genuine revolutionary statement should be made.

The myth that this strategy engendered, and that still persists, is that the blacklist was aimed at free-thinking liberals and not at the Communist Party. This was, of course, the "Party line," but, beyond the deceit, the myth obscured then, as it does now, the historical significance of these political events and not just in the United States. This is what our myths often do. They allow us to disguise the truth from ourselves.

The larger story that was taking place was far more important than the Hollywood episodes. As the Cold War began, the Soviet Union, joined by communist China, dominated much of the world, and even their strongest opponents felt some inevitability about the ultimate triumph of Marxist ideology. Yet at the very time of the Hollywood hearings, the Communist Movement was beginning to unravel. Within less than a decade, particularly following the exposures at the Soviet Party's Twentieth Congress in 1956 and the growing revolts in the Eastern Bloc, the international Left — Marxist, Leninist, Maoist — was starting to erode as a political force. More important, it was dying as a faith, a quasi-religion, that offered hope for the future.

The fervor in Hollywood over an alleged "witch hunt" averted our gaze from a painful reality, a turn of history with not only enormous political implications but artistic ones as well. To this day, many in Hollywood fail to acknowledge the moral and spiritual dimensions of this historic struggle against unbridled power, and, significantly, few Americans have ever tried to dramatize it on the screen.

The blacklisted writer in the central myth, then, isn't a communist following Party directives, but a self-sacrificing free agent. It is an admirable ideal turned into romance, something Hollywood does well. The truth is, it took courage to defy HUAC and the government, but it took perhaps even more courage for some at least to defy the Party. For the first, you lost your job; for the latter, you lost your friends and reputation. I chose the former course, didn't cooperate, and lost my job; so I'm not proposing a counter-myth, only the acknowledgment of unpleasant truths. Myths, in the long run, do a disservice to us all.

CHAPTER FIVE

The Path of Radical Romanticism

What I experienced in my mid-century "Jewish world" as a deflated political idealism was, I'm convinced, something very old by then. What we shared was a view of reality that began and ended as a rejection of "the world as it is." What we were experiencing was a spiritual malaise. There was something broken-hearted about it.

Philosophers have cited this rejection of a "given world" as increasingly common in modern times; but we need to make a distinction. To reject "the world as it is" could suggest either insanity or sanctity. Saint Francis and many other holy men and women rejected "the world" and sought radically different ways of life. What I'm describing is something between genuine idealism and a disabling illusion, and often a mix of the two.

This was far from being an exclusively Jewish disorder; but it had deep roots in Jewish hopes and, even more, in Jewish fears. Less than a philosophy yet much deeper than a mood, what we experienced, at its root, was a form of despair.

Because I believe there is something to learn from this, I'm going to risk a diagnosis — inadequate, to be sure — but one drawn from experience as much as the history books. But we have to start with some history.

* * *

Something restless and disquieting, beyond anti-Semitism, became pervasive at the very height of the modern era — that is, at the end of the nineteenth century and the first decade of the twentieth. Many in the intellectual and literary world, disillusioned with Napoleon's tyranny and resistant to bourgeois materialism, had turned against society and its norms. This modern alienation had been expressed in the Romantic Movement and later in literary forms such as Symbolism and Surrealism. Artists and poets rejected the narrow rationalism and materialism of the modern period and sought a deeper meaning of life. In some cases, they rejected rationality itself, exploring the unconscious, the spontaneous, and irrational, and found their truths in emotion, nature, and sexuality.

The most prominent of the early Romantic poets were initially Goethe, Schiller, and Heine in Germany, and Byron, Keats, and Shelley in England; they were later followed by Symbolists such as Baudelaire and Mallarmé in France. Beethoven, Schumann, Berlioz, and most particularly Richard Wagner expressed this passionate estrangement in music. The movement created what became a stereotypical image of the artist and poet as a doomed and isolated rebel.

The Romantic age saw a growing rupture in social and political life as well. As Marx predicted, with considerable overconfidence, capitalism by the 1890s was creating the seeds of its potential destruction. The peasant revolts and artisan revolts against industrialization, the Luddites, and others, gave way to even more violent upheavals among the industrial working class. By the end of the century, strikes were becoming frequent, and, more ominously, a worldwide anarchist movement incited assassinations of political leaders, including American president McKinley in 1899. An anarchist's shooting of Crown Prince Franz Ferdinand in 1914 ignited the First World War, beginning the dissolution of modern European society.

This many-faceted revolt would carve a path in the Jewish world that I call "radical Romanticism," an often extreme rejection not merely of the status quo but of any conceivable social order. The anarchist Emma Goldman admitted, "I cannot imagine any society which I could accept!" It is not difficult to perceive the underlying polarity in this sentiment — the rejection of a world that would never accept Emma.

The most significant and long-lasting such movement was begun by Karl Marx, a German Jew who briefly flirted with Christianity while at the university but then, in effect, founded his own religion, Marxism, complete with an anticipated apocalypse followed by an earthly heaven called "communism."

My own perception of "radical Romanticism" as the engine of modern revolution is not a theoretical argument but one based on my personal experience. However, commentators such as Isaiah Berlin and George Steiner have held similar views.

Among the more astute commentators on Romanticism as a historical development, Isaiah Berlin was arguably the pre-eminent Jewish intellectual of the late modern period. It was Berlin, an Oxford don, who pointed out Romanticism's deepest and most ironic contradictions. The Romantic Hero, exemplified by Napoleon as well as the poets, embodied a nationalist impulse that, in time, negated the Enlightenment ideal of universality. The failure of the French Revolution to establish either peace or justice resulted in the spread of an irrationalism more powerful and enduring than the cult of Pure Reason. Most ironically, the Romantic quest for unlimited personal freedom spawned both fascism and communism, twins separated at birth but united in their opposition to any genuine individualism.

Berlin concluded that "Romantic irrationalism" had, however, revealed that "the ends of men are many," unpredictable, and, in fact, incompatible, and that the concept of a "perfect society" is "incoherent in principle."

*   *   *

What I'm calling "radical Romanticism" has a long history. Over time, it became an outlook that negated the inherent goodness of creation, and this led, in turn, to an equally radical rejection of tradition and religion. Yet, paradoxically, this negation has its deepest roots in Judaism and Christianity, both sources of a desire for and anticipation of a "new creation."

The earliest Christians experienced the promise of a new and eternal life arising out of the resurrection of Jesus, and this was translated by many into an expectation of an immediate "end time" and the rejection of a fallen world. Similar Jewish apocalyptic visions can be found in their earliest literature, and the Kabbalists conceived a cosmic transformation taking place beyond human history.

The emancipation of European Jewry, on the other hand, led to a persistent tendency to translate Jewish traditional thought into modern idioms. To some degree, this development was in open competition with Christian beliefs. Rabbi Leo Baeck saw the Christian proclamation of Jesus as the Messiah as primarily "premature" and believed that, once corrected, Christians would accept the revelation as interpreted by Judaism. However, even in his formulation, the Messiah was still expected and would bring the promised redemption.

The familiar saying "The Messiah will come today if you will listen to his voice" expresses the traditional Jewish and Christian concept that placed the Messiah both within and beyond historical time. There had always been some conflict among Jewish thinkers, as well, as to whether the *Mashiach*, the Anointed One, indicated a specific person or the onset of a final age. In this respect, historical development and salvation were interwoven.

The Jewish messianic tradition has deep roots but was expressed most fully in the Middle Ages. While it was rarely voiced in terms of direct personal messianic claims, there were many revelations or visions that anticipated the coming of a messianic age. Linked to a need and demand for repentance, this was a theme in the work of the most notable spiritual masters, including Joseph Karo and the Ba'al Shem Tov. Two quite legitimate religious leaders, however, were perceived as near-messianic figures themselves — Rabbi Vital in the sixteenth century and Rabbi Safrin of Komarno in the nineteenth. These were hardly insignificant figures. Chaim Vital was an important disciple of Isaac Luria, who founded a major school of Jewish mysticism, and Rabbi Safrin was one of the recognized Hasidic masters of his time.

Later Jewish messianic sects expressed the persistent hope, as human as it is Jewish, for an ultimate deliverance. Some of the "Frankists," followers of the eighteenth-century self-proclaimed prophet Jacob Frank, even perceived Napoleon as the Messiah. Frank himself had claimed to be the successor to both King David and Sabbatai Zevi, the most controversial and destructive of the false prophets. Possibly suffering from what we would now describe as bipolar disorder, Zevi was a charismatic figure prone to deep depressions. His messianic claims drew great numbers to him in the seventeenth century, but, threatened with execution by the Turkish sultan, he converted to Islam. This naturally led to mass disillusionment and restrained further messianic claims among Jews for some time to come.

*　　*　　*

These messianic hopes, however, never died and, in my judgment, were the roots of what I'm describing as radical Romanticism.

The utopian politics of the modern era, and particularly the revolutionary ideologies which shaped the lives of those of us on the Left in Hollywood, found widespread support among European Jews while at the same time fomenting the ire of their enemies. In time, Jews would be attacked from all sides. Revolutionary socialists in France such as Proudhon and Lassalle, himself a Jew, denounced Jews as proto-capitalists, and Marx and Engels deplored "Jewish influence" as inherently supportive of entre-preneurial capitalism. In time, this "left-wing" antagonism would become as lethal for Jews as the racist barbarism of the Nazis, and the seeds were equally as deep. Nonetheless, the Jewish messianic impulse, inherent in the tradition, would be channeled into radical politics for much of the next century.

This messianic vision has always been related to a desire for a tran-scendent commonality. Jews, perhaps more than others, have sought a universality that would transcend yet not wholly invalidate Judaism. Rabbi David Novak identifies a quasi-messianic streak in German liberal socialism at the end of the nineteenth century, another effort to achieve a unity that could escape the problematic limits of Jewish particularity. The Jewish path, nevertheless, remains inescapably particular as a concrete communal experience.

What was significant in my time was that this messianic impulse was seldom if ever acknowledged as such, and certainly not in Hollywood. The "why" is obvious. The charge of Jewish complicity in modern revolutions, whatever the motivation, opened yet another door for condemnation and persecution. However, the recognition of "Jewishness" as an essential in-gredient in modern revolutionary thought, if seen in perspective, dispels the notions of conspiracies based on self-interest. Jews, more than anyone else, were the victims of this illusory vision.

Many who were hostile to the Jews, most particularly Hitler and the Nazis, were well aware of this vulnerability. To associate Jews with wealth and capitalism was a predictable and effective ploy on Hitler's part be-cause it played to popular prejudice. The attack on Jews was also advanta-geous for Hitler because it allowed him to suppress his radical rivals. One must remember that the Nazis were "National Socialists" appealing to the same deracinated mass base as the communists. A common saying during the 1930s, when the Nazis and communists fought frequent violent street battles, was "Scratch a brown shirt and you'll find a red one." Just as he had eliminated the early Nazi radicals, Hitler was dividing to conquer and us-ing the Jews to do so.

There were unique left-wing spins on this theme as well. Isaac Deutscher, Leon Trotsky's follower and biographer, wrote *The Non-Jewish Jew* in 1958, arguing that revolutionary Jews, such as Trotsky and Rosa Luxemburg, were in the true Jewish prophetic tradition. Deutscher ar-gued, furthermore, that Jews as revolutionaries now transcend history. In that this suggests surpassing the limits of class consciousness, it is a strange and contradictory thesis for a Marxist, yet is quite consistent with the underlying messianic impulse.

*   *   *

While there have been no worse tragedies to befall the Jewish people than the mid-twentieth-century Holocaust, the fate of Jewish communists in Russia and elsewhere has had a disorienting and disheartening effect of its own — one that has lasted long after Hitler's demise. This is a chapter of history that can linger, if unexamined, like a cataract clouding our view of past events and their meaning.

CHAPTER SIX

Red: The Color of Blood

The troubling problem that we face in confronting the charge that communism was fundamentally a Jewish movement is that it is largely true.

You can see why I'm proceeding cautiously. During my own days as a young communist in the 1950s, as I recounted earlier, anti-Semitic slurs were ubiquitous among the most ardent anti-communists. Opportunistic "red scare" literature often featured photos of Jewish celebrities linked to left-wing politics, providing their original Jewish names as proof of the existence of a subversive Jewish underground.

So let me be clear at the outset about what I'm not saying. I'm not suggesting a Jewish conspiracy — or any conspiracy, for that matter — as the source of the historical developments I'm describing. Conspiracy theories may be reassuring to those who look for some secret pattern or explanation for the violent vagaries of our times, but I'm not one of them.

As we have noted, most Jews in Europe and America were neither capitalists nor communists. The Jewish leadership in the radical anarchist, socialist, and communist movements was important — indeed, crucial — but for the most part it was short-lived and, far from serving Jewish interests, led often to tragedy and destruction for Jews as well as others. And, finally, as we shall point out, there were not only a significant number of Jews who opposed the extremists but many who provided the intellectual and moral leadership that defeated communism.

However, the price of the denial of the Jewish foundation of Marxism as well as its spread by Jewish revolutionaries is not just the vulnerability laid open by the facts but the fact that we miss the essential Jewish part of the story. That it is a tragedy is one of the reasons why it is so seldom related.

*   *   *

From Hope to Despair

Let's step back for some background to this sad story.

For many of the early Jewish communists, the rejection of capitalism was not just a theoretical issue. It had been spurred by conflicts within Jewry itself as Jews were often pitted against each other in industrial conflicts in Europe and then America. It was not uncommon, for instance, to find German Jews exploiting Russian Jewish employees. It is estimated that three hundred thousand German Jews had emigrated to America before the massive wave of immigrants from the Pale of Settlement.

Despite their achievements, particularly in banking and finance, German Jews remained vulnerable and continued to strive to retain their relative status in American society. This did not create solidarity with their fellow Jews. Whatever the serious deficiencies of Marxist analysis, and they were fatal, it is true that the "class war" among Jews themselves was a factor in creating a backlash against capitalism among the immigrants.

The central Jewish role in the rise of communism is clearly evident if one simply tracks the chief ideologues, revolutionary leaders, and propagandists. In some ways, communist ideology was shaped by a prolonged Jewish quarrel. Karl Marx was the founder of the movement, but his most vocal opponents — democratic socialists, Bundists, and liberals — were often Jewish as well. There were certainly non-Jews such as Lenin and Stalin who played pivotal roles, but the original cast of the communist tragedy is disproportionately Jewish.

At the time of the 1917 October Revolution in Russia, the three top leaders, the *troika,* who were greeted with banners bearing their images, were Vladimir Lenin, Leon Trotsky, and Grigory Zinoviev, the latter two Jewish. The mere recitation of the other major leaders of the October Revolution, such as Lev Kamenev, Karl Radek, and Genrikh Yagoda, makes it clear that the original revolutionary core was a Jewish one. Stalin and his lackeys were initially second-level, not much more than bit players in the drama.

Zinoviev, the most popular leader, replaced Lenin as the head of the Comintern, the revolutionary world organization, and held the highest position in the Soviet Party until Stalin made his successful attack on him in 1927. Zinoviev was finally convicted of "treason" during the notorious

Moscow trials and executed along with his comrades Kamenev and Yagoda in 1937. Radek was also convicted in a mock trial and sent to the Gulag, where he was murdered by the KGB in 1939. This, in effect, terminated the Jewish Soviet leadership.

Among the other Jewish Bolsheviks was "Iron Felix" Dzerzhinsky, the founder of the NKVD, the Soviet secret police, and one of the most prominent heroes of the revolution. His death, probably a murder, came in 1926 and, once he was acclaimed as a martyr, cities were named for him. He was the principal architect of the Soviet regime's "organized terror" and openly proposed a policy of "extermination on the basis of class." His ferocity was outdone only by Nikolai Yezhov, known fearfully as "the bloody dwarf," who became Commissar for State Security following Yagoda. Yakov Sverdlov played a major role in the October revolt, and in 1918 supervised the slaughter of the Tsar and his entire family. Sverdlov himself was killed by an angry factory worker in 1919, and a prominent statue of him was then erected in Moscow. His son became an officer in the KGB, the successor to the NKVD.

That virtually all of these figures were Jewish was undoubtedly the basis, at least in part, of Stalin's mistrust and the bloodbaths that he perpetrated in the 1930s. Stalin's purges eliminated nearly all of the original Jewish leadership. Stalin was a murderous paranoid and an anti-Semite since his youth, but the purges also served to eliminate his most serious rivals. Among the few Jews who remained loyal to him were the most bloody-minded, such as the notorious "Iron Lazar" Kaganovich, who was found guilty, posthumously, of supervising the Ukrainian genocide.

The Jews who remained loyal communists inside the Soviet Union were increasingly compromised and at risk. Golda Meir, the Israeli Prime Minister, made a visit to Moscow after Israel's independence in 1948, and Foreign Minister Molotov's Jewish wife made the mistake of affectionately greeting her in Yiddish. For this she was sent into exile, and the servile Molotov was forced to divorce her. The motherly Golda's warm reception by Jews at a synagogue alarmed Stalin. Golda had greeted them by saying that she was glad to see that there were so many people who still knew they were Jewish.

* * *

In that the Soviet Revolution promised a universality and identity beyond ethnicity, tribe, and class, it is easy to see why communism, for many Jews, became the greatest source of Jewish hope. In time, however, Jews also became among the most severe and effective critics of the Soviet regime.

Historian Yuri Slezkine's account of the growth of anti-Semitism in postwar Russia, which he experienced as a young man, illuminates Jewish attitudes as they hardened into deep anti-Soviet antipathy. To be a Jew in the USSR by the 1960s was to be a dissident, or at least to be viewed as one. Israel's Six-Day War was important to Soviet Jews, a turning point, in that the victory became a deep source of Jewish identity and pride. Soviet Jews became "anti-Soviet" by definition because their own worldview was now becoming as nationalistic as that of the Russians.

*   *   *

This admittedly relentless summary of the history of Jewish involvement in the rise of communism and the subsequent terrors it inflicted on Jews as well as others is necessary for two reasons. It is important for contemporary American Jews, particularly those young enough to regard all this as "ancient history," to know the complexity of the Jewish role in these modern events, and then to recognize that the admitted complicity of Christians in the Holocaust and the ugly Islamist extremism of recent times are not the only examples of how thwarted and distorted ideals can lead to violence and hatred.

*   *   *

Beyond my own political experiences, my personal insight into this deep-seated Jewish revolutionary attitude came from my close friendship with Ruth's stepfather, the extraordinary "Papa Sol," who outlived Ruth's mother by several years, and became our true *pater familias*. Sol's story was both typical and remarkable.

Born into great poverty in a small *shetl* somewhere deep in the Pale, he saw a favorite uncle murdered by Cossacks during a pogrom. As a very young man, he migrated first to Trieste, dealing primarily, as far as I could determine, in black-market goods during the post-revolutionary chaos. He then went to Romania before finally making it to America, where he toiled, literally, as a street peddler of toys and trinkets. Relatively uneducated yet brilliant — a master chess player — he came to California and became a wholesaler in toys and sundry goods, finally buying and building warehouses. His shrewd real-estate holdings made him a millionaire after the Second World War.

Papa Sol was an exemplary American success story, the poor immigrant who made more than good. Yet to his dying day, Papa Sol was a Bolshevik at heart. Not that he ever belonged to any party or even gave money to any cause, but emotionally his sympathies remained with the Soviets and their revolution of hope. He had financed the escape of two sisters, at least, from the Pale; but when much of the rest of his family later emigrated to Israel, he never really forgave them. His attitude wasn't rational, especially considering his own flight and the growing anti-Semitism at that time; but somehow his family had betrayed the dream by deserting the promised land.

Papa Sol and I were very close for many reasons. My communist background, though I never concealed my disaffection, gave me a distinction that others lacked. I had taken risks, though hardly on the level of his own. He enjoyed arguing with me, and I loved him too much to want to cut deeply into his illusions. I don't think he ever understood my religious leanings, and I never pushed it. He disdained religion, especially Judaism, as "all nonsense!" Sadder still, he viewed his own Jewishness as simply a misfortune that he had to overcome. He told me that he thought it was a kind of "mistake" that there had ever been a Jewish people because all it had led to was suffering.

As a young man, Sol had been in a crowd in Odessa that had listened to an oration by Leon Trotsky, probably then head of the Red Army. Sol wasn't interested in becoming a revolutionary, only in survival by escape. But I can imagine, at least, some inner conflict that was never resolved. The embers of hope that perhaps only the very young experience seemed never to have died in him.

*   *   *

Red Roses and Thorns

Radical Romanticism had a decidedly feminine face as well, and one that provided inspiration for many Jewish women in America, or at least shaped many attitudes, including most certainly those of women in Hollywood.

The challenge of assimilation often was felt most acutely by Jewish women. Men engaged in the workplace might learn to adapt and, as with

Ruth's grandfather, soon pick up some English, but the women at home often remained in ghetto-like isolation. Many of the younger women as they became educated naturally rebelled, and some few became highly radicalized.

One of the most charismatic and representative figures of the high modern era was the anarchist Emma Goldman, later romanticized by the radicals of the sixties as a proto-hippy liberationist. Goldman was all that and more. She held almost every anti-institutional attitude of the period and anticipated some to come.

Emma came to the United States in 1885 and was involved in revolutionary activities until deported to the Soviet Union in 1917. By the early 1920s she was so disheartened by what she saw there that in 1923 she wrote a book, *My Disillusionment in Russia*. This launched a new career for her as a lecturer, now lionized by upper-class intellectuals disenchanted by war, the Depression, and capitalism.

In some respects, Goldman is a model of the contradictions that overwhelmed radicals then and later. She rejected not just normative socialism but any conceivable form of government, proclaiming that "I can never work within the State!" Her personal life was a mess. Her longtime lover Alexander Berkman committed suicide, and she never again found a stable relationship. She loved primarily her own words, describing the experience of giving a "fighting speech" as "ecstatic." She borrowed terms like "life force" from Henri Bergson, but was never a systematic thinker, much less a philosopher. "If I can't dance, I won't join your revolution" is an oft-cited quote, popular during the years of the counterculture — an appealing sentiment for college radicals, certainly, but Emma never said it.

Her personal behavior and aggressive sexuality scandalized intellectuals such as Bertrand Russell and H. G. Wells, and many others also refused to accept Goldman's criticism of the still-idealized USSR. Goldman's own account of her meeting with Lenin reflected the deluded, gaga view of that systematic executioner as a "great man." Back in the U.S. in the early thirties, Goldman hobnobbed with the likes of H. L. Mencken, Edna St. Vincent Millay, and Theodore Dreiser. Her patronage by the glitterati of the time prefigured composer Leonard Bernstein's dreamy view and patronage of the "black power" militants a half-century later. When Goldman's offer to join the London dockworkers' strike was rudely refused, she consoled herself by taking refuge in heiress Peggy Guggenheim's villa in the south of France.

Goldman was, nevertheless, a serious revolutionary who embraced power and violence as the sole means of social change. Her ideas of anarcho-syndicalism proved more appealing than Marx's theories because they provided inspiration for movements as diverse as the Mexican revolution and Mussolini's fascism. Power and violence went hand in hand throughout the century. If such radicals opposed war, it was not because of its cruelty; they opposed it only when they saw it as an instrument of the "ruling classes."

It is easy to see the appeal of "liberation," the breaking free from all restraint. In time, however, the violence, the growing flow of blood, would begin to take its toll on the dream. Rosa Luxemburg, another Jewish "Red Rose" of the era, paid a much higher price for her revolutionary fervor. Following the failed "Spartakus" uprising in Germany, an attempt to forcibly create a Soviet-style regime in 1919, she and her companion, Karl Liebnecht, were executed. However, the "Spartakusbund" and its *Red Flag* newspaper provided the foundation of the German Communist Party. Like Goldman, Luxemburg became an icon for the radicals of the sixties, and German director Fassbinder once planned a film biography of her that was to star Jane Fonda.

While Emma Goldman and Rosa Luxemburg have been celebrated as heroines of the Left, it is illustrative of my contention — that the underlying motivation of this generation was more "radically Romantic" than political — to note the similarity in style and even personality with two other Jewish women of the modern period. They were both certainly "radicals" but, though in different ways, militants of the far Right.

Gertrude Stein, born in Oakland, California, to a prosperous Jewish family, is famous for her experimental literary efforts and, even more, for her generous support of American and other "Lost Generation" writers and artists during the twenties and thirties in Paris. She is less well-known for her support of the collaborationist Vichy regime. She was so ardent in her support that she and her famous companion, Alice Toklas, remained unmolested by the Gestapo during the war. Stein also openly admired General Franco of Spain. This is not to imply a sympathy for fascism as such, but to add a note of correction. Sometimes a rose isn't what it seems to be.

A better-known advocate of an ultra-conservative ideology is Ayn Rand, born Alice Rosenblum in St. Petersburg in 1905. Rand detested not only communism but all forms of liberalism, and voluntarily testified before the HUAC congressional committee investigating Hollywood. Like Emma and Rosa, she never considered herself Jewish, other than by accident of birth, nor was she religious in any way. Her flamboyant individualism, sexual adventures, and relentless self-promotion would have made it impossible for her and Emma Goldman to ever stay long in the same room.

*   *   *

The self-promoting theatricality of these few women shouldn't obscure the seriousness of what many Jewish women were facing and the growing dissatisfaction among women in general. It is important to distinguish the legitimate grievances from the self-indulgent veneer.

The feminist movement in postwar America was also led most conspicuously by Jewish women such as Betty Friedan and Gloria Steinem. The movement, however, had its own distinctly American flavor. After the Second World War, its primary appeal was to middle-class women seemingly caught in suburban torpor. Despite Friedan's Marxist sympathies, American feminism proved to be quite compatible with capitalism, emphasizing what would later be termed individual "empowerment" and stressing the need for equality in career opportunities far more than any new ideal of communal life. This embrace of entrepreneurial individualism, what my generation of radicals would have spurned as "careerism," led, ironically, to a kind of class warfare within feminist circles as upper-middle-class intellectuals claimed to represent the interest of working women with whom they had, in reality, little in common other than being pushed around by men.

Jewish women took the lead in the feminist movement, in part, because the role and traditional authority of Jewish men during assimilation was frequently undermined. This loss of male role models has resulted in the emergence of a type of young American male certainly not limited to Jews — bright, precocious, sensitive, and very vulnerable. What this new boy-man is *not* is a father.

The conservative critics, including women, charged the feminists with emasculating American men. In my experience, they have it backward. The feminist movement arose in reaction to this emasculation. Throughout the Industrial Revolution, men had been replaced by machines, and in modern America, then, by technology and bureaucracy. In the new technological America, there is no perceived need for masculinity, except perhaps in beer commercials.

This has confused gender relations for generations and produced anger and resentment among men, and their withdrawal from traditional male responsibilities. Women had no choice but to look to themselves for security and support. The gradual emasculation has also produced a pseudo-masculinity that indulges in sexual exploitation and violent games and fantasies.

The challenge this development presents — men unable or unwilling to assume adult roles — is obviously not just a problem for Jewish women or men, but is in many ways at the heart of the social dissolution we've all witnessed. To address this, however, we'll need a different understanding than the feminist rhetoric provides, or that of its critics to date.

* * *

The Dissidents

We need to complete this historical chapter, if not the story.

In chronicling the Jewish role in the rise of communism, we have recorded some hard truths, but they should be balanced by the long honor roll of Jewish leaders, intellectuals, and scientists who provided crucial leadership in the nearly century-long struggle that defeated communism.

Not surprisingly, many Jews disagreed with the revolution, the Party, the Soviet regime, and then often with each other.

Several of the early dissidents like Will Herberg and Isaac Don Levine were ex-communists who broke with the Party early and became its most feared and despised adversaries. Levine was among the first to expose Russian spy cells in the United States. Other staunch anti-communists were socialists and labor leaders such as Lee Pressman of the CIO and David Dubinsky of the Garment Workers. Over time, the number of Jewish political thinkers opposing communism as well as fascism grew, and many played central roles in the Cold War, including Arthur Schlesinger Jr., John F. Kennedy's advisor, and Henry Kissinger, Richard Nixon's architect of foreign policy.

Many kept their liberal credentials, though bitterly denounced by those clinging to utopian hopes, or still susceptible to communist propaganda. For the most part, the anti-communists were either praised or damned as "realists." Arthur Schlesinger played a major role in the formation of the Americans for Democratic Action, a staunchly anti-communist liberal coalition, and helped to derail Henry Wallace's bid for the presidency in 1948. Wallace, a Midwestern naïf, seemed utterly beguiled by Stalin's promises of peace. Schlesinger, the realist, reportedly remarked, "Henry seems to see Russia as a sort of Brook Farm community."

The philosopher Sidney Hook, one of the most tenacious of the American anti-communists, considered himself a genuine "Marxist" and, therefore, was detested by the Left. A self-styled "open-minded atheist," he nevertheless retained a sense of his Jewishness and noted wryly how the Jewish members of the Left-wing journal *The New Leader* could subdue the outspoken radical Dwight MacDonald, otherwise fearless, by just hinting that he was somehow "anti-Semitic." "It was the only way we could shut him up," one of them admitted.

*   *   *

Aftermath

As Teilhard de Chardin warned, it is as hard to know when something ends in historical terms as it is to fix a beginning. It is even difficult to determine what exactly is terminating.

As early as the end of the fifties, many of us had a sense of closure and wondered, after all the violence, what had been gained. Were there lessons discernible in the fading glow of the fires in Hiroshima and Nagasaki? Did the Holocaust and then the exposure of the Gulag archipelago reveal any new truth about the human condition? After a century of critical modern thought, what had we learned? Were we witnessing simply the end of the age of ideology, or sensing something more fundamental?

Few fully digestible ideas filtered down to us in Hollywood, and we ended up with attitudes rather than beliefs. But the sky wasn't falling, and we knew Chicken Little was un-American.

The postwar decades were a time of great accomplishment in the fields of civil rights and equal opportunity. Under the indispensable leadership of Martin Luther King, the Civil Rights Movement was a spiritual crusade that drew on the biblical roots of moral courage, particularly in the black communities. As did many, I spent years in the Civil Rights Movement and regret not a minute. But as we celebrated the attainment of equal rights, we were also sensing that America was teetering on the edge of a cultural and moral precipice. In many ways, it is still teetering.

In Hollywood, we used to call that a "cliff-hanger."

CHAPTER SEVEN

Movies as a Jewish Mirror

I hope I've now offered sufficient exposition and a setting for this survey. My Hollywood was a provincial company town and, for most of the time, a "Jewish town" as well, and yet it was a major force in shaping America's idea of itself. It did so by claiming to mirror American life.

But how much truth did these images reflect? Were they really fun-house mirrors that bent and distorted our self-image? For that matter, did the "Jewish town" honestly reflect the reality of Jewish life, or simply Jewish hopes and dreams?

Here's an "establishing long shot" of the movies.

*   *   *

Hollywood: Dawn to Decline

The movies were born when our families, Ruth's and mine, were still a long way from Hollywood; yet their hopes and desires were reflected on the screen from the beginning of this new art. Early movies often de-picted Christian faith and piety. Passion plays were among the first theat-rical events presented, and one of the first great silent movies, the Danish classic *The Passion of Joan of Arc*, provides a glimpse into Christian sensibil-ities following the First World War, a time of growing doubt and despair. A saint and martyr condemned by a corrupt church as well as earthly power, Joan glances up as she is consumed by flames and sees flocks of birds flying toward heaven. This is pure Christian iconography, a vision of faith in the face of a terrible death, brought artfully into the twentieth century.

The Jewish experience had also been on the screen quite early in now-forgotten Yiddish films, but, most significantly and potently in one of Charlie Chaplin's memorable short films, *The Immigrant*, which depicts in comic terms the desperate lives of the newcomers. Chaplin, an immigrant himself who had known great poverty, was not Jewish, as many of his later fans and critics assumed. He became, nonetheless, at least symbolically, "the wandering Jew" — the rejected perennial outcast. However, through his comic genius, Chaplin turned his "little tramp" into the most familiar and beloved figure in movie history. Chaplin's personal sympathies, even after achieving great wealth, remained with outsiders. When asked if he was Jewish, Chaplin replied pointedly, "I do not have that honor."

We should cite *Abie's Irish Rose* as, at least, a cultural and historical marker. While not successful in its movie version, for decades following the First World War, the play was the longest-running hit on Broadway. A grossly sentimentalized depiction of an interfaith marriage — Jewish boy, Irish-Catholic girl — the story didn't imply a loss of faith or tradition on either side. It simply resorted to stereotypes, *schmaltz* and *shtick*. Nonetheless, mixed audiences accepted it with good humor, while elite critics such as Robert Benchley detested its low-brow farce, and even more its longevity.

The silent era in Hollywood ended on a note of successful Jewish assimilation as Al Jolson, playing a cantor's son, depicted his own personal conflict between Jewish tradition and worldly success in the first acclaimed sound film, *The Jazz Singer*, in 1927. Equally as sentimental as *Abie's Irish Rose*, the film at least took the problem of assimilation seriously. Nevertheless, it concludes with Jolson on stage singing "My Mammy" to his Jewish mother in the front row. Jolson, as usual, was in blackface. One must acknowledge that "progress," while real, is often uneven.

(An addendum: Some decades later, my writing partner, Jim Buchanan, and I wrote the screen test for Neil Diamond, who recreated Jolson's role in Universal's *Jazz Singer* remake. Neil was an enormously popular singer, and a likeable personality, but though still heavy on sentimentality, the remake failed. I think the basic idea was still relevant; it was the *schmaltz* that had gone stale.)

The so-called Roaring Twenties in America was, in historical terms, a brief intermission between catastrophes. Though brief, this period of American prosperity saw an unprecedented burst of creativity, much of it guided by a Jewish sensibility; but this exuberance also blinded Americans to what was happening in the rest of the world.

Anti-Semitism, evidenced so nakedly in the Dreyfus affair, was again growing in Europe but wouldn't be directly confronted in a major film until the dramatization of that trial in *The Life of Emile Zola* in 1937. Dreyfus's chief defender, the Gentile writer Zola, portrayed as the movie's hero, was played by Paul Muni, and Dreyfus by Joseph Shildkraut, both distinguished Jewish actors from the Yiddish and European stage.

Hollywood was a place of business more than art, but controversies were not uncommon, especially if they mined box-office gold. The town's first major film was controversial and grew more so over the years, to the point that it was, in effect, banned in Hollywood. This was D. W. Griffith's *Birth of a Nation*, a misguided and dismaying portrayal of the post–Civil War Ku Klux Klan as heroic defenders of patriotic virtues. Griffith, a Southerner, the first real pioneer of film form, would try to make up for this prejudicial work with his subsequent epic, *Intolerance,* and the more lyrical *Broken Blossoms,* which boldly depicted racially mixed lovers with sympathy.

While mostly providing light entertainment, Hollywood would continue to produce challenging work that advocated racial and religious tolerance and, for a time at least, supported traditional moral values. Hollywood's Jewish pioneers, like many immigrants, were initially eager to embrace established mores.

Many of Hollywood's best talent, however, came from — or rather, fled from — Europe, where movie images were darker and traditional values openly challenged. The movie "glances" provided by the artistically innovative European films were either cynical and despairing — such as the German silent films *The Last Laugh* and *Metropolis* — or overt revolutionary propaganda from Soviet Russia. Among the most inventive of the latter were the films of Sergei Eisenstein, a Jewish director, who developed new cinematic forms and theories but remained largely in the straitjacket of Soviet ideology. All of these ideas and techniques were eventually exported to Hollywood, but, in the process, diluted — wine into Coca-Cola.

The devastation of the First World War was the subject of several notable Hollywood films, and perhaps the final shot in the Academy award-winning *All Quiet on the Western Front* provides the most poignant glance into the prevalent despair. A young soldier reaches out of his miserable trench to touch a butterfly, but, as he does, he is shot by a sniper and his hand falls lifelessly. The lament was not simply for a youthful death but for the loss of nature and beauty.

The postwar illusions of peace and prosperity came to an end in the 1930s when Ruth and I were born a continent apart. We grew up during the Great Depression and the Second World War, and these events, though viewed through the filter of movie sentimentality and melodrama, shaped our self-understanding.

While countless films have recorded the tragedy of the Holocaust, including powerful dramas such as *The Pawnbroker* and *Schindler's List*, I would contend that it was Hollywood's light entertainment over the years that offered the best and certainly most positive view of Jewish life and culture. The stature of early comics such as the Marx Brothers, Jack Benny, Milton Berle, and George Burns was more reflective of the growing acceptance and, indeed, esteem that Jews were attaining in American life than was the acclaim of more culturally prestigious figures such as Aaron Copland and Leonard Bernstein.

There is probably no work more celebratory of Jewish life in "the old country" than the musical *Fiddler on the Roof,* and few more enduring symbols than Marc Chagall's improbable fiddler. By celebrating "tradition" in song and dance, the infectious music and humor built a bridge of understanding that perhaps only popular art can provide.

*　　*　　*

Classic Hollywood reigned from the 1920s to the 1950s, with a legendary high point in 1939, considered by many the *annus mirabilis* during which films such as *Gone with the Wind, The Wizard of Oz, Mr. Smith Goes to Washington,* and *Stagecoach* were released. The forties and fifties — about the time when I first made my way through the studio gates — were, in my judgment, an even more remarkable era during which major directors such as John Ford, Frank Capra, and John Huston made some of their most memorable films — *The Searchers, It's a Wonderful Life,* and *Treasure of the Sierra Madre.* Hollywood, quite properly, never made distinctions between Jewish directors and others, but for our purposes we might note the distinctly Jewish humor as well as compassion in the work of Billy Wilder, William Wyler, and Fred Zinnemann, evidenced in *Some Like It Hot, The Best Years of Our Lives,* and *From Here to Eternity.* Zinnemann, married to a Catholic, would also direct *The Nun's Story.*

Things then quickly changed. Beginning in the mid-sixties, not just the movies but American life itself underwent a meltdown. The warm, fuzzy high of sixties' nostalgia still blurs this reality for many, but the hard facts are that divorce and crime rates doubled within little more than a decade, and a growing drug addiction problem soared into an epidemic. Racial conflicts flared, and political life became increasingly bitter and unstable.

This was also the twilight period of "Old Hollywood," as movies gave way to TV and a rapidly growing and inherently fickle "youth market." Postwar prosperity had fostered a huge mass entertainment industry, including sports, and ultimately shaped news and politics, in effect, into extensions of show business. Americans spent more and more hours a day being "entertained" — even by real disasters and tragedies.

The fade-out of Old Hollywood ended with the demise of the established studios — a cultural rupture that has been disguised by the subsequent vast revenues of the mass media industry. Old Hollywood was dead. What had died, however, wasn't simply a provincial town, but a dream.

While I would be ungrateful not to acknowledge the many advantages I enjoyed while working in Hollywood — a comfortable income and, most important, rich and lasting friendships — I've rarely been inclined to defend "our town." The moral confusion and excesses promulgated in films during the last decades made this increasingly difficult. I will now offer, nonetheless, a defense.

Hollywood, my "Old Hollywood" at least, advertised itself as the "entertainment capital of the world," not the center of culture or enlightenment. Hollywood was a settlement in early Los Angeles, not ancient Athens. I would suggest that Hollywood has been more honest with its customers, as well as itself, when it offered escape rather than analysis. There's nothing wrong with "entertainment" that allows us to escape for a moment from reality as long as we don't confuse the diversion with that reality. Chaplin and others may have touched at times on real poverty and hardship, but no one seriously set out to probe the problem of evil. Fred Astaire and Gene Kelly and so many others offered a musical make-believe world of innocent romance that you didn't have to believe to enjoy, and the best of the "screwball" comedies allowed us to laugh at our follies without suggesting a remedy. I see nothing to condemn in these offerings.

Hollywood has been most irresponsible when it has taken itself most seriously. Too often the industry has presented skewered, politically slanted, or at least wholly inadequate interpretations of history, war, and social injustice. The "realistic" depictions of violence and sexuality are usually the least accurate. Worse, the enactments of evil invariably trivialize it. To seek escape from pain and suffering, even through daydream and distraction, is humane — indeed, "only human"; but the movies should not indulge in attempts to escape evil by putting it in makeup and wardrobe and pretending to overcome it through special effects.

The Jewish dream of universal peace and justice, shared by all, was not brought about by the movies and never could have been. It was, nevertheless, an admirable animating impulse. That's the dream that has largely died. However, the death of a dream can either result in disillusionment or be a wake-up call. In Hollywood, it has been both — but which will prevail — disillusionment or a new clarity? We still don't know.

Another cliff-hanger?

*　　*　　*

Entertainment as Culture

To better understand Hollywood, whether as a "Jewish town" or as a global industry, we need to examine its anomalous roots.

A unique aspect of predominantly Jewish Hollywood has been its mixture of wealth, status, and, paradoxically, a persistently adversarial attitude. Why?

As many scholars have noted, the aspirations of European Jews after the emancipation were less about consolidating wealth and power than gaining acceptance in cultural circles. Given the intellectual and artistic attainments of Jews within their own tradition, especially their achievements in fields such as medicine, mathematics, and music, this is not surprising. As bourgeois society developed, however, new and less defined standards emerged. Public prominence became less a matter of commonly recognized attainments or of inherited status; it was increasingly associated with fame and personality.

The emergence of this popular "democratic" culture gave Jews an opportunity to express talents that had been latent for generations yet suppressed in isolation. Not only composers of the renown of Mahler and Schoenberg, but actresses such as Sarah Bernhardt and Ida Rubinstein were recognized as major artists and idolized. By the turn of the century, with the mass circulation of the press and then the gradual establishment of an "entertainment industry," the famous artist was being molded into the modern celebrity. Significantly for Jews and other minorities, it was now possible to circumvent the old cultural establishments and achieve a new kind of success.

It was not, as has been customarily noted, simply that the early movies were a marginal business and therefore open to Jewish entrepreneurs, though this was a factor; it was also that a new form of mass culture had appeared, one gradually divorced from an upper class and their patronage. The merging of a fading "high culture," particularly in music, with entertainment that would appeal to even uneducated crowds generated a vigorous and uniquely American synergism, and created the most distinctive and treasured forms of American popular culture — the Broadway musical, jazz, popular dance music, and the movies.

In time, the mass-manufactured products of this popular culture would transcend American limits and become truly international. It is not accidental that just as they had facilitated trans-national finance, Jews would play a central role in this cultural expansion.

The remarkable achievements of this half-century were so rich and lasting that they need no rationale, but there was a price to pay. No matter how great the public acclaim and financial rewards, there remained a high degree of artificiality in this largely manufactured "culture." It was increasingly designed to appeal to the largest possible audience, and that was the problem. What was personal, authentic, and spontaneous seldom remained so for long. Even the most accessible popular work of art was reshaped further into a standardized commodity.

What is amazing and worthy of praise is that so many artists and fine works managed to survive this process. The more lasting problem for many of the creative people involved, however, was that they themselves were also turned into products.

The inherent sense of estrangement experienced in the loss of control of an artwork, not dissimilar to the alienation of workers described by Marx, is even more profoundly felt if the "artwork" is yourself. This is the natural seedbed for the angry adversarial attitude that has always permeated Hollywood. This sense of exploitation and vulnerability is hardly limited to Jews, but their long history of social separation could only enhance it, especially if the celebrity persona was increasingly separate from some residual deeper identity. A highly competitive and inherently insecure business then further hardens an individual. He or she becomes as "adversarial" as everyone else just to survive. As I warned my writing students, if we stay in Hollywood long enough, we all become "angry old Jews."

*   *   *

Some Thoughts on Comedy

I have always felt that not only the most enduring works of Hollywood but, in their own way, the most penetrating were comedies, and this is, in large part, due to a Jewish sensibility.

I have an aversion to overly intellectualized views of humor in general and film comedy in particular, but I have to risk this hubris to dig out some insights. I'm not indulging in the lost art of film criticism, a sport now for movie buffs, or assessing the delightful silliness of my one-time hero, Danny Kaye, or the beloved Jack Benny, but referencing the more lasting work of comedy creators such as Ernst Lubitsch, Billy Wilder, and Woody Allen, as well as writers such as Paddy Chayefsky, Sidney Buchman, Morrie Ryskind, Neil Simon, and I. A. L. "Izzy" Diamond.

Commentators from Plato to Bergson viewed the underlying gap between the ideal and the real, or even the human and the divine, as a source of healing laughter — or at least laughter. As Paul Johnson has noted, comedy also often conveys a sense of "approaching catastrophe," whether in the form of a banana peel or one of Oliver Hardy's clever schemes. There is, therefore, some form of critical realism lurking even in the midst of farce. Comedy is telling us, at the very least, that we humans don't understand ourselves and that we're going to pay a price for our follies.

What made Hollywood's best comedy work, I believe, was the additional spice of Jewish pessimism. Charlie Chaplin and Buster Keaton could conceive of a happy ending, however fanciful, but not the Marx Brothers or Woody Allen. Billy Wilder might toss a bone to the audience, but the fatalism isn't far beneath the laughs. There was a conspicuous misanthropy among the comedy writers I knew, almost all Jewish, but without it I doubt that they would have been so funny. This is ironic, of course, because this talent made many of them rich and even famous. It is reported that Groucho Marx was once pressed about what he really wanted in life, and, replying in a rare note of seriousness, said, "I just want nothing to change!" This is a desire that barely conceals a fatalism, and is, naturally, a comic premise.

Mixed in with the slapstick and silliness, there was not infrequently social comment — indeed, criticism — that was sharp and pointed. This is true in some of the seemingly most flippant work of Lubitsch or Wilder and is quite evident in films such as *Ninotchka, My Man Godfrey,* and *The Apartment.* American film comedy is usually about sex, just as British humor is often about class, and this male-versus-female theme reached its height in the Spencer Tracy and Katharine Hepburn films of the 1940s — the best written by Garson Kanin and directed by George Cukor.

I have written more than once about my appreciation of Woody Allen, whose early films made him, in my judgment, the most significant filmmaker of my generation in that he caught the existential angst of otherwise prosperous overachievers. *Crimes and Misdemeanors* is a hilarious and at the same time deeply serious film that questions God's justice, and hence existence. Allen's despair often blinds him to the full dimensions of his own stories; but it is so honest that it provokes a deep laughter of recognition in all of us. Woody's comedy cuts as deep as the laughter, though, because it expresses the deep vulnerability of otherwise seemingly successful Jews, who might be described as Willy Loman's children. The tragic hero of *Death of a Salesman* committed suicide rather than admit failure, but his kids got the insurance money.

Over time, however, angst can become tiresome. Perhaps it might have been relieved had Woody known a less diluted and more challenging Judaism. As I concluded some years ago, I just wish that Woody, for his own sake and ours, could have had the chance to meet Jeremiah.

Woody's occasional assaults on religion, especially his own Judaism, now seem rather benign in retrospect. His cynicism was perhaps more corrosive than his critiques. Humor, in any case, is always most justified and salubrious when it attacks our pretensions and hypocrisy. The problem in Hollywood has been that we tend to expose other people's vices rather than our own.

Hollywood often tries to sell its comedies, particularly those aimed at the young, as "irreverent." This is based on the questionable assumption that some things in movies are still held in reverence. This worn-out appeal hasn't made sense since Ben Hecht wrote *Nothing Sacred* in 1937. Nonetheless, there are "sacred cows" in Hollywood nearly as untouchable as those in India.

My friendship with Mort Sahl, the pioneer of contemporary political humor, was quite brief but enjoyable — and instructive on the subject of Hollywood's own hypersensitivities. I was halfway out the door, just departing the business, when we met, and Mort was slipping into a kind of career limbo. While still admired and very funny, his humor, once considered the epitome of "irreverent," was discomforting many in the "New Hollywood."

Mort had been an enormous success. He had his own TV show, was one of the few comics to be on the cover of *Time* magazine, and eventually became a member of the show-business circle around President John F. Kennedy. Ruth and I had delighted in his early stand-up work both at the Hungry I in San Francisco and at the Crescendo on the Sunset Strip. His meteoric rise and subsequent decline illuminated the precarious role of serious humor in the popular entertainment business.

Jim and I met Mort through actor Dick Crenna, both hometown L.A. boys, and Mort reminded me of the bright, funny Jewish guys I knew at Fairfax High, though he was obviously brighter and funnier. Despite his perceived countercultural stance and political activism, we found Mort to be as much a part of "Old Hollywood" as we were. He greatly admired Bob Hope, from whom he had derived much of his own technique. Mort had been badly shaken and disillusioned by the Kennedy assassination, and perhaps that trauma had somewhat shifted his perspective; but I detected the Jewish moral sensibility beneath the hip, cool exterior. The target of his later quips became the new Hollywood establishment, and his infectious laugh didn't disguise the sharpness of his bite. He was scathing about the new elite's hypocritical endorsement of the dubious "new" sexual morality, which he called "social democratic sex." If he had stopped there, he might have been safe, but he didn't.

Hollywood, as much as any other industry, traditionally had excluded women from key positions. Ruth had encountered this discrimination in the animation field, where, in her day, virtually no women could rise above the ink-and-paint department to become animators. Similarly, our daughter Teresa was among the first generation of women to be fully accepted as makeup artists, thus overcoming a kind of discrimination as absurd as it was indefensible. Clearly, the struggle of women for equal, just treatment was a good and necessary effort. However, comedy is supposed to puncture even our most lofty pretensions. The folly of self-conscious virtue is as much a universal comedic theme as the ignorance born of vice.

Mort's keen eye had observed the misuse of the feminist stance by some of the town's most ambitious women, who were aggressively carving out personal careers in the name of equality. "Have you ever noticed," he asked audiences, "how much the 'new women' resemble the old men?" This was an unforgivable taunt in those PC days, and Mort never regained his once-high status. In Hollywood, as elsewhere, you have to be very careful about what you consider "irreverent."

I would still contend that the richest achievement of American films has been in comedy, because our comedies have been our most accurate and honest mirror. By the 1980s, however, some critics were observing a streak of cruelty creeping into popular comedies, and this has been followed by the assault humor of ferociously partisan "political" comics. Curiously, some of these so-called commentators are taken with a seriousness that ignores their clown makeup and baggy pants. The concept of humor as potentially unifying and reconciling now seems as incongruous in our day as Chaplin's humanism, with its sentimental merging of "tears and laughter."

We laugh because we must to survive, so I would never want to step on a laugh line or kill a joke. But at some point we should be careful about how we mock others. Some insults might be forgiven, but ridicule, never. Perhaps, for the present, we can afford our increasingly abusive humor — but only as long as our thick-skinned insulation lasts.

CHAPTER EIGHT

East of Hollywood

The blacklist left me unemployed, bitter, disillusioned, and desperate. It was also one of the best things that ever happened to me.

For a brief period, through a new friend, a talented writer who later would become my partner, Jim Buchanan, I found a job in local television.

Jim and I had met at an unusual party, a kind of literary gathering hosted by Anaïs Nin, the avant-garde writer and confidante of Henry Miller known for her free-spirited lifestyle. She was older when we met her but still flamboyant in manner and certainly in dress. Jim later described her as wearing "some kind of a birdcage on her head." We had both been invited by another writer friend from McGowan's workshop. Ruth and I and Jim and his wife, Ellie, found each other quickly because we were decidedly not flamboyant and therefore conspicuous.

Anaïs Nin, who collected and encouraged young writers, was very gracious, even extravagantly so. She introduced everyone as either "published" or "not published" and made it clear that the latter category was the most admirable — it suggested artistic integrity. Jim was working in the casting office at Twentieth Century Fox at the time, having moved up from the mailroom. Both of us were decidedly "unpublished," and we hit it off immediately.

Jim was later one of my friends quizzed by the FBI about my loyalty. Though scared and puzzled by the interrogation, he defended me and was further willing to risk his own livelihood by finding me a job I desperately needed.

The position was working with Jim — the two of us were "front men" for a quiz-show executive. We were employed as "producers" of a live quiz show on a local TV channel, a test run for a network slot. The real producer was a fugitive, so to speak, from the "quiz show scandals" of those years — the exposure by Congressional investigators of highly rated but rigged network quiz shows. Some of the "fixers" went to jail; but our new employer somehow dodged the subpoenas and ended up in Hollywood. After Jim and I were long gone, he found success with his own network show. I presume it wasn't rigged.

The job as pseudo-producer paid well, but the hours were awful, and the atmosphere was oppressive. Our boss's attitude toward the contestants and the audience — and us, for that matter — was one of cynical contempt. The hours were made worse by his insistence on convening staff meetings after the show that would last into the early morning. This also provided him with opportunities to further "interview" our young secretaries, or at least those seeking rapid advancement. Jim and I knew we wouldn't last. We were both either too honest or too dumb, or both, to survive in this manipulative world. Ruth, despite knowing our financial situation and being eight months' pregnant, kept after me to quit, and, exhausted, I finally did. Jim, also a new father, left to teach school. I took a civil-service exam and, satisfying the limited requirements of that era, became a social worker. Even though we pursued different "day jobs," Jim and I decided to write together, and we would continue to do so for the next twenty years. That's a happier thread in this story.

Despite the brief financial relief from work on the quiz show, Ruth and I were still close to being broke. I was willing to take any social-work job that was immediately available. I was even ready to become a counselor at Juvenile Hall — perhaps appropriate, considering my own minor delinquency — but didn't like what I heard about having to discipline angry, six-foot-tall adolescents. So when I was informed that if I were willing to work in the heart of the gang- and drug-plagued East Los Angeles *barrio*, I could start immediately, I agreed and went to work the next Monday.

* * *

Inside the *Barrio*

It is not false modesty that has prevented me from ever claiming that I was a particularly talented writer. I think that, whatever my accomplishments, they were due to hard work and good fortune more than talent. The good fortune was that Jim, my partner, was a born writer who had the writer's equivalence of "pure pitch," particularly when it came to dialogue. So with my modesty now established, I will unabashedly state that I think I was a very good social worker.

In the nearly three years in East L.A., I was, first, a family case worker, overburdened at times, as were all of us, with a heavy caseload of impoverished, largely Mexican single mothers. I helped several to be trained as typists or electronic assemblers and to become independent. I then specialized in cases of "deprivation due to drug addiction," which meant dealing with families torn apart by the heroin abuse that was epidemic at the time. I worked with parole agents and did group work with a psychologist to help men coming out of prison. A couple, I realized, were *jefes*, major drug dealers, who were far beyond our reach, but perhaps others might have been helped.

Much of the work was arduous but gratifying, though often a difficult mix of accomplishment and pain. Blind Julio was a case in point. This was the name the neighborhood gave this older man, my "client," a known drug dealer who had, in fact, partial vision. I learned about him from irate neighbors, all women, who called me as his social worker and demanded action. This was unusual for East L.A. and particularly for this neighborhood, notorious for its poverty and crime. But these irate women demanded, in often broken English, that I do something to stop Blind Julio from continuing to use his children, all under the age of ten, as drug runners. I had not visited the family yet, but was naturally appalled at the prospect of this abuse. Several of my clients, perhaps most, were affected by — if not directly involved in — the then-heavy heroin traffic plaguing the East Side. Blind Julio's behavior, however, crossed the line.

I made several house calls promptly, but, other than confirming that Blind Julio and his passive wife were highly suspicious and uncooperative, I didn't observe any criminal behavior, and it was unlikely that I would. The phone calls persisted, though, and so I went to a friendly cop in the Sheriff's Department, whom I knew from another case, and talked with him. He was thoroughly knowledgeable about Blind Julio's drug-dealing and assured me that it was just a matter of time before he was busted. Nothing happened, however, and I took to making quick, unexpected house calls, pounding on the door. I never expected results other than what I achieved — the sound of a toilet immediately flushing. I have no idea how much my unwelcome pounding cost Blind Julio in heroin. But, after some time, nothing had happened, and I still received angry phone calls.

I consulted with my agency supervisor, an old pro, who advised me to consider legally removing the children from the home — in other words, placing them in foster care. I saw the necessity, if for no other reason than that the house and the kids were unusually neglected and dirty even by the standards of this extremely poor neighborhood. I reluctantly took the first step by requesting Blind Julio's criminal records. I would have to prove to a judge that he and his wife were unfit parents, and I couldn't do that just on the basis of hygiene or even relative physical neglect.

As I expected, Blind Julio's arrest record was extensive, and his thirty years of criminal history included a thirty-year prison sentence. I guess that his wife and kids were a late addition to his life. But then I discovered something in the police records that I didn't expect.

In recent years, Blind Julio had been arrested, always for possession of narcotics, in several locations close to East L.A., but in different municipalities. In every instance, he was not only *not* prosecuted; he was released to the Sheriff's Department, and then the charges were dropped.

This wasn't hard to figure out. Blind Julio was an informer for the Sheriff's Department. He had, in effect, a license to deal as long as he helped control the traffic by snitching on others. I wasn't indignant. I knew from my past police experience on the *Nightwatch* show that this was the way the game was played — devious but necessary in the real world. It also explained why I had been stonewalled by my friend at the Department. Nothing was going to happen to Blind Julio. I had no choice but to act.

With his criminal record and my reports about the child neglect, it wasn't difficult to get the court order, and we removed the children from the home. I think there were three of them. Blind Julio and his wife were probably so drugged themselves that they displayed little emotion as I led the kids out of the house. But as I put these children, all terrified and crying, into the placement worker's car, I felt wretched. I have no doubt that this was the only thing I could have done, and clearly in their best interests, but it remains a painful memory. I was still learning that life offers few neat or clear solutions.

I had to remove children from their parents one more time, but that was easier. I had found mama and papa, both stone alcoholics, unconscious on the floor, while the oldest girl, perhaps six, was trying to cook a meal for the others. She could barely reach the boiling water on the stove. This required immediate action. This situation was easier because we were able to place the kids with family members.

Another client of mine, a young woman, a heroin addict with two small children, came to an even worse end. She and her children were murdered during the night. The word on the street was that she was also an informer or perhaps threatening to become one. The house had been filled with gas from a stove jet during the night and then set on fire. I'd like to think the killers didn't know the kids were there. In any case, I had to testify at the coroner's inquest about the woman's state of mind. This could have been taken for a suicide. But I knew that this woman wasn't suicidal and certainly would never have killed her children. I had visited her just a week before and watched them together — another memory that comes back now and then.

In another neighborhood, I formed a self-help support group of single mothers that broke the isolation of several of these lonely women. I was then ordered by a high-ranking agency supervisor to cease and desist in this activity because it violated the "confidentiality" of my clients by introducing them to each other — a judgment so absurd that, while I had no choice but to comply, infuriated me. In response, I refocused my energy and, using some of my communist training, helped to organize the first social workers' union west of the Mississippi. Angered by the bureaucracy and red tape, social workers demanded conditions that allowed us to do effective work. I was proud to become the union's first full-time organizer.

*   *   *

Whatever I accomplished, the truth is, I was the beneficiary of those years in East L.A. I had experienced real poverty as a child, but there I encountered a deeper deprivation — not the abstract exploitation posited by the Marxist notion of a "proletariat," but a suffering that could not be alleviated by mere economic or professional help. It was a deprivation that came primarily from the loss of love and trust.

I was, in short, introduced to the human condition, unfiltered by preconceptions. I learned that the worst suffering was not an affliction as defined by philosophy, but something far deeper, and I witnessed it in flesh and blood. This suffering could only be addressed, I came to realize, by faith and a source of healing beyond the best of human efforts. It took me a long time — years, even decades — to figure this out, but the process began in the barrio.

*   *   *

The Exiles: The Movie

It was during the blacklist years that I worked with Kent Mackenzie, a friend and talented filmmaker. Kent's idealism was inspiring. I had met him during my last year at UCLA, but it wasn't until I was blacklisted that my unwelcome free time and a high degree of frustration led me to commit to help him make his film, *The Exiles*.

A feature-length documentary, shot on 35 millimeter black-and-white, *The Exiles* had the feel of a dramatic story. It depicted one long day and night in the lives of Native Americans — or "Indians" as they were then called — living on L.A.'s skid row. The two saloons that were our primary locations, fancifully called "The Ritz" and "The Columbine," served as the exclusive meeting places for Indians. This was an extraordinary "shoot." Given the equipment of that era, it was necessary at times to use a dolly and even "lay track" in these chaotic, crowded, and sometimes violent bars.

My function was working as assistant director, but mostly what I did was help Kent assemble the narrative soundtrack, edited from hours of interviews he had conducted with the three principals. Looking back, I think my real role was as a sounding board for Kent's developing ideas, or, maybe, just as a friend.

The film took several years to complete, and at great emotional and financial cost to Kent. It immediately won some critical praise — especially from Pauline Kael, then-critic at *Esquire* magazine — and a top prize at a European festival, and then just as quickly disappeared.

The Exiles would be discovered a half-century later, belatedly hailed as a classic American documentary and placed in the permanent collection of the Library of Congress. Justly celebrated for its remarkable cinematography, *The Exiles* was Kent's work, his personal vision and accomplishment. I was simply fortunate to be among those who helped him.

I met Kent and his friends at the USC film school in 1956 when we joined together to protest the firing of his teacher, Andries Deinum, who had refused to answer the questions of the House Un-American Activities Committee. Despite our protests, he lost his university position. A scholar and social analyst, Deinum had been a colleague of a prominent communist documentarian, Joris Ivens, and although I attended the hearings, I know nothing about his political views at that time. Kent was not a political partisan then and, to my knowledge, never was. On the other hand, I had only recently broken with the Party. Despite my disillusionment with communist ideology, I still considered myself "on the Left" and circulated petitions defending Deinum and others. Deinum found another academic position and declared himself "a refugee from occupied Hollywood."

Kent and I became good friends, and, as proof of that, he somehow managed to sneak me into Jean Renoir's "master class," a workshop for USC graduate film students. This was despite the fact that I wasn't a graduate student and was studying at UCLA. Renoir, the great humanist filmmaker, was a significant influence on all of us, and my gratitude to Kent would be profound if his friendship had provided nothing further. But, of course, it did. I think it was Kent's integrity even more than his talent that drew me and others to him. I admired his short film, *Bunker Hill,* but the vision that led to *The Exiles* wasn't yet fully formed. We were on similar paths — more than we realized — beyond just theorizing about films.

Our friendship was too brief, eventually cut short by Kent's untimely death at the age of forty-eight; but our wide-ranging discussions were his lasting gift to me. Our explorations of film form and technique (the early "cinema verité" approach) were meaningful but perhaps less important than the seeds of a shared determination that was close to hope. Our increasingly intimate talks, often late at night when editing the narrative tracks, reflected a shared sense of our own "exile" from the dominant culture, including Hollywood. We recognized that we were both seeking something beyond movie-making. As I say, only seeds were planted then, but I doubt that it is coincidental that, though we discussed neither religion nor faith, we both became Christians.

Kent's remarkable film portrays not just Native Americans lost in the urban jungle, at risk of losing even the remnants of their culture and identity, but our own sense of drift and uncertainty at that time. It is very gratifying to know that, though it took a half-century, others now recognize his talent and remarkable accomplishment. Even more, I hope it will be recognized that his poetic images convey a spiritual if not prophetic truth about those times and our own.

CHAPTER NINE

Inside the Gates, or, Hollywood, Here I Come — Again

In time I went back to Hollywood. As much as I admired Kent's integrity, this is where I and my first dreams were born — so maybe that was inevitable. I still retained my determination to become a writer and filmmaker. Still, during the blacklist years, working in the *barrio*, that seemed a fading dream.

I was also finding social work satisfying despite the bureaucratic red tape that ensnared our efforts. My second child, Bethe, had been born, and with some help from Ruth's family, we had bought a modest home. I was seriously beginning to consider a life outside of show business. Looking back, I don't think it would have been a bad one.

Jim and I continued to write together, exchanging ideas and rough drafts, almost every weekend. We were beginning to find, through collaboration, a style that was our own, a blend of our different talents. We shared an enthusiasm for the best of Hollywood's past work — especially John Huston's films, but also those of John Ford and Preston Sturges. We were also stimulated by the new forms coming out of Europe, particularly the films of François Truffaut and the "nouvelle vague" in France. The Italian "neo-realists" such as Ermanno Olmi and Francesco Rosi were also exploring an innovative poetic sensibility.

My loyal agent, Ilse Lahn, now represented us as a writing team, and we found occasional work, though at Guild minimum. Larry Peerce, son of the famous tenor Jan Peerce, was just beginning his career as a director and hired us to work together on a script. The results, though never produced, pleased everyone, and confirmed our strength as a team.

A published short-story writer and later a novelist, Jim was well-educated in classic literature and history. Not having been tutored by the Great Muse or the Communist Party, Jim's range was far wider than mine, and his erudition would benefit us for years to come. It was his idea to convert into a contemporary screenplay an amusing episode in Julius Caesar's life. Caesar was abducted by pirates but charmed them into becoming his collaborators. Our "Caesar" was a Miami gangster.

Paul Kohner, the head of his own "Tiffany" talent agency, was an elegant Viennese Jew, as was our motherly agent Ilse, who ran his literary department. Kohner represented Ernest Hemingway as well as our artistic heroes, filmmakers such as Huston, William Wyler, and Orson Welles. Kohner had accepted Jim and me, though we were clearly on the very bottom of his writers' list — so low, in fact, that, on occasion, Ilse had to reintroduce us to him as his clients.

Kohner was, nevertheless, a legendary "super agent," and after reading our script — as he later recounted — he made only one phone call. It was to Sam Spiegel, who had recently produced *Lawrence of Arabia* — and he bought the script. Spiegel, at the height of his power, was creating, in effect, his own mini-studio and turned the project over to others. Our screenplay was then made into a mess of a movie in an effort to make it "hip." Nevertheless, our original screenplay, a rare form in those days, sold for so much money that it made the front page of *Variety*.

We were inside the gates. Now, if we could only manage to stay there.

*   *   *

This kind of overnight change of fortune can be so disorienting that it can cause you to lose your equilibrium and good sense. With one phone call, it seemed that Jim and I had gone from being, respectively, a fifth-grade school teacher and a social worker in the *barrio* to employable screenwriters. Fortunately, our wives, Ruth and Ellie, kept their heads. Ruth, ever cautious about our inherently insecure future, allowed me to exult and strut for a while, but insisted that we bank the money. She would consent to only a few new purchases. She agreed, I remember, that we could buy some new trash cans. I think she felt we had been embarrassing the neighbors with our old ones.

For the next few years, Jim and I were considered a promising young team and would work for several major studios. A new life had begun for me. What's amazing is that I survived it.

During my first years as a social worker, Ruth and I were blessed to have two daughters, Terry and Bethe. I don't think my little girls ever knew how Ruth and I struggled to overcome the anxiety and insecurity of the blacklist years, but they might have sensed something, the way kids do. My personal behavior became increasingly reckless, I suppose, as compensation for my loss of control and hope. It was a very tough time for Ruth as well, and her prudence and patience were the keys to our survival. Yet, looking back, this was the closest I ever came to living what others would consider a "normal life": living in a house in the San Fernando Valley with a wife, two children, and a dog, and driving across town to work every day. Once I resumed the life of a Hollywood writer, our income grew (though often I endured long stretches of unemployment); but our life was hardly normal. I would never again know where or if I'd be working for more than weeks at a time. It was temperamentally the life of a riverboat gambler.

While Austin and Buchanan, known for years as "the boys," were finally inside the gates of Hollywood, it wasn't the Hollywood we imagined or expected. The creative problem we faced was that Jim and I were of a generation inspired by the classic Hollywood films. Jim, more literate, admired the sophisticated dialogue of Ben Hecht and the collaborating duo of Billy Wilder and Charles Brackett, while I was drawn to great performers such as my first hero, Chaplin, and Bogart. We were a good pairing, but, unfortunately, we wanted to resuscitate the fading movie magic of our youth. We wanted to make the kind of films that John Huston, John Ford, and Preston Sturges made. Lamentably, they were already considered old-fashioned.

The mass audience, moreover, increasingly younger than we were, had little nostalgia for the strong adult characters and the genre stories that inspired us. Our screenwriting careers went rather rapidly from promising to quixotic. I always wanted to please audiences. This was somehow "in my blood," and this desire — and the necessity of supporting our families — led Jim and me to a career of prolonged compromises. In the end, Jim and I never did the work we wanted or hoped to do; but at least we were well-paid. And, I must admit, we often had a very good time — that is, if we kept our sense of humor.

*   *   *

Revolt in Berkeley: The Musical

Jim and I certainly did our best to adapt to the changing times and what was becoming the "new Hollywood."

In the mid-sixties, we were sent on a research trip to Berkeley to observe the student revolt that was just erupting on that prestigious campus. These were among the first and the most publicized of the student demonstrations that would eventually sweep the country. Our assignment was based on the absurd idea of our boss, a producer at Columbia, that a student rebellion was potential box office, if for no other reason than the abundance of sexy college girls or "co-eds," as they were then called. Though he had never been to college himself, he had once been a dance director on one of the popular "college musicals," probably at MGM.

This ridiculous premise led to Jim and me, as the youngest writers at the studio, being paid to wander around the sprawling UC Berkeley campus looking for a story, presumably one that could feature sexy "co-eds." What we witnessed was one of the first major campus protests. Wielding my big, clumsy tape recorder, I managed to stand next to Mario Savio, the curly-haired rebel leader who would soon achieve national notoriety, as he gave one of his first, quite eloquent speeches. Far from appearing as a wild-eyed radical, young Mario, a mathematician, had the studious style of the junior faculty.

The "co-eds" we encountered were more angry than cute, and stylistically they were the pioneers of what was to become the radical fashion of bib overalls, no makeup, and unkempt hair. These were the minority, of course. The sorority girls still looked like, well, "co-eds," but they weren't protesting. The crowds grew larger, and the chanting and marching soon led to clashes with the police, though at that time with minor consequences.

It is a fact largely forgotten today: The original focus of these demonstrations was not the Vietnam War or civil rights but resistance to increasingly impersonal and regimented university procedures. The first protest signs read "Do not fold, bend, or mutilate," referring pointedly to the IBM computer cards being used for class registration. Students now seldom knew the professors or received personal guidance. There were no more "Mr. Chips" to offer calming counsel, and the kids felt increasingly like punched IBM cards themselves.

The "Free Speech Movement," or FSM, as the Berkeley demonstrators called themselves, was part of a generic cry of a generation facing a depersonalized, seemingly indifferent world, whether in government, the military, or on campus. The demand for "free speech" was really a test of university regulations, which were, in fact, reasonably liberal. This quickly degenerated into the "filthy speech movement" that channeled the anger and frustration into futile bleats of obscenities.

In any case, there wasn't a movie in it, certainly not a musical, and nothing that would appeal to Columbia Studios. Jim and I were paid for this folly and had some good meals in San Francisco, but were soon out of work again. We had been selected for this bizarre assignment because we were still referred to as "the boys," but we were, in fact, getting dangerously past thirty, then still young for established writers, but a chronological turning point that would, in time, become perilous if not fatal for Hollywood screenwriters.

*   *   *

Package Deals

An incident in the MGM commissary in the summer of 1969 revealed how much further Hollywood's greedy pursuit of the youthful *zeitgeist* had downgraded into a farce. An old friend from the Left, a talented comedy director, rushed up to me one lunchtime in great excitement to announce that he had "landed the rights to the Black Panthers!" What he meant was that he had somehow secured the TV and movie rights to depict that ultra-radical and often violent "black power" group. "And, what's more," he exclaimed, "the Morris office is going to package it!" Translated, this meant that the William Morris Agency, then the largest in Hollywood, would represent the Panthers and all the rest of the "talent" as a package deal, taking a commission, of course, from everyone.

I trust that you'll believe that I didn't make this up. I couldn't. My imagination was never that rich. Paddy Chayefsky did depict such an arrangement in a hilarious scene in *Network*, directed by Sidney Lumet. My friend's Black Panther package never materialized.

The "Old Hollywood" was dying, but the "New Hollywood" was even more opportunistic and shallow. What's more, some of the studios were being taken over by "foreign interests." In time, they would be run primarily by corporate executives from other industries with assistants who held MBA degrees and provided a "bottom-line" assessment of the value of actors or scripts. The steady profits would flow mainly from TV, while movies would become even bigger gambles.

Aging Hollywood made a desperate effort to look young, and paunchy producers wearing bell-bottoms could be seen dancing the latest frenetic gyrations with their younger second wives, losing decorum while risking cardiac arrest. But some things never change. New deals with new talent were cut, but the bookkeeping would remain mysterious, and, as in Vegas, with the odds always in favor of the house. Even the most conspicuous box-office successes would still pay the talent perhaps fifty cents on every dollar owed.

$$* \quad * \quad *$$

Tom Swift and Buffalo Bill

After the Berkeley fiasco, Jim and I worked for a pugnacious but very bright producer at Fox named Saul David, who hired us to write a screenplay based on the Tom Swift stories, the tales of adventure popular with youngsters early in the century. It was a dream assignment that allowed us to spend weeks researching the era when American optimism was symbolized by young Tom Swift's ability to fix almost anything with the right screwdriver.

Saul was designing the project to be a two-hour-plus road show that would feature a giant dirigible capable of floating around the world. Mike Todd's *Around the World in Eighty Days* had been a big hit as a road show, but Saul wasn't an imitator. He admired only Todd's profits. He pushed us for something original.

The Swift books, credited to a fictitious "Victor Appleton," had, in fact, no real author. They had been put together by an assembly line of writers that provided healthy adventure stories for young boys. The same literary factory produced the Nancy Drew series aimed at girls. This was about the time that the Boy Scouts had become an almost obligatory activity, and wholesome behavior was joined to the excitement of new mechanical discoveries.

Our version, commissioned by Saul for Twentieth Century Fox, where he was producing the "Our Man Flint" movies starring my old City College chum, James Coburn, reflected our own increasingly cynical times. A disillusionment with the initially exuberant sixties with all its

86

mindless excesses had, in fact, already set in, and we sensed a swelling balloon of drug-induced illusions that would soon pop or deflate.

The underlying idea of our story was that Tom Swift would discover what couldn't be fixed with a screwdriver. In other words, our story turned dangerously ironic. The head of the studio, Daryl Zanuck, would later denounce our final script as a satire. Satire, as translated in Hollywood, meant "box-office poison."

We had young Tom and his mates encounter Freud, femme fatales, anarchists, and rabid Irish revolutionaries — all of whom left the young, idealistic Americans in a state of discouraged bewilderment. This was, of course, our point. The world was clearly not susceptible to being "fixed" by Tom's ingenuity any more than peace was going to be achieved in our own day by free love and LSD.

Despite Saul's track record as a successful producer, his pugnacity and our satirical approach doomed the project. After reading our latest draft, Zanuck put the picture on hold. Frustrated, Saul, a former New York publisher and a highly sophisticated man, retaliated with a juvenile prank. He recruited Jim and me as conspirators in his own "project comma."

Twentieth Century Fox had just emblazoned a new logo on its main building: "Think Fox!" Saul paid someone in the prop department to manufacture a plastic comma in the same color, which at night Jim and I helped to paste in the middle of the logo. When Zanuck and the execs came to work the next morning, they were greeted with the public admonishment "Think, Fox!" We were never detected as the culprits, but Saul left the lot soon after, and then, naturally, so did we.

*   *   *

Jim and I next went to MGM, where we worked for an old friend, an award-winning producer, Bill Froug, later to pioneer the "how to do it" screenwriting books, though he was not a screenwriter. Bill was a charming, lively man who presided over one of the last of the "writers' tables" at the commissary, which gave Jim and me the opportunity to meet some of our most illustrious and talented older colleagues, such as Walter Newman and Bill Bowers. Froug presided at these jolly lunches and seemed to know everyone in the business. Adopted as an infant, Bill never knew his birth mother, but, raised by a Jewish family, he "felt Jewish." So did I, but I knew I wasn't.

Jim and I were engaged to do an adaptation of a biography of Ned

Buntline, P. T. Barnum's colorful and equally unscrupulous competitor, who, in effect, "invented" Buffalo Bill and the Wild West Show. William Cody had actually been a young frontier scout with remarkable abilities as a horseman, but, as "Buffalo Bill," he eagerly allowed himself to be turned into a show-business phony and persuaded his friend, the frontier gunman Wild Bill Hickok, to do the same. Jim and I naturally treated this material ironically, and with the same fatal results.

I did have the opportunity, while researching both projects — Tom Swift and the Wild West Show — to study the turn-of-the-century period thoroughly. I studied "Buffalo Bill" not as a scholar, mind you, but as a fellow entertainer. My insights, if any, were, again, "from the inside." If the rebels of the sixties had so quickly turned into show-business entrepreneurs, I was wondering if history itself wasn't a vaudeville show. This, of course, only reflected my own cynicism.

I wasn't ahead of my times. Federico Fellini, Ingmar Bergman, François Truffaut, and other filmmakers were already dissecting a European society that had spiritually collapsed. The American-financed postwar reconstruction had rebuilt industries, but it couldn't manufacture a renewed spirit. And now we Americans seemed in need of a spiritual transfusion.

*   *   *

Writers, Thinkers, and Me

Jim and I then did a few more scripts for Saul David (hard to find a more Jewish name), who had moved to Universal. Despite his acerbic nature, Saul was a helpful and generous mentor. He was rare in being a Jewish political conservative, and, as such, he offended so many of his Hollywood contemporaries that it isolated him. Quite successful as a major film producer, he was nonetheless eventually blackballed and ended his life in a kind of exile. In fairness to those he angered, he was an oppositional personality who took much delight in antagonizing others. Saul's uncompromising logic, so very Jewish, was his gift to me. Although I seldom agreed with him on most matters, he gave me a good and necessary shaking up. My regret is that, without any real faith, and certainly with no religious convictions, Saul was ultimately lost to cynicism and despair — but that, too, was a lesson.

I remember Saul, Jim, and me celebrating with relief Israel's military victory in 1967 after some tense and fearful days. Our hope, and that of many in Hollywood, was that the victory would lead to peace. It was a vain hope, as it would be again in 1973, but I came to recognize that realism — even a realism that might lead to armed conflict — was a form of moral demand for Jews. Only those whose very existence has never been at serious risk can afford to abstract morality from circumstances.

Israel might be surviving, but it seemed to me that America was falling apart. The assassinations of King and the Kennedys, riots and political resignations, drugs and violent crime — all seemed part of an ominous tide. The radical posturing of the "counterculture" warriors had degenerated into wardrobe displays, and, far from posing any serious challenge to the status quo or providing alternatives, they had simply become a new conformism, the "conformity of dissent," as the astute Jacques Barzun described it. The "real thing," the brave Soviet dissident Alexander Solzhenitsyn, spoke at Harvard and alienated Americans by chastising us for debasing our own culture. He then exiled himself, this time to the woods of Vermont.

Solzhenitsyn said something that stuck with me. Interviewed by the BBC immediately following his expulsion from the Soviet Union, he had been asked what he had learned from his many hard years as a prisoner in the Gulag. He replied that he had realized "that there is a real difference between good and evil." I wasn't used to people using those terms.

*   *   *

Studio writers in those days took long lunches even when their offices were on the lot. Work — that is, actual writing — usually began after phone calls, lunch, and reading the trades. Jim and I spent many hours during those years discussing the meaning of life, a subject made all the more confounding by being in a world of costumes, makeup, and sets. But we were interested in life beyond Hollywood.

We debated the relative merits of Sartre and Camus, the French existentialists who, despite being fashionable, were asking appropriately hard questions. Jim took Camus's part and won. Sartre's political inconsistencies were perhaps forgivable, but his philosophical despair was not mine. Camus was, at heart, a poet and an utterly honest man. His angst seemed less reasoned and thus less self-justifying. It came out of the destructiveness of war and the disillusionment that followed. I had paid no

89

such price for my anxiety, but it was as real. The possibility that these French intellectuals raised — that human life was essentially meaningless if not worthless — seemed, from my point of view, a reasonable conjecture, given how bad movies and music had become. Being well-paid only increased what Sartre had warned us about: living a life of "bad faith."

The questions were inescapable, and I had the good fortune — or, as I would later see it, something more than that — to hear a man who not only deepened the questions but pointed to some answers, although ones that were strange and new to me. This was the Christian philosopher Paul Tillich, who spoke on two occasions at my alma mater, UCLA. I attended both. The thoughtful integrity of Tillich, white-haired and frail, just a few years from his death, kicked a door open for me. I still doubted the relevance of Christianity, at least for me, but I realized that it was the unthinking blockage of my past, even an arrogance, that made me deny the intellectual force and depth of the Christian tradition. I wasn't considering faith or anything "religious" at this point — only philosophical answers to the perennial questions. Tillich was an intellectual as rigorous as Sartre and as honest as Camus. The title of his best-known work, *The Courage to Be,* suggests the core of his insight that faith and courage are inseparable.

I wanted more and sought it. But I took my time.

CHAPTER TEN

Dancers and Other People

One of the advantages of "making it" as a writer in the last days of the major studios was the opportunity to work with some of the most talented — indeed, legendary — performers of the "Golden Age" of Hollywood. Chaplin was naturally my first hero and often entertained at our Circle Theater cast parties with hilarious improvisations. At times he also lectured us young actors on technique, although, in truth, his genius lay in performance, not theory.

Buster Keaton had no theories and was strangely self-deprecatory. Fortunately, he proved genial about reminiscing, and his stories spurred our imaginations. Melvyn Douglas and Walter Pidgeon, major stars in their day, were thoroughly professional and easy to work with, as were veteran character actors such as Jack Gilford, Mike Mazurki, Cliff Osmond, James Whitmore, and "Cookie" (Elijah Cook Jr.), as well as fine actresses such as Marjorie Bennett, Nanette Fabray, France Nuyen, and Naomi Stevens. Working with these "pros" reminded me why I loved the theater and admired good actors.

But if there was any reason, other than pure chance, that led me to work with great dancers, I can't figure it out. I guess I was just lucky. In any case, Fred Astaire, Gene Kelly, and Sammy Davis Jr. were undoubtedly the best hoofers in movie history, and over the years I was engaged in projects with all three.

Fred Astaire, Gene Kelly, and Sammy Davis Jr.

I didn't learn anything about dance from these men, but I had the chance to see all three of them as human beings. In a sense, these relationships, like my earlier glimpse into Jerome Kern's elegant life, demystified these famous men.

One of those uncanny moments, when you feel like you're in a movie, occurred at Fred Astaire's home. We were in the middle of a story conference, and Fred pulled me aside to ask my advice about his dramatic performance. Jim and I had always referred to Fred as "the greatest living American," our tribute to his style and class, but recognizing something more: a rare integrity. Fred had introduced many of Mr. Kern's best-known songs as well as those of Irving Berlin, George Gershwin, and Cole Porter. So here he was, asking my advice — Einstein asking me to help him with his math. I made some suggestions and then, even more strangely, ended up having to repeatedly assure one of the world's greatest entertainers that he would do well, and not to worry. Fred was among the most gracious men in the business, but I don't think he was just trying to make me feel good.

Gene Kelly was, if anything, even less secure. Gene wasn't just a wonderful dancer and singer; he was one of the major innovators in movie musicals. Gene, also an established director, was put in charge of the re-scheduled "Tom Swift" production and supervised Jim and me as we did yet another rewrite. The rewrite went poorly, and the movie was, as they used to say, "unrealized" — that is, finally abandoned. This was neither our fault nor Gene's. Fox was about to go broke.

Despite our assurances that we respected his judgment even if at times we disagreed with some of his ideas, Gene remained hypersensitive and defensive, as if he were the untested newcomer, not us. I think he sensed the changes in the business and must have felt the ground slipping from under him — a nasty metaphor, I know, for a dancer.

Jim and I wrote a TV pilot project for Sammy Davis, or Sam, as he preferred to be called, and, for a while, whether we liked it or not, we became part of his entourage. This was usually a large number of people — including agents, musicians, and even other celebrities — who attended his nightclub performances and partied into the morning. Sam and his charming wife, Altovise, a beautiful former model, also insisted on having us to dinner, and I think Ruth and Ellie (Jim's wife) enjoyed the experience. Sam joked pointedly with Ruth about their both being Jewish — he had converted years before — and she took it in stride. She didn't know how seriously to take Sam as a Jew. He didn't seem very observant, but she found him charming.

I later directed Sam in an episode of *Charlie's Angels*. Our relationship was somewhat strained by his wanting the same preferential treatment as his mentor, Frank Sinatra. Legend has it that Sinatra once responded to a movie producer's complaint that they were "ten days behind schedule" due to Frank's laxity by picking up the script, tearing out ten random pages, and then announcing, "There! Now we're back on schedule!" Unfortunately, this was TV, and Sam wasn't Sinatra, and I had to insist on his complying with our even more demanding schedule.

On one harrowing day, we were shooting in a hotel ballroom with a band, a dozen showgirls, and fifty dress extras when Sam announced that he was tired and was going home early. I literally pleaded with him until he relented and finished the scene. This unreasonable demand for special treatment indicated an inexplicable underlying insecurity. At another time, when I expressed my genuine appreciation for a suggestion he had offered, this multitalented show-business legend looked at me appreciatively and said, "You know, I really am good!"

There were other performers, some almost equally as famous and successful, whose insecurity brought out behavior so bizarre that I'm not going to identify them. The worst form it took was deliberate cruelty in their attitude toward others, usually the "little people" on the set. It almost never happened to me, but it was still hard to watch, much less forgive.

I wish, looking back, that I hadn't been so insecure myself. Perhaps I might have understood these talented and famous people better. I know this is a strange comparison, but in my later years, working with addicts as a prison chaplain, I began to see some parallels. I realized how deeply addictive the desire for fame could be. This addiction was actually a longing for something more than success or recognition. It was a desire for a kind of immortality, to be remembered, and yet still more.

Gil Bailie, an astute observer of the changing culture, once suggested that I introduce myself in a lecture by saying, "I've spent most of my life in Hollywood — but then so have you." The mass media has become all-encompassing, resulting in a pervasive exaltation of celebrity. As historian Daniel Boorstin observed a half-century ago, the celebrity is now a person simply "famous for being famous." I was around for much of that half-century, perhaps long enough to let my eyes adjust to the glare. I saw the nature of fame change.

I doubt that Fred, Gene, or Sam were aware of how their status as "celebrities" or simply "famous people" was changing. I'm sure they were concerned about age and diminishing abilities, as anyone would be, though particularly an entertainer, but I doubt that they thought much about fame itself.

These remarkable men had achieved their status primarily because of truly exceptionable abilities, all three world-class dancers and entertainers. This recognition was consistent with traditional fame in that ancient figures, whether kings, conquerors, or "geniuses," were renowned for their abilities as well as for the "virtues" of courage, physical beauty, or benevolence. However, beginning in the fifties, the basis of fame in Hollywood began to shift rapidly. There were several reasons for this development, but in Hollywood it had to do with commerce. Losing the adult audience to television, the movie and music industries consciously cultivated a "youth market" of teenagers as an alternative consumer group. Highly imitative and dependent upon peer approval, teens were devoted to their own fashions, and ideal repeat customers.

This kind of commercial stampede is characteristic of Hollywood, yet this new gold rush overlapped with the decline of the "Old Hollywood." Welcoming change, some of us initially held out hope that an adult audience might be retained. This promise was most evident in the best of the music of the sixties. Again, many of the major artists were Jewish, such as Bob Dylan, Paul Simon, and Leonard Cohen. An old friend from the Left, Marv Mattis, became a prominent executive in the music business, and we had several conversations about how to integrate what we saw as the radical new "urban folk music" into movies. Unfortunately, the studio's interest was in profits rather than revolution, artistic or otherwise, and led to a mindless pandering to the young rather than lasting innovations. In time, both Marv and I jumped the wall and headed for the desert.

I liked kids, just as I loved my daughters; I just never thought they should control the market.

This marketing strategy led, in time, not just to a new group of idols but eventually to a change in the nature of fame itself. The older screen stars had been, for the most part, adults who, like Fred, Gene, and Sam, displayed remarkable talents; or they were iconic men such as Duke Wayne, Bogart, and Gable; or idealized female stars such as Bette Davis and Loretta Young. These were not just glamorous figures, but symbols of heroic courage, beauty, virtue, and, occasionally, danger.

In time, such icons were replaced by very young personalities such as James Dean, Elvis Presley, and Marilyn Monroe. The new iconography was that of the angry, sullen adolescent male and the sexy girl-child; this would create the celebrity models for the rest of the century.

The media industry successfully created an assembly line of almost identical rebels, exotics, and bad boys and girls, as replaceable and temporary as shelf products.

We all seek recognition; it's only human. But what we really want and need is to be accepted as we really are and were meant to be, not as imaginary products. Fred, Gene, and Sam wanted to be admired for what they truly accomplished. Did they sense this change in "fame," already impending when I knew them? I hope not.

*   *   *

Politics, the War, and the Russians

During those last years in Hollywood, I still retained some sense of political commitment. I just wasn't always sure to what. Nevertheless, Jim joined me in several causes — primarily raising funds for civil rights organizations and Cesar Chavez's farm workers union. This gave us the opportunity to meet Chavez, a genuinely humble man, as well as Luis Valdez, the talented founder of the *teatro campesino*, the innovative union theater company. We also drove a truckload of supplies to the striking workers in the Central Valley, and for a brief moment, I felt that I was back in a "real world."

I remained leery of any partisan involvement, with one exception. Bruce Geller, the creator of the *Mission Impossible* series for which Jim and I had written several scripts, was later the director of one of our better but still unsuccessful movies. We all forgave each other for our sins and became good friends. Committed primarily to the defense of Israel, Bruce involved me in my only partisan political activity of that time: primarily supporting Democrats committed to Israel. This gave me an opportunity to meet Senators Henry "Scoop" Jackson, a powerful voice in the Senate on foreign policy, and Daniel Patrick Moynihan. Jackson was running for president, Moynihan for a Senate seat in New York.

Senator Jackson struck me as a nice guy, solid, but too stolid to be TV-friendly, which was increasingly essential for a presidential candidate. Bruce was producing some of his campaign ads and filmed him at the UAW headquarters, speaking to auto workers. Moynihan, on the other hand, was a notoriously witty conversationalist, and a unique combination of intellectual and political street fighter. We spent some time with him at a fund-raising party, the kind of "A-list" Hollywood affair we rarely attended.

Moynihan was also known to be a hard drinker and proved it that night, talking a little too candidly, I thought, for a politician. What struck me was how deeply pessimistic he was about the future, including the prospective outcome of the Cold War. He deplored the cynical policies of the Soviets, but, like Solzhenitsyn, perceived a lack of resolve in the West, particularly in Europe. Perhaps this was an exaggeration, and Moynihan was simply unburdening himself with friendly strangers. His perspectives may have changed later, as did mine, but the doubts about the devolving American character of this most perceptive observer, a renowned sociologist, revealed the darkening mood of that time.

Moynihan would be elected New York's senator that fall, and we were happy to have contributed to his campaign. He later became our very able American representative at the UN and wrote an insightful book about that experience, aptly entitled *Maximum Feasible Misunderstanding.*

*   *   *

Jim and I were also active in the anti-war movement, which, in elite Hollywood circles, meant attending cocktail parties, particularly at The Daisy, an exclusive club in Beverly Hills. It was a unique show-business form of militancy, combining drinks and flirtations with anti-war ingénues eager to meet producers — all of us, of course, committed to peace and justice.

We did do our share of marching, however, and were in the crowd when violence erupted at a "peace rally" outside the Century City Hotel, where President Lyndon Johnson was staying. "Hey, hey, LBJ, how many kids did you kill today?" was the collective chant in those days. I approached the growing crowd tentatively, with good reason. I had gotten a phone call from an old leftist friend the night before warning me that there would be violence at the rally because he and a band of militants were going to start it. Jim and I and some companions from the studio had been having drinks on the roof of the executive building at Fox before joining the march and were by that time more tipsy than militant. The Fox lot was so close that we had hoped to get a bird's-eye view of the event, but we had been chased off the roof by the Secret Service.

I spotted my friend and his comrades — dressed in what was then the style of Japanese rioters, bandannas around their heads — as they trotted by, a phalanx headed for the police lines. I put my group into a quick-march retreat as the violence broke out. The media was snookered into portraying the incident as an over-reaction by the Los Angeles police. It was, in reality, what you might call just another form of show business. Fortunately, there was no serious damage to anyone — except the reputation of the police.

My anti-war activities at times brought me into contact with some of my old comrades on the hard Left; however, I made a concerted effort to distance myself from anyone that I suspected had an agenda beyond ending the war and extending civil rights. This attitude and my unwillingness to lend support to their faction eventually led me into conflict with what remained of the old Left in the Writers Guild. A definitive break and, I fear, some ensuing enmity came when I joined the director Arthur Hiller in initiating a campaign on behalf of Jewish writers in the Soviet Union who had been denied the right to emigrate to Israel.

Our campaign in Hollywood on behalf of the so-dubbed "refuseniks" was inspired by the arrival of a delegation of Soviet writers as part of a cultural exchange with our Guild. This was, in fact, one of the last desperate attempts of the Soviet leaders to use a policy of "peaceful co-existence" to sustain their increasingly unstable regime. Some of our Guild members, including our former president, my good friend John Furia, had previously visited the Soviet Union, and now it was the Soviets' turn.

I was on the Board of Directors of the Guild, and despite my outspoken "anti-communist" opinions — a highly relative position within ultra-liberal Hollywood — I was made part of the American team to greet the Russians. I immediately contacted my Jewish "refusenik" friends, writers who had managed to get out of the Soviet Union and make it to Hollywood. A couple of them had been successful filmmakers in the Soviet Union before running into trouble because of their Jewishness or their honesty, or both. I asked them to brief me about the group soon to arrive.

The Soviet delegation was headed by a distinguished older man named Alexei Kapler, who was a story in himself. Jewish by birth but I doubt by conviction, Kapler was a legendary figure due to his sad personal history. As a young man he had briefly been the lover of Stalin's daughter, Svetlana, then also quite young, and this had cost Kapler years in the Gulag. How he survived was the mystery. He was eventually rehabilitated, and, now a benign, white-haired "Father Christmas" in appearance, he became the leading film critic on Soviet television.

The real leader of the delegation, it became clear, was a big, burly man named Metilnikoff, whose reputation as a writer was based on his war stories, several of which had been made into movies. The other two writers seldom spoke, always deferring to Metilnikoff out of respect or perhaps fear. Two things became clear about Metilnikoff. He was a Party propagandist, and not particularly subtle about it, and he had an agenda. Someone had clearly briefed him on the composition of the American delegation, which had been announced in the trades. Several of us had been blacklisted, but I was the only Gentile in the group, and Metilnikoff clearly concentrated on me. He was the proverbial Russian bear, but, with me at least, a friendly one. His English wasn't very good, but his message was plain. He would put a big arm around me and say, "Ron . . . these refuseniks . . . no good people!"

Ruth and I hosted the Russians one night, taking them to a Mexican restaurant in the downtown area and deliberately driving through some poorer areas so they could see the wide range of American life. For the most part, they had been hosted in the lovely Beverly Hills homes of our successful members or taken on studio tours. We passed a group of African-Americans entering the Music Center for a concert, and the Russians seemed astounded that they were allowed to do so freely. Apparently, they actually believed their own propaganda.

At the Mexican restaurant, Metilnikoff, a bit drunk, drew curious looks from the Latinos when he loudly toasted Pancho Villa with a shot of straight tequila. It was a familiar place for Ruth and me, because we had lived in the neighborhood during my college years, but we were the only non-Mexicans in sight. When I described this, in my quasi-Marxist terms, as being "working class" — which it certainly was — Metilnikoff snorted with disbelief. These Mexicans could not possibly be "working class," he asserted, because they were all too well-dressed.

His dismissal had to be rendered into English for us by the group's official translator, Bella Epstein; she and Kapler were the only Jews in the Soviet group. Bella was a charming, highly literate, and sophisticated older woman who had traveled widely in her official capacity, attending film festivals and other cultural events throughout Europe. She had begun her career doing simultaneous translations of American films at the Kremlin for Stalin and his confrères. Bella was particularly friendly with Ruth and gave us a small gift of Russian folk art when she left.

This is a story with a sad ending. When we learned the identities of the Soviet delegation, our refusenik friends explained that at least one of them would either be from the KGB or have the assignment of watching and reporting on the others. They had no trouble identifying that person in this delegation: Bella Epstein had played this role for many years.

Ruth and I found her so open and charming that we didn't want to believe this. However, after our night out at the Mexican restaurant, we returned with Bella to the home of Michael Blankfort, one of the elder statesmen of our Guild, who had visited the Soviet Union in the 1930s and spoke some Russian. Alexei Kapler was an old friend and had remained at the Blankforts for dinner. He was apparently speaking rather frankly about conditions in Russia when he heard Bella's voice as she entered. He quickly signaled to Michael that it would no longer be possible to speak freely.

There's another, even sadder footnote. Some years later I got a call from David Rintels, our Guild president, who had written the TV drama *Sakharov*, about the noted Russian scientist and human rights activist. David told me of a private communication from Bella Epstein. She was exploring the possibility of defecting. This was just a few years before the Soviet Union dissolved; but no one could have guessed then how quickly that would happen. David and I discussed the possibility of securing a book deal for Bella as a means of assisting her. David reported later that, unfortunately, serious illness interfered with her plans.

Looking back, I realized why my "refusenik" friends had expressed so little condemnation of Bella, even though she had undoubtedly harmed others in the past. We have no way of knowing what terrible circumstances might lead people to compromise their principles, or what "lesser evil" might have been chosen when no good choice was available. I realized that I was in no position to judge anyone other than myself.

Our campaign on behalf of the "refuseniks" had been quite successful, culminating in full-page ads in the trades signed by notable liberals such as Henry Fonda and Barbra Streisand, and many respected writers such as Paddy Chayefsky and Edmund North. Arthur Hiller called me sometime later to tell me that we had succeeded in getting the release of at least one of the "refuseniks" we had identified, and he and his family were now safely in Israel. However, this effort and my continued criticism of hypocritical communist "peace initiatives" led some of my colleagues in the Guild to characterize me as a "conservative," a damning label in Hollywood.

The damning truth was that I wasn't as conservative as I was increasingly cynical. I didn't care about my image. I just didn't like what was happening to me.

CHAPTER ELEVEN

Facing the Tube

From Film to Television

Jim and I didn't know it at the time, or want to know it, but the death of old Hollywood was also the demise of our dreams as screenwriters. We would continue to get studio assignments while still trying to sell our original scripts, but they were meant for another time and a past industry. We might be romantics, but we could count; we could see how much we didn't have in our bank accounts. We considered our options. Jim could go back to teaching school and I could go back to doing social work, or we could go into television. It was a painful but otherwise easy decision.

Sadly, the move to television meant leaving our always supportive agent, Ilse, who had made only half-hearted tries at entering TV-land. This sophisticated lady, as well as most of Paul Kohner's elegant clients, were declining in several ways, including becoming legendary. We regretted leaving Ilse, but we were fortunate to have been approached by Frank Thompson, a highly literate literary agent who had solid television contacts.

Frank — or "the Ace," as his many friends called him, a nickname he had earned for his academic achievements rather than card-playing — was with one of the major agencies more adapted to the times than Paul Kohner's shop; but, in many ways, Frank was a throwback to the charming, sophisticated agents of an earlier generation, a rapidly disappearing breed. Insightful, always dapper, and wonderfully quirky, the Ace had given up the promise of an academic career, after having earned a Phi Beta Kappa at Harvard in American history, to return to Hollywood, where he and I were once classmates in junior high.

Frank had been influenced by an incident as odd as his choice to become an agent. When he was growing up, his family lived in the plebian section of the Hollywood Hills, where very early one morning his mother heard a knock at their back door. It was Humphrey Bogart.

Bogart, who apparently lived someplace at the top of the hill, had been on a binge that night that ended in a row with his then-wife, Margo. He had wandered into the foothills, and as the sun rose and sobriety kicked in, he desperately needed a cup of coffee. Frank's mother gave him one. Frank remembered his younger brother shaking him awake with the whispered announcement, "Mama's having coffee with Humphrey Bogart!"

Frank and his family subsequently became occasional guests on the sound stages of the gracious-when-sober Bogart, and Frank caught the show-biz bug. A college classroom, even at Harvard, couldn't compete with Bogie's world of improbable adventures, and not just on the screen.

Truly an Ace, Frank immediately found us work in television, where we would toil for the next decade, first as writers of "episodic" and then "long-form" TV movies and pilots, and finally as producers. Jim and I worked on many different TV projects, mostly crime and suspense dramas, but some comedy, as well as the first TV movie about the new gadget called "the computer." While this versatility was financially profitable, I think it also arrested our career. A network executive, a friend and genuine fan of ours, once introduced us as writers to a new producer by saying, "You should know these guys — Austin and Buchanan — they can write anything!" Being able to write "anything" really meant, I fear, "nothing in particular," a verdict fatal to a hope for distinction.

The failure of our feature-film projects thus first forced Jim and me as writers into television; but then, out of self-defense, we became producers. We achieved some success working as what would later be called "showrunners," basically hired guns who produce other people's TV series. We also wrote some highly rated TV movies and were frequently employed in "development," which meant being well-paid to come up with ideas for series that, for us at least, were never successful. I think by this time Jim and I had become as tone-deaf to the mass audience as Jim, a former jazz musician, was to rock and roll.

Our engagement as show-runners on the original TV series *Charlie's Angels* probably provided our most lasting Hollywood credit in that the show became what *Vanity Fair*, the fashion journal, called "the hottest show on planet earth." This extravagant claim was based primarily on the show's introduction of hairstyles and lip gloss. The critics were often less kind. Clive James, writing in *The Observer* in London, lamented that the show "has succeeded in uniting the population of the world like nothing since the common cold."

Not surprisingly, the work proved stressful due to the endemic insecurity that quick success produces, and not just in the performers. Jim and I were summoned to replace a couple of early producers, quick casualties of anxieties and clashing temperaments. Our boss, Aaron Spelling, looked to Jim and me to bring things under control. I think what we provided in calming that storm-rocked ship had less to do with our show-biz skills than our experience as battle-tested fathers of teenage girls. Jim and I certainly contributed nothing to the advancement of lip gloss.

The show, in any case, was a big hit, and it pulled some spectacular ratings, the only bankable measure of a TV show's status in Hollywood. The opening show of the second season, a two-hour spectacular that we shot in Hawaii, introduced Cheryl Ladd as Farrah Fawcett's replacement and featured ample beach-and-bikini scenery. Cheryl surprised us with a welcome flair for comedy, the beautiful Jackie Smith did a graceful dance on the beach, and high-spirited Kate Jackson got into the mood and even did a hula. The night that it aired, this extravaganza garnered nearly 50 percent of the great American audience. The TV critics, a frustrated lot by nature, snarled, but, thanks to the overnight numbers, Jim and I were the overnight darlings of the studios and networks, and even remained so for about a year.

I guess you could say that I was a success. At least I had attained the immutable symbols of Hollywood success — a private secretary, a private john and designated parking space, and my name in the *Variety* crossword puzzle. I had made it. What "it" was, however, was increasingly uncertain.

I was succeeding in ways uncomfortable to me, and I was doing work that seemed meaningless except, of course, for the comfortable income. But I had delightful friends, mostly writers who were wry and lively conversationalists. Jim was like a brother to me, and we gave each other mutual support when needed — which was often.

You can stay stuck in that kind of situation for a long time, and I did.

*　　*　　*

During my nearly four decades in the Writers Guild, I spent more than two-and-a-half years on strike. My role in these Guild battles ranged from picketer to picket captain, and then from negotiating committee member to negotiating committee chairman, each step contributing to a potential ulcer and a much thicker skin.

I'm fortunate that my Writers Guild experiences of long labor strife and bitter internal disputes were the closest that I ever came to succumbing to a war mentality. The Hollywood writers of my time were a contentious lot, and anyone attending a Guild meeting, especially at strike time, would have quickly been disabused of the naïve idea that education alone produces rationality. There were many difficult and disheartening times, including my being publicly denounced as a traitor to the cause when I attempted to mediate strike issues. I can no longer remember the issues, and I doubt that anyone else can either, but it was hurtful.

Yet what I remember best is the feeling of solidarity and especially the comedy. I once frantically trailed after the comedienne Lily Tomlin, a Guild member, as she fled from a picket line outside Paramount. The media were after her to make a statement, and, as a Guild spokesman, I was trying to impose on her the need to be supportive. Lily wanted neither my advice nor the media attention, and ran from all of us.

On another occasion, while in New York during a particularly bitter and divisive strike, screenwriter Frank Pierson and I, representing the West Coast writers, were met with more hostility than fraternal greetings. We were angrily denounced as Hollywood elitists during that evening's contentious meeting. The nastiest attack came from one of our own West Coast members, a prominent bi-coastal comedy writer, a woman known equally for her talent and her vitriol.

Again, I can no longer remember the issues. They probably had to do with the frequent pay inequities in the "soap opera" field. Even though the meeting was tense, everyone flocked as usual to the bar afterwards, and it was nearly one in the morning before the last of us trailed out. Unfortunately for our angry adversary, the sharp-tongued comedy writer, there were no cabs in sight, and this was during a time in New York City when neither male nor female felt safe on late-night streets. She had no choice but to ask Frank and me to walk her to her hotel, which, naturally, as elitist gentlemen, we did. The conversation en route was a little strained — even for three people who wrote dialogue for a living.

*   *   *

London Days

In 1981, at the end of another long and bitter Writers Guild strike, Jim and I were asked to co-produce a series to be shot in London, and we jumped at it. It was essentially a British series, but would star the fine American actor Sam Waterston, and the head of the company was John Hawkesworth, whose work we greatly admired. John had produced *Upstairs, Downstairs* and the *Duchess of Duke Street*, and would later create the Sherlock Holmes series with Jeremy Brett. John flew to L.A. to meet with us, and it was arranged that I would go to London to work with the Brits and Jim would stay in L.A. and develop scripts with American writers. In other words, it would be an American-British co-production — which meant that it would never work, and it didn't.

The series was called Q.E.D., after the initials of the central character, an eccentric American inventor living in England in the early 1900s, whose brilliant logic often prompted the Latin exclamation *quod erat demonstrandum*, or, "Q.E.D. — it's obvious!" The idea of a title for a series rooted in Latin should have suggested the inherently limited nature of its appeal, but, at that point, I didn't really care. I was eager to get away from Hollywood. Sam Waterston was excellent in the lead, and a thoughtful and sensitive man — not always the case among even talented actors. (A few years later Sam and I tried to initiate a production of Walker Percy's novel *The Thanatos Syndrome*, and I think we might have had a chance, but, unfortunately, it was just at that time that both Ruth's mother and Sam's mother became seriously ill.)

Q.E.D. was a delightful period adventure-comedy, and Hawkesworth provided the high-quality production values for which the Brits were well-known. However, the show's sensibility and sense of humor remained very British as well, and thus were predictably foreign to the American mass audience. While never confident of the show's success, I was pleased to work with John and Sam, and even more pleased to be able to live in England for over a year. I visited the village where my father's family had lived for centuries. I even found a distant cousin still residing there who showed me the shell of an eighteenth-century house where a common ancestor had once lived. Apparently, at least some of the animals had dwelt inside with the family. It was clear that I was not from a noble lineage.

For most of our stay, Ruth and I lived in a delightful section of London near Hampstead Heath, and she was able to spend days at the extraordinary museums, particularly the National Gallery and the Tate, as well as study at the Hampstead Art Institute, where she refined her watercolor skills. I was happy to drive her to "Constable country" to contemplate the nature which that great painter caught on canvas. His burial place was in a little churchyard in Hampstead, and we would pay homage while on our frequent walks. For the rest of her life, Ruth would pursue the beauty of nature in her own work.

It was a very pleasant life. We went to the theater or the opera almost every weekend and explored every corner of London. But, of course, I had not left my anxieties and doubts behind. Nevertheless, in a new environment that broke the spell of the familiar, I started to see the world more clearly.

I began to attend mass regularly for the first time. For a short while, we lived within walking distance to the Brompton Oratory, the church of St. John Henry Newman, where I could go to daily mass as well as attend lectures and concerts. I also had plenty of time to read and even think.

The reason for this leisurely life was that my British colleagues really didn't want me around. They were personable, some even friendly, and genuinely solicitous, making sure that Ruth and I found a nice place to live and providing me with a good car. But they were talented and highly experienced professionals, and I had been forced upon them by CBS. A Yank who knew the American temperament was the network's prerequisite for green-lighting the series. The ratings of *Charlie's Angels* and some of my other credits offered assurances that I had the popular touch, but, for the Brits, it was no guarantee that I had any real ability or knew what I was doing. Jim was a safe distance away in Hollywood, and they clearly wished I were there as well.

So, over time, "perfidious Albion" went into action, and I was systematically excluded from key decisions and then, whenever possible, from the production process itself.

I was delighted. I discharged my responsibilities by giving Hawkesworth extensive notes and whatever advice he sought, seldom followed, and occasionally conferring with Sam. I had no desire to run the show or to interfere in it. It was a strange, utterly unacknowledged arrangement of mutual convenience. I would be sent to look for distant locations in other parts of England, or do research at the British Library. (Hawkesworth, whose wife was titled, secured the otherwise unattainable pass.) Safely out of their hair, Ruth and I would take off on what for us were most pleasant paid vacations, including trips to Malta, Scotland, and Ireland. I spent days at the British Library, where I had access to one of the world's greatest collections of works in English. (I wondered which desk Karl Marx had used.) I came up with some ideas for the show, knowing that they would never be used, and then spent hours reading for my own edification.

*   *   *

I had decided while in England to write a play about Thomas Merton, the well-known convert to Catholicism and author of the spiritual autobiography *The Seven Storey Mountain*. A Cistercian monk, poet, and peace advocate, Merton wrote perceptively about contemplative prayer, a new subject for me. While impressed by his writings, I was more intrigued by his life, which, in some ways, was similar to my own. He had lost his mother at an early age and had been a political radical while in college, and, disillusioned, sought the religious life. I responded to his temperament as much as to his faith.

To understand Merton, I decided to read his sources. (This was possible thanks to my increasing leisure time; *Q.E.D.* began to sink as soon as it went on the air.) Merton was a classically trained scholar in English and French, and many of his references were well beyond my grasp; others were not only accessible but, in time, transformative for me.

The most significant figure I discovered was Jacques Maritain, the French philosopher. Maritain, an anti-fascist exiled in America during the war, had influenced many American Catholics, including Dorothy Day, the founder of the Catholic Workers, whom I also admired. I devoured Maritain's philosophical works, particularly his Thomistic analysis of art and beauty, and even understood some of it.

I felt that I had found in Merton, Day, and Maritain a genuine radicalism that went beyond politics. It was a commitment to the poor, but also suggested an authentic way of life. I was looking for something that answered Ruth's concerns, and, in truth, my own, that I wasn't simply searching for another utopia or some new "answer to everything." What I was seeing in the *imitatio Christi*, the imitation of Christ, was a commitment that didn't depend upon ideology, power, or even results.

The Merton play, once completed, was a one-man performance piece, and Father Elwood "Bud" Kieser, the only producer of Catholic programming on TV at that time, was eager to stage it and then put it on television. Only later did we discover that a codicil in Merton's will expressly forbade any such performance of his work or depiction of his person. Apparently, when his *Seven Storey Mountain* first appeared, a noted Hollywood actor wanted to buy the rights so that he could portray Merton. A good Catholic, the actor was better known for his charm and musical abilities than for his acting skills, and Merton, fearful of the results, made sure that no such fate would befall him even after death.

I was disappointed, but in preparing the work I had, in effect, taken a crash course in Catholic literature, both devotional and theological, as I probed Merton's extensive sources.

I had received my first catechism, even if it was my own.

*   *   *

Going Home

Jim always said that I went to London and never came back. In a way, he was right. When I returned to Hollywood after the predictable demise of *Q.E.D.* — which drew ratings lower than public television — I had changed, and, close as we were, Jim knew it.

By the 1980s, I wasn't the only one changing. In many respects, the whole world seemed in flux. I was now consciously "cutting myself loose" from my past life, but the world seemed even more adrift. When Ronald Reagan became president, I was uneasy, but this was based primarily on my understandable prejudice against show-biz people in politics. Clearly a sincere and decent man, qualities undetected only by the intellectuals, he became an effective leader, particularly in foreign policy, guiding policies that led to the remarkable defeat of the Soviet Union without a war.

Ruth and I passed through Reagan's hometown — Dixon, Illinois — during the period of his presidency, and visited the modest museum in his childhood home. We were touched by the interior, with its small kitchen and linoleum floor, because it reminded us of our own childhood during the Depression.

Reagan had made a valiant effort to return America to these simple roots, the Norman Rockwell, small-town America of traditional values and neighborliness. It was a commendable effort to "go home again"; but as Thomas Wolfe could have told him, it can't be done. The Reagan Revolution may have succeeded in many respects, but not in the way he probably most desired. Americans didn't "return home" to the old values. The truth is that, for many, there was no longer a home to which to return.

*　　*　　*

Jim and I had kept an office on the Sunset Strip, which we used when we weren't working at a studio. It was directly across from one of the venerable industry watering-holes, the Cock 'n Bull, where we presided for several years at a backroom writers' table. Our agent, the inimitable Ace, and several genial, witty, and even successful writers would gather regularly for collective therapy derived from denouncing the town and the business. Our discussions were less about world politics than about Writers Guild affairs and when we would next be out on strike. Those were the good times.

It was an odd life even for Hollywood. I was deeply committed to the Guild, the only defense that writers had against exploitation, but I was also living my version of a "fast lane" life. I was lucky to have a patient wife and such good friends, but I was not pleased with myself or with the life I was leading.

Once, as Jim and I were taking one of our periodic strolls on the Strip, weaving our way down the now-fading but once-glamorous boulevard, I told him that I felt somehow lost. He was sympathetic as always, a brother as much as a friend. I remember telling him that I didn't know who I was anymore.

I was beginning to realize that I was going to have to find out.

ACT TWO

A New Life

CHAPTER TWELVE

Conversion

Father Tony, smiling, blessed and doused me.

We were in a side chapel, and Ruth and our girls and Jim and his wife, Ellie, were there, along with a few of my closest friends, probably less than half of them Catholic. I was entering the Catholic Church. I was nearly fifty.

Ruth had patiently accepted my new Christian convictions, though not without some misgivings. This was not so much due to her Jewish identity, or even the painful memories of her days in Brooklyn, when she had suffered discrimination and even some animosity from her Catholic neighbors. Her best friend in her early teens had been a Catholic girl whose mother would not allow Ruth to attend her daughter's birthday party.

Ruth was more concerned about me. Was this another pursuit of some unrealizable ideal, or, possibly, even a substitute for my lost radical utopianism? There is no shortage of examples of secular radicals or even communists becoming Catholics. Both Merton and Dorothy Day had taken that path. Was I again looking for some absolute, all-encompassing answer to life's dilemmas?

After we had returned from London, she had asked me to wait and to test my beliefs. She didn't have to point out to me that my commitment to Christianity, to date, had cost me nothing. She had seen and was encouraged by some changes in my personal behavior — less drinking and fewer explosions of judgmental anger — and there were other changes that she didn't know about but may have sensed. But I was still living a comfortable life, reading more about prayer than praying.

I knew she was right. She usually was, especially about me. By asking me to first test my faith, my Jewish wife was pointing me in the inescapable direction of a genuine Christian life.

*   *   *

Old Friends, New Friends

When I returned to Hollywood after the London sojourn, I actually knew very few Catholics. Perhaps in an earlier generation I might have found them, but in the "post-countercultural" Hollywood, there were few identifiably religious people of any kind. They certainly hadn't been hanging out at the Cock 'n Bull or strolling the Sunset Strip. Our old friend and mentor, Shimon Wincelberg, was the only religious Jew that Jim and I had encountered. A fine writer, Shimon was respected by his colleagues, but also the source — though never the butt — of humor. Writers all delighted in the story that he had refused to take a call from Daryl Zanuck on *Shabbat*.

In time I would come to have several good Catholic friends, including John Furia, a former president of the Writers Guild, and Jack and Patt Shea. Jack, who had gone to Fordham with John, then served as the president of the Directors Guild, and Patt wrote for *All in the Family*. I also sought out Father "Bud" Kieser again; he was producing *Insight*, an award-winning TV series with spiritual and moral themes. A big, persuasive man, he could have been a success in Hollywood on his own merits, probably more easily without the collar. Father Bud had wanted Jim and me to write a script for him, but it never happened. A real producer, he enticed us with creative freedom. "You can write about whatever you want," he said, confident of this appeal. "The war, civil rights — anything!" But I was heading down a road that he didn't expect. "I'd like to write about original sin," I told him. Father Bud was puzzled, particularly when he realized that I was serious. But he remained my good friend and counselor for some time to come.

In my last years in Hollywood, I did work on a couple of shows that had a "Catholic spin," but little truly Catholic content, other than wardrobe and props. The best was the *Father Dowling Mysteries*, produced by an old friend, Dean Hargrove, one of the most successful TV creators during that time. Dean and I had known each other since the old studio days, and he used me as his "relief pitcher" on several of his shows, writing and fixing scripts during the last hectic months of the TV season. Father Dowling was played by the talented Tom Bosley, who was Jewish (not that this mattered). A genial man, he made a genial priest. It was a good, tight show, as were Dean's other productions, *Matlock* and *Jake and the Fat Man*, and I worked on both of those as well. I'm not sure that the audience ever noticed that the plots of these three shows, all mysteries of a sort, were at times interchangeable, but as long as Father Dowling remained just a detective, there's no good reason why they shouldn't have been.

*   *   *

Another priest, Father Anthony Scannell, who would become my first confessor, then asked John, Jack and Patt, me, and a few other Catholic professionals to resuscitate the annual Catholic award show and mass. This had once been a top event in Hollywood, when stars such as Bing Crosby, Rosalind Russell, Fred MacMurray, Loretta Young, and Irene Dunne attended.

We had no such luminaries now, but under Father Tony's guidance, a new organization, Catholics in Media, was launched and sponsored a Catholic awards show that once again became a popular event. Cardinal Roger Mahony celebrated mass, and Catholics such as Gregory Peck, Carroll O'Connor, and Rosemary Clooney were honored, as well as many others not of the faith. Steven Spielberg graciously came to accept an award for his film *Schindler's List*, but there were some nominal Catholics who kept their distance even when their work received recognition. Being a Catholic who actually supported the church was still something that not everybody wanted to advertise in Hollywood. But under the leadership of Father Tony and the Sheas, Catholics in Media grew, and more Catholics came out of the closet.

One of my first roles in the cast of "usual suspects," those of us known as Catholics in Hollywood, came quickly and unexpectedly. Joop Koopman of the *National Catholic Register*, a respected Catholic weekly, knowing my Hollywood background, asked me to cover a press conference with the new archbishop of Los Angeles, Roger Mahony, known for his strong support of the farm workers. I welcomed Mahony as a leader and, by and large, so did most Catholics, especially political liberals.

So it was astonishing to discover that the archbishop, soon to be Cardinal, was announcing his support for a new "code of conduct" for Hollywood. This was, in effect, a new "production code" concerning content, or, to Hollywood ears, "censorship"! Mahony, it turned out, had been snookered. A Protestant evangelist known for his attacks on Hollywood instigated the proposed "code," and the new archbishop, then unaccustomed to such big-city manipulation, had been persuaded by some of his inherited staff to endorse the effort. It was a public relations disaster and, I understand, led to a couple of staff people getting the episcopal axe.

I joined the press corps as we listened to Mahony make this ill-advised endorsement and was as stunned as anyone. I knew how this would go down, and "down" was the predictable direction. "Censorship" is a boogieman word in Hollywood that is applied to anything more critical than a frown of disapproval.

In many ways, this hypersensitivity to censorship was based on real fears, but it also reflected an uneasy collective conscience. Hollywood, in fact, imposed its own form of censorship, one far more effective than any outside authority or pressure group could have managed. Writers had no control over their material, and even the most distinguished directors had to fight for the right of a final cut, and seldom got it. The studios and networks had the final say, and the criterion was anticipated public reaction — as unpredictable as it was arbitrary. In other words, box office and ratings — in other words, anticipated revenue — sat in the judgment seat. What was permitted was what paid.

The archbishop had wandered into a swamp of bad publicity, but, to his credit, recovered quickly. This is why I was summoned by my friend, Guild president John Furia, along with fellow Catholic "usual suspects" Jack and Patt Shea, to an emergency meeting with our new leader. The archbishop closed the door to his office and said bluntly, "I've made a big mistake, haven't I?" I admired his openness. We confirmed the calamity and then went to work. By the next week we had assembled a select group of industry people — not the top brass but the "creative community," those most fearful of censorship and outraged by Mahony's proposal. They included the current presidents of the talent guilds as well as some top producers, almost all Jewish. Mahony hosted an unpublicized closed-door breakfast meeting at the California Club and explained that he had no intention of endorsing any form of censorship, and, what's more, that his office would be open to all present at any time if they had any concerns. His obvious sincerity and candor carried the day.

The archbishop's future friendship with industry leaders such as Lew Wasserman and his repeated affirmations of creative rights and the freedom of expression made him, in time, a popular prelate even among Jewish liberals, despite his precarious start.

*   *   *

The relationship between Hollywood — particularly "my Jewish town" — and the Catholic Church had always been complex, and often tense. I had some insight into the past because of my friendship with Jack Vizzard, an ex-Jesuit who had been one of the "censors" at the Breen office. This was the successor to the original organization, the "Hays office," which the industry had invited before the war to review films prior to release. This was the industry's idea of self-governance, an effort to avoid threatened government oversight following public criticism of growing sexual explicitness in movies. The situation had been aggravated by several well-publicized sex scandals, and, far from a serious examination of effects on public morality, the whole operation was basically public relations and damage control.

Curiously, the Jewish leaders of Hollywood had, in effect, called on the Catholic Church to help bail them out. Perhaps there was some sense of solidarity between two groups that had both experienced social discrimination. This alliance followed on the heels of a study of the problem commissioned by the industry and authored by the distinguished philosopher Mortimer Adler. Entitled *Art and Prudence,* his scholarly study drew more on classical moral philosophy than religious precepts and was quite reasonable, though, I suspect, a bit academic for Louis B. Mayer or Sam Goldwyn.

Adler confirmed the obvious — that art did have effects on people's perceptions and that even art should be balanced by prudent judgment. I have no idea if Adler's report prompted the relationship, but the Catholic-run Hays office went into operation and then, under Breen, lasted until the 1950s. It is interesting to note that Adler, a Jew, wrote primarily as a noted Aristotelian philosopher but later converted to Catholicism. Hollywood really didn't care where the ideas came from as long as they didn't damage the box office.

Jack Vizzard's book *See No Evil,* written after his retirement, tells the amusing tale of the often-bizarre conflicts that plagued the so-called censors as they negotiated sometimes over single words and glimpses of flesh, or even the positioning of beds. Jack related how the Breen office lost its final battle to preserve Hollywood's purity in a bitter conflict over the word "virgin." Somehow it's fitting that the studios ended self-censorship by acknowledging, though not necessarily endorsing, virginity. But then you have to be from Hollywood to follow the logic.

*   *   *

Following my new commitment, my first inclination, not surprisingly, was to involve myself in the church's peace and justice activism. In addition to committing myself to direct work with the poor, I attended some meetings of a Catholic peace advocacy group, but it was a commitment of short duration. I found these good Catholics, several of them religious sisters, sincere but extraordinarily naïve. The end came when one of their speakers was none other than "Irv," now old and bald but still recognizable as the romantic figure who had approved my entrance into the Young Communist League. My old comrade was now preaching "peaceful co-existence" but with the familiar left-wing spin that left no doubt that the warmongers were American. An older priest and I exchanged a look and then a few words as we departed. It was clear he wasn't coming back either.

I quickly learned to stay away from the politicized extremes within the church. Some of the conservatives were arguing that American capitalism was the natural ally of the church and were eager to make this a kind of social gospel for the rest of the world. It seemed clear to me that the increasingly amoral free-market system was no more compatible with Catholic social teaching than Marxism. But I didn't want to make enemies, or even debate. There was plenty to do without arguing about it.

*   *   *

A New World of Thought

My associations over the coming years with Catholic intellectuals and publications turned out to be more positive and enriching than contentious. I had some parting of the ways with old friends over the best way to deal with dissent in the church; but it was increasingly characteristic of the times for people to bash each other.

I found the Christian intellectual orbit to be much wider than I had realized, and while many Catholic and other Christian social critics have been largely ignored by the academic guilds, the work being done is lively and stimulating.

Some of it was significant in providing a critical context for my own experiences in Hollywood, both in the entertainment industry and later with the young street guys. Christopher Lasch's *The Culture of Narcissism* remains indispensable for understanding the impact of the mass media, and *Dancing in the Dark*, a collection of essays on youth culture edited by Quentin Schultze, offers a keen understanding of American pop culture.

The most significant scholarly work for me, however, has been that of René Girard, which concerns the nature and origins of violence, and it provoked me to reconsider how we depict conflict in the mass media. A member of the *Académie française*, Girard offers insights that are strongly supported by Hebrew as well as Christian scriptures. The Gospels, unlike mythology, confirm the necessity of Girard's perspective, which is that of the victim of violence rather than the rationalizations of its perpetrators.

Much of my own movie and TV work dealt with crime and violence, and while Jim and I had some sense of moral responsibility, I don't think we ever grasped the full effects of what we were depicting. My later assessment of the media has convinced me that Girard's study of the causes of conflict is now essential reading if we are to break the endless cycle of "blame" and accusation that perpetuates violence.

* * *

Girard's pioneering work also confronts the difficult and painful subject of genocide. His analysis reveals this impulse as having a universal character related to the need for the condemnation and killing of a scapegoat. Slogans such as "the war to end all wars" and even "never again," however understandable, run the risk of promoting the self-deceiving concept of some ultimate conflict that could resolve violence.

In referring to any scholarly approach to the study of genocide, we must be aware that a long-held and understandable concern among Jews has been that comparisons made between the *Shoah* and other modern genocides could relativize the Jewish tragedy by folding it into the perennial nature of war and state terrorism. The unique historical aspect of the persecution of the Jews must be recognized in order to be fully understood, yet a neglect of prior and later genocidal campaigns runs the risk of ignoring the nature of genocide itself.

As with anti-Semitism, genocide in our times is a disturbing aspect of modernity. The systematic attempts by governments to exterminate whole populations and the ideological justifications of these murderous campaigns cannot be dismissed as merely a continuation of "man's inhumanity" or compared to barbaric invasions with their bloody plundering. Nor do the religious wars of the past, though characterized by fanatical condemnations of heretics or aliens, compare to the quasi-scientific methodologies and rationalizations of the modern era.

Prior to the *Shoah*, the Ukrainian genocide, the forced starvation of perhaps seven million people — 25 percent of the population and as much as 80 percent of Ukrainian intelligentsia — was conducted by relentless ideologues, not barbarians, in this case communist rather than fascist. A Maoist version of this ideology was used decades later to justify the slaughter of millions in China and Cambodia. In Armenia, the genocide was similarly rationalized by radical Turkish nationalists. In the later part of the century, genocidal killings such as those in Sudan and Rwanda took millions of lives — and some are not over yet.

What all of these collective horrors revealed, first, was a *de facto* indifference on the part of the major powers and certainly no serious attempts at intervention. There have also been deniers and debunkers in the aftermath eager to use the lack of reliable statistics to deny the full reality of the crimes committed. The deeper denial, however, may have been on the part of world leaders, unwilling to recognize what they were confronting.

There are two central issues raised by the modern genocides. The first arises from the argument that there is nothing new in this kind of mass killing other than the methodology and the scale. One might then ask, How is it possible that such savage aspects of human behavior remained so vigorous after the benefits of the Enlightenment and modern advances in knowledge? Whatever happened to "Progress"?

The second question is even more troubling. If there is something distinctly modern in the pseudo-scientific rationalizations of genocide, then the very concept of "development" might be questioned. Sudanese historian Francis Deng and author Gabriel Meyer, a journalist who covered the violence in Bosnia as well as Sudan, point to the distinctly artificial nature of modern identities such as "Aryan" or "proletarian" as clues to the origins of modern genocide. These highly tentative if not fictional concepts of national distinction — "Sudanese" or possibly "Iraqi" — are a source of such anxiety that this itself promotes violence against any group who by their "alien" presence challenges these fragile, artificially constructed identities.

In light of these later tragedies, we should consider a final question: Might our well-intentioned efforts at "modernization" actually be creating the deracinated identities and despairing conditions that lead to war and genocide?

The insights of René Girard are, I believe, essential for a deeper understanding of these modern genocides — not that anyone has a theory that will prevent war and violence. We do, however, have models to guide us in the effort to mediate violence: Buddha, Socrates, Isaiah, Jesus and the saints, as well as modern figures such as Bonhoeffer, Stein, Gandhi, King, Mandela and Tutu, Pope John Paul, and the Dalai Lama. Whether we will learn from them or not is yet another question.

*   *   *

Traveling Mercies and Saving Grace

All of this intellectual stimulation was rewarding, but was this expansion of knowledge the basis of my conversion? I don't think so.

There are many stories of conversions. I wouldn't compare myself to St. Paul or any other saint, for that matter, except as a set-up for a joke. If St. Paul's or St. Augustine's conversion took place in a decisive moment, in minutes or seconds — Paul is struck down on the road to Damascus, and Augustine reads some lines of Scripture — mine took almost twenty years. This is one of the reasons why I've never been able to explain it. I'm reluctant to admit, I guess, that I'm such a slow learner. The other reason is that I don't know yet quite how it happened. I think it has something to do with grace.

Ruth and I had also taken trips to Rome and Israel, and perhaps these experiences had affected me.

Ruth's extraordinary closeness with her mother, Alma, a single mother for much of their life together, made Alma's death quite devastating for her. This was eventually eased somewhat by a trip to Israel with her stepfather, our Papa Sol, and some of his family; during the trip we donated an ambulance in Alma's name to the *Magen David*, the Israeli Red Cross. This memorable journey allowed Ruth to visit Jerusalem and the Western Wall and to meet some distant family members who had emigrated directly from Russia.

She also had the experience of being in a world where, as she exclaimed with amazement, "Everybody's Jewish!" It also provided the opportunity for me, the only Christian in our tight little group, to visit many of the holy sites, including Bethlehem and Nazareth as well as the Church of the Holy Sepulcher.

It was a trip that deepened my understanding of how profoundly Jewish were both Jesus and my wife. Ruth wept several times. At the dedication of the ambulance, of course, but also at the Western Wall and, more inexplicably, at the first sight of the Mediterranean. She was also bewildered by this extremely emotional reaction. All she could say was that somehow she felt that she had "come home." I had a similar experience when first exploring the English countryside where my ancestors had lived. I'll let the psychologists ponder this, but I think there's more to these feelings than we can know.

* * *

In the past I attempted to write about the nature of religious faith and discovered that I could, at best, articulate only some of my own personal experience. In my case, faith came at the end of a very long road. I think for most of us faith arises from some often-inexplicable experiences. These are experiences of grief, loss, peace, and joy, and sometimes a strange mixture of all of them. I discovered that these experiences were shared by others, and affirmed by the teachings of a tradition.

Many seeds of faith and "saving grace" were planted in my life, but the most significant of all was simply Ruth's abiding love. True to her biblical namesake, she was forever one with me in spirit. Without this experience of a love that engenders faith and trust, I'm not sure what the word "God" would have meant to me.

Only after all these explorations over a dozen years would I formally enter the church, with Father Tony performing the baptism.

Better late than never.

* * *

I gave up show business. I knew that's what I had to do, but you're not supposed to do it on your own. That's almost cheating. The business is supposed to give you up, to dump you once you've failed or grown too old.

The hardest task I faced was telling Jim. I was sure that it wouldn't injure our friendship, but dissolving our long partnership could put him at risk professionally; we were, after all, an established team. I think Jim was bewildered by my decision. I couldn't really tell him then how I was going to change my life — because I really didn't know. Despite his concerns, however, Jim accepted my decision, and would, in the coming years, not only remain my closest friend but my strongest supporter.

Ruth was still nervous. We were Depression babies, and she never lost her fear of impending financial distress. She knew, however, how unhappy I'd become with myself and sensed that a new life for me might benefit her and our marriage as well. Again, she was right. Our daughters, Terry and Bethe, had begun their own independent lives — Terry starting a successful career as a makeup artist, and Bethe graduating that year from college after majoring in English and the classics, much to my delight. My familial responsibilities seemed to have been largely met, and the two people closest to me, as well as my daughters, gave me the support I needed. If I was going to change my life, it was up to me. I couldn't blame anyone else if I failed.

I told my current agent, now a top guy at Creative Artists Agency (the Ace had quit the agency to become a writer himself), that I was retiring and would no longer be seeking work in the business. I had only just returned from London, and I don't think there was any extraordinary demand for my services as there had been after *Charlie's Angels* — so he didn't go into shock. A short time later, however, he called to offer me another assignment: producing a TV show in Australia. When I turned him down, he paused and said, "You really mean it, don't you?" He wished me luck, but I suspect he concluded that I had just flunked a sanity test.

I then went to a Catholic church in Hollywood and offered my services. I'm not sure what I thought they needed or what I could really offer; but I had social-work experience, and the streets that I had known as a boy were now filled with addicts, prostitutes, and runaway teens. The cocaine scourge was turning into the even-worse "crack" epidemic, and this parish was right in the center of the action. The priest referred me to the central Catholic Charities office downtown. When I walked into the office of Father Padraic, the director, and told him of my past experience and that I was willing to go to work, he smiled and said in his lilting Irish brogue, "Ron, where have you been? We've been waiting for you!"

CHAPTER THIRTEEN

Mean Streets

I looked around in disbelief. I had grown up on these streets. I had delivered newspapers just below the Sunset Strip and would take the "red car" trolley or ride my bike to Hollywood Boulevard just past Vine to see an afternoon of Westerns at the "Hitching Post" theater. The Hollywood of my youth was never as glamorous as people supposed, but it was safe, and you might occasionally see a famous face. Tourists waited outside the Brown Derby on Vine to get autographs or would gather in the evening at the Grauman's Chinese Theatre or Egyptian Theatre to watch the stars arriving for movie premieres.

I was still going to be working in Hollywood, but it was a different Hollywood than I had ever known.

*　　*　　*

For the next eight years, following my conversion, I would work for Catholic Charities as a volunteer social worker and co-director of a residential program for homeless men. "Homeless" was actually a gentle euphemism for addicts, small-time drug dealers, and sex hustlers. These were to be my "clients," and my new Hollywood office was an adjunct to a church.

I can't remember entering a Catholic church before I was a Catholic — or, for that matter, why I was there. I think I attended my first mass at the old Saint Joseph church in downtown L.A., but how I got there still puzzles me. But I went back a few times, always sitting in the back like an interloper. Sometime after a trip to Rome, when I was working at MGM, I began leaving my office at noon without telling my secretary where I was going. It was assumed, I imagine, that I was sneaking out for a "nooner," as a daytime rendezvous was called back then, but I was actually walking to a nearby church for mass, again sitting inconspicuously, almost secretly, in the back.

The first time I approached the altar was at a church near Fox. It was Ash Wednesday, and I assumed that receiving the mark of ashes on my forehead as a sign of repentance wasn't going to commit or compromise either me or the church. I have only recently determined that the priest I approached was undoubtedly Father Charles Cummins, who was, in time, transferred to a beautiful mountain valley in Utah where, decades later, he would be my pastor.

Now, beginning in a new life, I would walk from my new office next door into the Blessed Sacrament Church to pray each day. This was perhaps the first time I actually thought of myself as a Catholic.

* * *

In the mid-eighties, Hollywood Boulevard was drab and dirty, and the side streets were risky at night. The drug epidemic, following a decade of disintegrating American family life, had drawn kids, many of them runaways in their early teens, from all over the country. Girls as young as thirteen were learning quickly how to "turn tricks" or simply exchange oral sex for drugs. "Crash pads" piled with filthy mattresses were filling up old and abandoned houses. Drug dealers of all races created a street market so open and thriving that traffic on certain streets would be stopped until a deal was concluded. Many of these dealers were kids, strung out themselves, but others, older guys, were bold, threatening, and dangerous.

There were customers for drugs and sex continuously cruising Sunset Boulevard, particularly on the weekends, and on certain corners the "working girls," as they preferred to be called, would parade their wares. They would stand on display in groups of two or three, many wearing the high boots and leather coats that were the fashion. Other nearby areas were favored by gay hustlers, many of them young boys. Across from the Goldwyn studios there might be twenty or more smiling and waving at the older gentlemen, the "chicken hawks," as they were called, who slowly cruised by in their nice cars.

Added to this grim mix was a horde of lost souls known uncharitably as "street crazies." For years, the aging area's old mansions had been converted into convalescent homes and halfway facilities for the mentally ill.

Now, as the "de-institutionalizing" process emptied the mental hospitals, many former patients wandered back to these neighborhoods. "Off their meds," they became confused, helpless, and, occasionally, even more dangerous than the drug dealers.

Finally, there were the innocent but just-as-lost young people who came to Hollywood, as had throngs before them, to seek fame and fortune as movie or rock stars. Not a few carried guitars, looking if not sounding like whoever was the current rage in pop music.

*   *   *

I had reported for duty, so to speak, at the Catholic Charities office next to Blessed Sacrament Church, a handsome old edifice, which once had as parishioners the movie people living in the hills above the boulevard. It was now primarily a Latino parish, with many members from Central America, and was near the epicenter of the drug-and-sex trade. The church rectory had become what the street people called a "spot," a term used for generations by vagrants indicating a place where they might possibly "score" something — bus tokens, a cup of coffee, anything. So to relieve the priests and parish staff, Catholic Charities had opened a social service office on the property. The full-timer was a cheerful Filipina social worker named Astrid, who somehow kept her pleasant disposition, despite the fact that the waiting room was swamped daily with poor Latinas and their kids, druggies, panhandlers, and the mentally ill.

Initially, Astrid didn't quite know what to do with me and was too busy to think about it. There was no shortage of work to do. The question was where to put me.

My first assignment was to be part of a nightly patrol along Hollywood Boulevard, trolling for the most vulnerable. Social workers from support agencies worked in teams of two. Most, such as the Children of the Night or Teen Canteen, were on the lookout for runaway girls. Others, such as Hollywood Mental Health, would attend to the most obviously helpless of the mentally ill. Many in both of these groups would often resist or even flee from the help offered.

My target group was single men, the largest and most difficult to categorize. The majority were addicts or older alcoholics, and there were few facilities for any of them; but if I located a young guy out of his element and at risk of being mugged, I could put him up for a night or two at a shelter or the YMCA.

Hollywood Boulevard must have been a shock to the tourists, many foreign, who arrived, cameras in hand, expecting to find glamour. They were often hustled by the panhandlers, runaways, and druggies, and I came to their aid more than once. But they still made the pilgrimage from Grauman's, with its cement handprints and footprints of the movie greats, down the promenade to Vine Street. The sidewalk they trekked was marked by more imbedded memorabilia — metal stars bearing illustrious names from the glorious past. I was always reluctant to step on them. It was a bit jarring to see nostalgic names such as Greta Garbo and Rudolph Valentino embellishing the now-drab storefronts. I remember respectfully stepping over Eric von Stroheim.

Our night patrols worked out of the "Sally" — what the street people called the Salvation Army soup kitchen. We'd get a few hundred people — mostly regulars every night — who would line up for dinner. The line was monitored by older men, veteran street guys themselves, who usually managed to keep order; but at least once or twice a week fights would break out; sometimes tables were overturned and food was wasted. Those of us from the agencies were identified, and, after dinner, people would then get in line to talk to us. As the Catholic representative, I was usually just asked for prayers. There wasn't much else I had to offer.

During the day I'd help Astrid with the always overflowing appeals for help, and I became familiar with the regulars, including the male hustlers and female hookers.

The sex business was usually brisk along Sunset Boulevard right down the corner from the church; but sometimes when it turned tough in the face of periodic police sweeps, several of the working girls began turning tricks in the back pews during the night, so we had to start locking up early.

I seldom dealt with the working girls. I think they were reluctant to mix with the street guys and crazies and maybe a bit self-conscious about coming to church, so to speak, under these circumstances. But I do remember a couple of them coming into my office. One was pencil-thin, undoubtedly a hard-drug user, who attempted to make her appearance more acceptable to me, assuming that I was a priest, by buttoning her worn black-leather coat over her tight slacks and flimsy blouse. Her companion, by contrast, was overweight and wearing an absurdly tight skirt and spike heels. The thin one made her pitch for some money with a rapid, nervous stream of words. When I explained that we didn't give cash, her friend responded with some openly obscene suggestions. She quickly realized that this was even more futile. I knew that they were desperate, so I wasn't offended. I even tried to offer some encouraging words about us all being God's children, but, under the circumstances, I fear that my pitch was as futile as their own.

The only hooker that I directly tried to approach often stood on the curb just outside our office, looking into passing traffic for customers. What concerned me wasn't that she was young and still unspoiled in appearance, but that, as I learned from the others, and from one brief and bizarre exchange with her, she was clearly psychotic and delusional.

I often wondered, as I saw the johns jerk their cars to a halt at the sight of this fresh young body, what they encountered when they were alone with her in one of the cheap motel rooms a few blocks away. Did they care that she was crazy? Did she somehow weave them into her psychotic fantasy life? Of course, I never knew.

One of the most benign but exasperating of our mentally ill regulars was a young man I'll call Arthur. We were his SSI payee, which meant that his disability check was sent to us for safekeeping and disbursement. Arthur had experienced a psychotic break several years before and was diagnosed at different times as schizophrenic, bipolar, and manic-depressive. In any case, his family had given up on him.

Arthur was clearly delusional, but in his own unique and not always convenient way. He was often demanding and, forgetting when or how much we had given him the day before, would hang around the office demanding money or at least attention; he was prone to temper tantrums. He didn't like this arrangement, but it kept him from being institutionalized, which he liked even less.

He had the habit of leaving demanding notes on the door always signed in the same way: "*Dr. Jethro, MD, PhD, Harvard, Yale, Princeton.*" This was Arthur's usual signature. Even the most casual notes bore the same credentials. After some lapse in his regular visits, Astrid asked me to check on him in his room in a nearby welfare hotel. He wasn't there, but the note on his door read: "Gone for more beer. Back soon. *Dr. Jethro, MD, PhD, etc. etc.*"

Arthur was overweight, near-sighted, and had a perpetually childish face. From what Astrid knew, he had been a brilliant medical student on a scholarship at one of the universities listed on the note, but, of course, not all of them. He had acquired a strange, affected accent, perhaps from an old Boris Karloff movie, and was prone to offer medical advice to strangers. One of the problems we faced was that he liked to answer phones. Our

Spanish-speaking secretary, Julia, was often tied up dealing with the Latinas and their kids, so if she didn't get back to her desk in time, Arthur would answer in a haughty voice: "Dr. Jethro speaking. May I help you?" One of us would have to take the phone from him before he could begin his medical diagnosis.

Another of my own regulars was a tall, handsome young man who, when I first interviewed him, was wearing a suit and tie. I'll call him Tom. He was from the Midwest and had come to Hollywood to become a movie star — not an actor, mind you, but a star. He had a car, he told me, but had just lost a job as a salesman, and asked for some temporary assistance. There was something that didn't seem right about him, but I was still pretty new at this kind of assessment. I was able to give him a voucher for some gas at a local station.

The next time I saw him, Tom was clearly going downhill. I guess you could say he had decided to play the part of a "sheik," like the venerable Valentino. I discovered that he had started lounging on street corners, seductively smiling at girls while wearing something like a turban. It was, in fact, a large bath towel that he had rather skillfully wrapped into a turban-like shape, the corners falling over his broad shoulders. He was so handsome and his smile so genuine that I gather he was quite successful in drawing young women into conversation at least. I never knew how he explained the towel or what they made of it.

It took some time and consultation with the pros at Mental Health for us to determine that I was dealing with the most severe case of narcissistic personality disorder that I or any of them had encountered — and this was in Hollywood, the world capital of narcissism. Tom had invented not just himself as a movie star, but a whole career, including a movie about to be released. Before he had run out of money, he had paid for a professionally printed movie poster showing himself as the lead and listing a real director's name. (I forget the movie's title.)

Clinical narcissism, I learned, comes from a painful inability to grow up, which leads the sufferer into an increasingly subjective and largely imagined world. If you were lucky and lived in Hollywood, you could turn this disability into a pretty good living, as I had. If you had some talent and training, turning daydreams into something coherent at least was possible. Otherwise, you were just lost in your dreams, like Tom.

The bizarre behavior, almost comic at times, of Arthur and Tom — and they were just two of many — made it difficult to see the human beings inside the mental illness. Others who raved and cursed us senselessly were even more difficult to accept. Yet in rare moments, their need to touch others became apparent. Arthur's fantasy of offering medical advice and Tom's manic desire to be loved and recognized were, however "crazy," deeply human.

*   *   *

During these years, the streets of Hollywood once again became my home, though certainly not my playground. In the old days, two "Buffalo Bills," in fact, walked Hollywood Boulevard, white-bearded men in full Western gear; they picked up a few bucks by posing for photos with tourists. Over time, the boulevard could boast at least a couple of Vampiras, a Marilyn Monroe, and a variety of aging Little Rascals. But during the plague days that I've described, even I, with my show-biz imagination, was unprepared for some spectacles.

One was the "Virgin Mary." Obviously as a Catholic, I'm disinclined to use this name in any irreverent way, but that's what she was called. Perhaps it's the name she preferred. She was very old, over eighty, and wore a dingy, once-white cape. Periodically and unpredictably, she would fling open her cape and expose her naked body. This usually produced a considerable start among passersby. I witnessed her theatrical display only once, from a distance, and watched a passing couple almost jump into traffic. The old woman then closed her cape and maintained an expression of considerable dignity, as if she had just bestowed a favor on an unworthy flock.

An even sadder figure was a fixture on one street corner that I passed frequently. He would stand as motionless as a monument. He was an African-American man of middle age in worn but not unkempt clothes who stared, expressionless, at the passing traffic. His face was painted white, and not with makeup but with what was clearly house paint. I never understood either the pathology or the message he was trying to send, but I always spoke to him. He would never reply or acknowledge my presence. I suspect my existence was not on his radar.

Strangely, one day as I passed, I realized that the African-American painted white was not the same man. It was, again, a black man with white house paint covering his face, but definitely not the same individual. Was he a copycat, a fellow traveler in the same strange land? This man at least looked at me, but he said nothing, and I continued on my way, forced again to accept my limited understanding of human suffering.

*   *   *

After a time in this desperate world, I realized that homeless single men lacked a reliable support system. Many were fleeing to Hollywood from the downtown skid-row area, also overflowing with drug users and alcoholics, and becoming increasingly violent. I consulted with Astrid, and we received permission from the Catholic Charities director to start a program aimed at single street guys.

I think I actually missed the nightly strolls down the boulevard. I had become friendly with many of the regulars working the boulevard, including a panhandler named Noel, who, over the months, always gave me the same pitch, as if we'd never met. I also got to know some of the transvestites who had their own corners for hustling johns who were so inclined. Most were men in drag, but one I took to be a young woman in short hair and men's clothing who said she'd had a sex change and was now called "Myron." Myron was a gentle, even sweet person, and as we became friendly over time, Myron confided to me that the sex change had become troublesome. She — or rather now he — confessed that after becoming male, he thought he might be gay.

I had committed myself wholeheartedly to this work, and I guess it must have showed. When I terminated the "night patrol" assignment, one of the supervisors from a mental health agency asked if I would consider going to work for them in a paid staff position. I was a volunteer for the church, but I don't think she knew this. I turned the position down, of course, but it was perhaps the most satisfying job offer I ever had.

*   *   *

Climbing Jacob's Ladder

I think it was more than a coincidence that Astrid and I came up separately with the same name for our new program — "Jacob's Ladder," a biblical reference to Jacob's glimpse into a heavenly life. We weren't going to offer any kind of heaven — far from it — only some place better than skid row or the cold cement of a storefront doorway.

Jacob's Ladder started and ended modestly. Given Astrid's many responsibilities, she more or less supervised my daily management of the program. Initially, we offered emergency shelter and food, but our goal was to provide long-term rehabilitation. We couldn't handle mental illness or severe alcoholism or addiction — there were other groups trying to cope with these problems — so to enter Jacob's Ladder a man had to be theoretically able to work. The director approved the program based on the condition that it be financially self-supporting, so we knew that in addition to our raising funds, some of our guys would, in time, have to pay at least some rent. This turned out to be largely theoretical.

Our small apartments were located in a squalid building on a street hardly conducive to rehabilitation, but it was close to the church, and it was all we could afford. This street was so dangerous at night that the locals called it "glass alley" because of the amount of broken glass from burglarized cars, probably left by unwitting tourists who couldn't find parking any closer to the movie houses on the boulevard. After our weekly night meetings, "my boys," as I came to call them, would insist on walking me to my car.

The guys were required to attend a weekly meeting at night in one of our tiny apartments, the occupants taking turns in preparing dinner, invariably spaghetti. We would sit in a tight circle, and someone would offer a blessing, often the "Our Father." Most of the black guys were Protestant, the Latinos were Catholic, and the others went along. We would then assess the week and how the individual "plans" were working out. Each man had to have a short-term and a long-range plan and a budget. Thinking ahead, much less with hope, was a big step for most of them. They weren't always at ease with reality. I remember one guy announced that his long-range plan was "to win the lottery." He wasn't kidding.

Keeping the guys off the streets was one thing, but there were also constant fights, even an occasional arrest, and I was sure that a couple of them were dealing drugs from this safe haven we had provided. But some good things happened. I was able to get some of the sex hustlers tested for HIV, and some broken teeth fixed by an altruistic dentist, and even got some of them jobs. But there were far more failures than successes, and some were particularly painful. A Puerto Rican kid, all the way from New Jersey, armed only with a great smile, was with us for six months. We got him off drugs for the first time, he told us, since his early teens, and then he killed himself. I never knew where he got the gun.

Two of my boys were called Big Mike and Little Mike, though these were superfluous distinctions because there was no possibility of confusing the two. Big Mike was big and black and had a rather ferocious expression and a shaved head. Little Mike, on the other hand, was small and white and usually had a genial if somewhat cynical smile on his face. Both appearances were deceiving.

Big Mike was, in fact, the gentler of the two. An illegitimate child of a single mother, he had been dishonorably discharged from the Marine Corps for drug use. He then went to UC Berkeley, where he studied mathematics until, lapsing back into drugs, he had a nervous breakdown. He ended up on L.A.'s skid row, where he was found living in a box by a friend of mine. Lew was a saintly skid-row social worker who later survived being stabbed by one of his many mentally disturbed clients. A fellow Catholic, he and I met one morning at one of the homeless meal programs and became good friends, so it was no imposition when he asked if I could help him get Big Mike off the row. His concern was that even though Big Mike had a usually gentle disposition, when he "lost it," he would become violent, even murderous.

Big Mike's story had some holes in it, but the part about his being a math major at Berkeley, which I originally questioned, was later confirmed when he enrolled in a UCLA extension course in calculus and pulled the highest grade in the class. He wasn't delusional. In fact, he was brilliant, some kind of math genius. We became good friends, and once he was on SSI, he would occasionally bring me gifts demonstrating some scientific principle, such as a vial of liquid that would respond to your body temperature. He was bright, funny, and amiable, but still potentially dangerous.

Big Mike was, I think, one of our success stories. With his SSI income we were able to finally place him in his own apartment in public housing. After a couple of years of stability, we were able to persuade him to contact his family in the Midwest, and then, finally, to return there. Of course, I have no way of knowing the outcome. The day he left, he told me that he would not be in touch with me again. He realized that he had to make a clean break with his past, including us. I think he was right.

He had once been attacked — "cold-cocked," as he put it — from behind by a fellow denizen on skid row, and had vowed to seek revenge by murdering the man. This was his thinking pattern at the time that Lew found him and got us to take over. We were able to help him deal with these bursts of anger that came from his exaggerated sense of shame and vulnerability. Because he was smart enough to be insightful, eventually his good nature prevailed.

Before he left, he told me, while smiling gently, that for some time he had nursed his desire for violent revenge and, for a short period, had considered the alternative of killing me. I think it was good that he told me this, but I admit that even after our warm farewell embrace, I was left with a slight passing chill.

Little Mike was also a success. Again, I have no way of knowing the end of his story following the five years he was with us, but I would call even surviving that interval a success. His family background was even grimmer than Big Mike's. His father had gone to prison for molesting his sister; his mother had abandoned them; and his brother once tried to kill Mike before committing suicide. Mike then tried to kill himself a couple of times and ended up institutionalized. By the time he came to Hollywood, he was a cocaine addict and a small-time dealer with the street moniker "Alabama," his home state. He was good-looking, and his soft Southern accent added to his charm, but he was deeply disturbed and still suicidal. He had been living in a storefront when he came to us on his own, bearded and filthy.

Little Mike boarded with us off and on — we had to expel him from the program for drug use more than once — for about three years. Then we had a turn-around. After he served a stint in a lock-up residential drug program that we arranged — and I appealed to a judge to let us have him again rather than give him more jail time — something seemed to change. Maybe we had worn him down by our refusal to give up on him. I don't know.

I knew that he had a deep fear and an abiding suspicion of other people but that he loved animals, and so I helped him find a job in a kennel. It worked. Two years later he was a supervisor of people as well as dogs, had his own apartment, pickup truck, and two German shepherds. The last time I saw him was when I was leaving town, not him.

*   *   *

I considered both Mikes to be friends, but the guy I called "my man" was Joe. He was both older and wiser than the rest, and at times wiser than I was. I came to count on him for help. He first turned up in the social-service line some months before with a filthy beard and wearing foul-smelling clothes. He had been sleeping in doorways, he told me, for a couple of months, but his back was hurting him, and so he decided to ask for some help, maybe just a night or two in a shelter.

Joe was a New Yorker with an accent to prove it, Italian, and a real Catholic. He'd been an altar boy and knew the liturgy, and even some Latin. I trusted Joe because he played it straight from the beginning, asking for what he needed without offering excuses. He wasn't a drug user, but he was a lifelong compulsive gambler whose addiction had cost him a family and several years in state prison for assorted fraud and white-collar crimes.

He had come to L.A. after his release, "looking for greener pastures," and told me that he had retained the look and smell of a "street crazy" because this was the safest persona to assume on these streets. No one figured you had anything worth taking, and you might be crazy enough to fight back.

Once we offered to help him, Joe cleaned up amazingly well. He had some stained teeth from his other compulsion, smoking, but other than that he was a reasonably presentable man with kind and intelligent eyes.

Joe became a kind of house manager for our program, settling disputes with a calm manner and an authority derived from a penitentiary stretch, a status most of my boys had yet to achieve. Joe thought that Astrid and I were crazy to offer help to most of the guys off the street. Twice a felon, Joe was what you might call a social conservative. He viewed bad habits and self-destructive behaviors, including his own, as signs of character weakness. Original sin wasn't even an excuse, though Joe was a pretty conservative Catholic as well. He ridiculed any excuse the other guys offered, whether it was poverty, discrimination, or parental abuse. To him, these were all just alibis. He was never really unkind in this judgment, just definitive.

Joe's keen intelligence was evident in his quick wit (he once told a loud and demanding new guy that he was as "persuasive as a hemorrhoid"), and so it was heart-breaking to hear his contemptuous view of himself.

He had separated from his family years ago, but his ex had sent him photos of his two children when he was in prison, and he had an address. He had started to compose a letter several times, and had asked me to read the pitiful effort. Given Joe's intelligence, I was surprised at his crude handwriting and poor spelling. But the worst of it was that he couldn't bring himself to express any real feelings. Perhaps it was an impossible task, trying to write to two young children and explain why you, their father, had barely seen them and never supported them.

"What am I supposed to say?" Joe agonized. "That I'm sorry?"

"What else can you say?" I replied. "At least they'll know you're alive and thinking of them."

He shook his head. "Maybe it's better they think I'm dead."

He almost shuddered in self-disgust. "Why am I doing this? I'm just trying to make myself feel better. It's all bullshit!" He crumpled up the letter and walked away. He would try again, but the letter was never written.

And after over a year with us, during which time he found a job and even a steady girlfriend, Joe disappeared. He left a message on my answering machine in his unmistakable accent, but in a voice strangled with emotion. "Sorry, Ron. . . . I love you guys. . . ." He couldn't continue and hung up. I never saw him again.

*   *   *

Astrid and I ran Jacob's Ladder for almost eight years. When we closed the program, our final statistics were strangely symmetrical. We had accepted over a hundred guys — a third of them white non-Hispanic, a third Hispanic, and a third black. A full one third didn't last more than a month, and another third eventually dropped out, though some after more than a year. I don't know what happened to any of them. Close to a third, however, stayed with us long enough to become self-sufficient. Some, like Little Mike, stayed for several years, and others came back at times to visit us.

This may seem a dismal result — maybe thirty guys stabilized over eight years — but I learned that, compared to other programs, it could be considered a success. But "my boys" weren't statistics to me, and the experience was deeply personal. Each young man, whether a "success" or a dropout, remains a distinct, even unique person in my memory.

*   *   *

Looking Back

During these years — more than a decade — Ruth and I lived somewhat distinct lives, much as we had during my studio career. She had her own art studio and, able to paint every day, refined her work. She was accepted into several watercolor shows, and finally won a major award in Los Angeles. As for me, instead of heading in style to a studio, I wore modestly drab clothes and drove an old car to a poverty center. My years in show business and some prudent investments made it possible for us to live a comfortable life, though hardly an extravagant one.

During the Thanksgiving and Christmas seasons, when our poverty programs appealed for volunteers, Ruth usually helped out, often in a soup kitchen. She never visited me "at work." Nevertheless, she accepted my new life, and, in truth, these were some of our happiest years, because I was finally working at something I found meaningful.

We had only one awkward incident. On one holiday occasion Ruth came to volunteer at a walk-in center for the homeless and, before I could warn her, sat down on the dilapidated couch in the reception area. I got her up quickly, but it was too late. She was appalled to find that, for the first time in her life, she now had lice. Because I worked there regularly, from then on I had to undress on the porch before she would let me into the house.

*   *   *

I wasn't sure at any time during these years how much good I was doing for anyone else, but I was learning about the necessity of a prayer life. A Columban nun, Sister Margaret Devlin, also ran a Catholic Charities poverty center, and we formed a support group for ourselves and others working with the poor and homeless. We met weekly at a pizzeria and called ourselves "the People of the Pizza." We prayed together, of course, but also drank some wine and laughed a lot. We knew we needed each other.

As my religious life deepened, I also discovered the spiritual value of periodic retreats and the need for spiritual direction. I would be blessed by having several gifted spiritual directors. These relationships enabled me to continue on my path. I would never have been able to do so without them.

These were rewarding years — not so much despite the constant confrontation with suffering and despair, but because of it. I was discovering that what lay beyond the darkness and fear that enveloped me was not just faith but what I can only call freedom.

*   *   *

This part of my life came to an abrupt end with Ruth's sudden death from cancer. Her death at age fifty-nine shattered my whole world, including the new one; yet, in time — a long time during which I drifted in a numbed state — this darkness also lifted, and I, again, found light and faith.

I will tell the story of Ruth's death in a later chapter.

In the year after her death, I considered returning to the poverty work in Hollywood, but the office had closed for financial reasons. I didn't have long to wait, however, before I sensed another calling. I was asked to enter into prison ministry and become a chaplain.

My memory now has to stretch back and overcome some resistance in re-entering another and, at times, even darker world.

CHAPTER FOURTEEN

Touching Glass: My Life in Prison

We were never allowed to touch, not in the flesh. So we put our hands to-gether on each side of the glass. It was a way of saying good-bye, even better than a handshake.

The glass separated me from an inmate whom I'd known for some time. He'd "caught the chain," as they said, which meant that he was head-ing for San Quentin or Folsom. Like all the men in this maximum security prison, he was considered too dangerous for me, even as a chaplain, to be in his presence without glass and steel between us. I don't remember his crime, if I ever knew it. I never asked or checked. I had to learn how to know these men simply in the moments we had together. It was better that way: I wasn't strong enough to ignore or forget their criminal pasts, espe-cially if they had been violent or murderous.

I was one of several Catholic chaplains working there; I was assigned to a couple of the five housing units and one with the highest security. We were in what was called the "Supermax," part of a complex of county facil-ities that incarcerated several thousand inmates. It was on the edge of the desert outside the city, so this meant a wearisome freeway drive, but prison ministry had proven so spiritually valuable that it was worth it.

As many times as I had been there, the huge Supermax structure, hid-den in the hills and lit up like a power plant at night, always gave me a chill when I drove up. Fortunately, I had my own parking space, just like in the old studio days — only this one was "reserved for chaplain" — and so when I was held up by the clot of city traffic, I could still manage to get through security, slap on my ID badge, follow the colored line directing me down the long stretch of empty corridor, knowing the TV monitors were watching me all the way, and reach my housing unit in time for my daily service.

As I walked a colored line, passing a long, moving row of inmates, occasionally one would surreptitiously wave a couple of fingers, and another might whisper "Orale, Padre!" — "Pray for me!" — and make a quick sign of the cross over his heart with his thumb. These were risky gestures because in this facility discipline was tight and all inmates were required to walk next to the wall, keep their eyes down, and remain silent. Greetings were against regulations, but, to their credit, the guards didn't hassle inmates when the gestures were for me — or rather for Whom they hoped I represented.

At the very end of several long corridors, I would be buzzed through the sally port — the thick, steel double-doors — into my high-security lockup. As the doors ground open and slammed shut with a clang, I would often hear the guard in the control room announce over the PA system, "Chaplain aboard." This was an inside joke, using an expression from the days of prison ships, and also a warning — not for the inmates but for the other guards to clean up their acts, or at least their attitudes.

I would step into the control room and open the satchel I carried, in routine conformity with rules that made sure there wasn't a gun or drugs among my rosaries and prayer cards.

The lone guard monitoring a panel of a dozen TV monitors that surveyed every cell in the unit usually gave me a welcoming smile. He would then announce my presence to the inmates over the PA system, and anyone wanting to speak to me would push a button in his cell, and red lights would light up on his control panel. I'd jot down the units and then make my rounds. As I approached the heavy steel mesh, some buzzing would sound and, first, the inmate in the bare recreation area would have to return to his cell, and then, after another buzz, a cell would open, and the inmate who had requested to see me would emerge.

My day had begun.

*　　*　　*

Our senior chaplain was a remarkable man whom I'll call Brother Al. His background is so extraordinary that I'll leave it up to him to reveal it fully. In his youth, Brother Al had been a heroin addict, a burglar, and, as a convicted felon, had once been an inmate himself in a Southern state penitentiary. He had lost a girlfriend, also an addict, to an overdose while he was inside, and that might have been the turning point.

He returned to his Catholic faith, briefly became a monk, or at least a novice, and then found his vocation as a prison chaplain. I had received diocesan training and had passed the tests for the chaplaincy, but Al's experience, combined with his spirituality, made him an invaluable mentor, and, initially, I simply assisted him with his duties. He then asked me if I would take over the top-security unit.

I had been there only once. Suicide attempts were not uncommon, particularly in that unit, and in the wake of a successful one, I had accompanied Brother Al to offer what might be called emergency services. On this rare occasion we were allowed to be physically present with a couple of the badly shaken men who had been adjacent to the cell where a young guy accused of child molestation had hung himself. We prayed with them and then with anyone else seeking our help. It was a long, difficult night.

Practically speaking, the top-security unit was time-consuming, and Al, along with two other part-time chaplains and some volunteers, was ministering to thousands of inmates. There was little time for the meticulous procedures that high security mandated.

I was, in fact, pleased that Brother Al had this confidence in me, and I accepted the responsibility.

*   *   *

In the high-security unit I wasn't allowed to do a confidential "one on one" in an interview booth without having the inmate placed in cuffs and shackled at all times. These were men who had nothing more to lose, mostly lifers, some on appeal from death row, and an assault on staff was always a possibility. I never worried that any one of those who asked to see me would confuse me with a guard, but there were a few whose hold on reality was shot, and, in any case, those were the rules.

Most of my ministry was "through the bars," which meant, in fact, speaking through heavy metal mesh. My presence was always at the request of the inmates, though many times I could never figure out what they really wanted. I don't think they always knew. Some just needed to talk to another human being.

The procedure was to send a written request, a "kite," asking to see the Catholic chaplain. Many who asked to see me weren't Catholics and were just "fishing," looking for angles to get something for nothing. I was used to it. They might ask for a rosary, though it was clear that many didn't really know what this was. Everyone wanted one, but only a few, even among the Catholics, really knew how to use it in prayer. Eventually I discovered that rosaries were being used at times for gang identification, so I stopped giving them out in any color other than black.

The housing units, or blocks, were divided into different sections. One of my groups included the men called "pro-pers," those who chose to defend themselves in court. Another unit was the "snitch block," the special lockup for inmates suspected by the others of being informers. I didn't like the designation because it was often based on unfair or trumped-up charges; but some in this group were, in fact, perpetual informers, trading information for whatever they could get. I struggled with it, but it was hard not to feel something of the contempt most prisoners felt toward these men who routinely betrayed others as part of their livelihood. I prayed to overcome this aversion as well.

I couldn't pray enough. Seeing a pile of kites, the many request slips in my intake box, could easily spur a sense of futility. I had to remind myself of my own repeated failings, and then kick myself into action.

*　　*　　*

I had several murderers in the high-security unit during the years I was there, and I got to know a couple of them pretty well. You could even say, I guess, that we became friends.

As a Catholic chaplain, I'm not a moral relativist, and I don't think I let these relationships, however friendly, blur the distinction between good and evil. As my sympathies grew, I reminded myself that while I'd come to know these men as human beings, I had never known their victims.

Carlos was the first man I counseled who admitted to murder. He was a sort of professional, a *soldado*, a soldier for *La Eme*, the Mexican Mafia.

Carlos wasn't in my high-security unit. He was next door, where the men lived together in a dormitory block and weren't always confined in their cells. He was a "three-striker," which meant that he was looking at a life sentence for being a repeat offender. He was in the process of appealing the "third strike," the aggravated felony that would put him away for good. Carlos asked to speak to me privately. He wanted help in his examination of conscience, the preparation for confession.

Carlos implied that the grave sin with which he was struggling was that he had killed more than one man. There was nothing either of us could do to bring back his victims, and legal justice wasn't the issue. These murders were unknown to the authorities; he hadn't been charged with homicide, and likely never would be.

My own struggle was somehow to turn Carlos's face from me to God. I told him that, not being a priest, I couldn't offer absolution; but, in any case, he had to stand face-to-face before God, not just a priest, and truly consider his crimes. I can't take any credit for this, but, over the months of our talks together, something began to happen.

Carlos was one of the most feared men in the three-striker unit and, thus, the most respected. He was a "shot-caller," prison slang for the boss of his dorm.

Most of the shot-callers were violent gang leaders who had the power — unofficial, of course, but recognized by the guards — to regulate the inmates' lives. He could tell them where they could sit at meals, which drinking fountain to use, or when they could use the collect-call pay phone. I had to be careful in handling the shot-callers because they might also forbid inmates to come to our services.

Carlos had the power to do all of this. Older than most and wearing horn-rimmed glasses, he was still a formidable physical presence, his powerful body covered with scars and tattoos. The fear and respect he commanded among the inmates allowed him, in answer to my prayers, to become a peacemaker.

"I'm doin' major time, Padre — probably life," he said, calling me "Padre" as so many did even after I told them I wasn't a priest. He continued: "So I might as well finally do some good with it. Way I see it, I got two choices — go crazy and start howlin' an' throwin' my shit through the bars, or head your way." He grinned at me through the iron mesh. "Hey, you don't have no women or money, or anyway, you're not supposed to!" Again, he was assuming that I was leading a vowed life of celibacy, and as it happened, I was.

The staff suspected his motives at first, assuming that he was following some *Eme* strategy. But when he began to restrain violence between the races, and to offer wise, even compassionate counsel to the younger inmates, we realized some real change was taking place. Carlos would sit most of the day reading his well-worn Bible, and my services began to be better attended, with the younger men now following him.

The hardest test came when Carlos was overtly insulted by a new and younger Mexican inmate who was perhaps hoping to "make his bones" by shaming the older man. The prison code called for one of them to die or lose face. I knew how difficult it was for him, but Carlos turned the other cheek, and the effect on the other men, however short-lived, was remarkable. Until the time of his transfer to the state penitentiary, there was peace and harmony in that unit.

The last time I saw Carlos was in an interview booth. He had asked to see me to say good-bye. We said a prayer and "pressed glass," flattening our hands together on the opposite sides of the heavy glass partition.

*   *   *

Lloyd, on the other hand, was easy to like at first but, ultimately, frightening. A small, neat, boyish white man in his thirties, he was in my locked-up unit to keep the other inmates from killing him.

He had confessed to molesting and murdering several children. Eventually, after months of legal appeals, Lloyd would be sent to a forensic hospital, a place for those the movies call "the criminally insane." To me, he appeared as coldly rational as anyone else, or more so.

Lloyd not only admitted his murders; he told me how much he deeply regretted and deplored them, and repeatedly assured me that he knew that it was best for everyone for him never to be released. So he said.

The frightening thing was that none of us — me, the staff shrink, or anyone else — believed a word of it. It was as if Lloyd was a brilliant actor playing a difficult role — the charming, sincerely remorseful serial killer. The day he was transferred out, he even thanked me for offering him the hope of God's forgiveness.

"I know I don't deserve it," he told me, "but I've placed myself in his loving hands, and, if I am sincerely repentant, I know he'll never drop me. Can we pray together?"

He used phrases like that more easily than I did.

None of us knew how to penetrate the intense darkness in which Lloyd lived. Yet he never seemed doubtful or confused. It was as if he was the only one who knew what to say and how to say it. There was something profoundly unnatural about that.

*   *   *

The murderer I knew best, after Carlos, was Chuey, also a kind of professional. He had been a gunman for an organized gang of *narco-trafficantes* on the Texas border before fleeing the state to avoid a warrant. He was appealing extradition, but he knew he didn't have a chance.

Chuey and his brothers had shot rival dope dealers for years, but, like Carlos, he wasn't charged with homicide. He was facing only a "nickel," five years for possession. The moral problem he brought to me was that his wife and her lover had informed on him.

Chuey was so heartbroken about his young wife's betrayal that he admitted that he had been suicidal. I knew the staff psychologist was giving him medication, however, and, though depressed, he seemed under control.

His dilemma was a difficult one. His "people" — meaning the drug lords he worked for in Texas — knew what happened and adhered to a strict code. Any snitch was to be killed. In this case, this meant both Chuey's wife and her lover. But the call was up to Chuey. His people wouldn't kill a man's wife unless he agreed to it.

Chuey came to my services regularly and prayed with sincere devotion, often with his eyes closed and his fists clenched as if he was preparing to fight his inner demons. He wasn't as big and muscular as Carlos, but he had a pockmarked face with black stubble and long, stringy hair. He would have been the ordinary citizen's nightmare in a dark alley. But Chuey was a deeply compassionate man. He didn't have Carlos's intelligence or stature, but, strange as it seems, the heart that had been broken was a good one.

Chuey's problem was further complicated, he admitted, by the fact that if he refused to allow the drug lords to avenge him by killing his wife, then they would cut him off — in effect, disown him. He was heading for the penitentiary, where he would be "green-lighted," meaning that there would be long-standing enemies waiting for revenge, and he would have no one to cover his back.

He told me all of this quietly, in private, and always with a passive acceptance, but when speaking of his young wife, he often turned away so he could weep without anyone seeing.

In the end, Chuey told me that he had made what we both felt was the right decision. He would not let them kill his wife, and he would accept the consequences.

"It's okay," he said with that disturbing indifference. "I just need to learn to sleep with my eyes open, that's all."

I know he meant what he said. I have no way of knowing if that's how it turned out.

So murder, increasingly, was not an abstract horror that happened to the inhabitants of a netherworld. I came to understand it as more human than inhuman. I can't claim to fully understand the impulse, any more than I can grasp evil itself. But while murder is never wholly rational, sometimes it makes its own ugly sense. Murder is trying to kill what is painful. It is negating the good that seems to be lost or denied. It is trying to kill God in others, and sometimes in yourself.

*   *   *

One of the aspects of prison ministry that frustrates volunteers is the lack of clear results. It's difficult to know over the years whether or not you've had any effect on those to whom you minister. After a time, they're released or transferred; in some cases, you get a letter or a card later, but most just disappear. You learn to appreciate any sign of a stirred hope or change, and settle for very small steps.

I had one particular success in prison that was small but gratifying. A regular in my "three-strikers" group was a tall Navajo with ink-black hair flowing down to his shoulders. He was, in fact, a transvestite who had fled the reservation to live on LA's skid row. It isn't usually understood that transvestites can be among the most violent inmates, often out of self-protection, and he had numerous assaults on his sheet.

He told me that his family was Catholic, and that he had been educated by priests and nuns. But there was clearly something troubling him about his faith. I once asked him about his reluctance to take communion, and he was evasive. I assumed it had to do with his sexuality, but I was wrong. Finally, when I asked him again, he blurted it out.

"It's all those Jewish kids," he said that night after our group session. "I don't like what the church says. I don't go along with that."

I was, of course, astonished. I indicated that I didn't know what he was talking about, and I didn't.

"The Nazis in the war. I've read all about it. They killed all those Jews, and little boys and girls, too. And the Catholic Church — it says that all those little kids are going to hell because they don't know Jesus, and that bastard Hitler — he gets off! That don't go down with me!"

I was delighted to be able to tell him that the church teaches no such thing. I tried, but probably failed, to explain the theological concept of the baptism of desire, and our belief that the innocent, Jews as well as others, are as loved and accepted by God as we are.

He didn't need to grasp the theology. He received this news like a birthday present. His eyes lit up with relief, as if he had been a Jewish kid himself, waiting in purgatory.

How and why this stranger in his own land had come to identify with Jewish kids in the Holocaust, I could only guess. But we both left happier than before.

*   *   *

If you have trouble with the metaphysical concept of evil when you begin this ministry, in time you learn that evil is very real and tangible even if it is hard to define. The inmates are seldom inhibited about religious ideas and language, and they openly speak of the devil or Satan, and the traps he sets for them.

I never thought, however, that he would personally introduce himself to me.

"Look, you believe in Satan? I mean, you think the devil's real, right?" The inmate addressing me was young and very intense, but I couldn't detect any signs of psychosis. He'd asked to see me for the first time and started out with this question. I wasn't prepared for this ploy, whatever it was, and didn't respond. He went on, his eyes fixed on me. "I know he's real! I used to lead the Bible class in the last joint I was in. I got a certificate." I wasn't impressed. He went on.

"I want to ask you. Maybe you'll think I'm crazy, but do you think it's possible that I'm Satan?" He still didn't seem crazy. I heard him out. "I don't mean just evil, 'cause we're all evil. I learned that. I mean, am I the devil himself, in the flesh? Because if Jesus came to us in the flesh, then you have to figure the devil can do the same. Why not me?"

I had the oddest sensation. It was one of those moments when you see yourself from a distance. I was having a theological conversation with a man who thought he was possibly the devil. I finally responded.

"I don't think you're the devil. No. Do you want to be?"

He actually thought about it. "I don't know. Maybe . . ."

I wondered if being the devil might seem better than feeling that you were nothing. His voice had changed. Now it was dull and hollow.

"One time in the joint, this crazy dude — I mean crazy-crazy — he was going to throw me off the top tier. I mean, down onto the concrete. And that big son-of-a-bitch could have done it. But I prayed and he didn't. And I prayed to the devil." He looked at me defiantly, and then went on.

"Okay, I know you believe there's a God. I don't know. There's no way of figuring it out. No way. Look, I know I'm crazy. I been crazy a long time. I do things. I can't help it. So what do you think, Father? Maybe I'm him?"

He assumed that I was a priest and would have the answer. I told him that he wasn't Satan and that he was just a human being like the rest of us. It was a futile argument. He just kept shaking his head. I don't know if he heard me, but I doubt that he believed me in any case.

*   *   *

I met few Jewish inmates over the years — only three that I recall. One was a middle-class Jewish guy who got busted for dealing drugs and was having a nervous breakdown in prison, and my friend, the psychologist Jim Carolla, who later replaced me as chaplain, made a special effort to help him — and his family — to survive the ordeal.

Another Jewish inmate, close to fifty, was clearly mentally ill. Believe it or not, he had been convicted of "terrorism." What that meant wasn't anything political. He had threatened to blow up a major insurance company with which he had a dispute. The charge — not to mention the long sentence he faced — seemed harsh, but I learned from him that, unfortunately, these threats were a habit. In any case, he should have been in a mental institution, not a prison. Small and defenseless, he was put in my high-security unit for his own protection. His father had died recently, and he asked me to "sit shiva" with him because there was no rabbi available. I couldn't fill that role, but I said some prayers with him, and he chanted them in Hebrew.

The other Jewish inmate that I recall was an Israeli-born hoodlum, probably part of either the Russian or the Israeli mafia. He wasn't very big, but he was so tough and self-confident that he never wanted my help or apparently needed it. All he wanted from me was an occasional chat. I think he was just bored.

*   *   *

Life in prison is, of course, a matter of deadly, relentless routine, and it tended to be that for me as well. At times I felt overwhelmed. I had an endless stream of prayer requests in broken English and Spanish, written on small cards that I provided, most tied in with court dates. The men who were facing the death penalty or who had just received life sentences I always saw and prayed with personally.

Preparing an inmate over forty for his first communion, discussing the nature of evil with a gang leader down from San Quentin's death row, or listening to my "pro-pers," mostly black, sing a gospel song with a joyful spirit that must have evoked memories of childhood — these made up for any tug of tedium. And so, in a very sobering way, did the not-infrequent suicide attempts, and the occasional ones that succeeded. Men desperate over life can be ingenious when it comes to finding ways to end it. When that happened, my hardest task was usually to address the now-deepened misery of those still living.

Being in prison — and chaplains are confined as well as the inmates — can clarify things, at least for some of us. It strips away the ego protection and some of the illusions of self-sufficiency. Old friends often asked me whether it wasn't tough on me emotionally to go from a privileged life in the Hollywood studios to my self-sentenced jail time. I told them, honestly, that prison in some ways was easier. You come to know just how broken you are. Hollywood was a world of illusion; in prison, I had no choice but to face a world of hard truths.

CHAPTER FIFTEEN

After Ruth

His name was Jesus. That's all I remember.

He was a tall, handsome Latino. I think he had a moustache. He was a doctor, and he was telling me that Ruth had a brain tumor. He paused. "More than one," he corrected himself.

I remember the cold wall at my back. I leaned against it so that I wouldn't fall.

I had seen that look on doctors' faces before. When Ruth's mother was in a coma, and then when her husband, Papa Sol, suffered a fatal stroke. It wasn't fear on their faces so much as bewilderment. There was nothing more for them to do or say. I actually felt sorry for them, but it wasn't appropriate for the family to be comforting the doctor. I just wished they wouldn't try to conceal what they so obviously felt.

Our family doctor, who was older and Jewish, had reacted with grave concern, but he had said nothing when he examined Ruth in the ER. While playing tennis, she had experienced dizziness that had increased to the point where it was hard for her to walk straight. We were both alarmed, but I told myself it was some severe flu. Our doctor's barely concealed anxiety had warned me, and now Doctor Jesus was confirming the worst. A brain tumor. No, "more than one."

The cancer would spread so quickly that Ruth would live less than six months. The first nights after the diagnosis, I slept on a cot next to her hospital bed. We wept and held each other. There was nothing more to say except to reassure each other of our love. I told her that it would last forever, but I'm not sure I knew what I was saying.

She returned home under hospice care after chemo and then radiation. The doctors, now specialists, never concealed the gravity of her condition, and finally one estimated (correctly, as it turned out) that she probably had only a few months left. He was a decent man and offered us only statistics, never really closing the door.

Ruth's distant cousins, a wealthy couple back East, graciously made inquiries about the present state of research and treatment and insisted that we see yet another doctor, an even more renowned expert. Again, he was caring yet straightforward. He really couldn't offer any hope. He simply advised us, the family, the girls and me, not to agonize over "why" because there were so many possible causes of cancer in the modern world that no one could ever really know its cause. Was it secondary smoke, the chemicals Ruth had used for years in the animation field, or perhaps even the paint fumes from creating her very own art? It really didn't matter.

*   *   *

Jim and Ellie and many friends gathered around us and remained a constant comfort. There were again tears and embraces, but, though many of us were writers, there were no words. A new friend, Paul Wolff, became my instant "Jewish brother," offering some of the spiritual strength he had been given following the death of his young child. Ruth's cousin, Rabbi Lewis Warshauer, was a source of consolation for Ruth, as he was for all of us. Though Ruth was never religious, Lewis was family. A friend recommended a therapist who had a special gift for caring for women with terminal illnesses. To my surprise, Ruth welcomed her presence, and they spent some hours alone together. Clearly, she brought Ruth some degree of peace and reconciliation. I learned only later that the therapist was — given the sad history, I'm tempted to say "of all things" — a Polish Catholic.

In time I would seek out Father Ralph, a Franciscan at the Serra Retreat in Malibu, who would offer me lasting peace and comfort and would be my spiritual director in the future. At the time, I didn't feel that I had a future.

While taking chemo, Ruth met an old friend from the YCL — in fact, it was the ex-wife of my comrade Gershon. She herself would live little more than a year. She came to Ruth's funeral, and I visited her a few times later as her health declined. She told me that she was surprised to learn that I had become a Catholic and asked Ruth how she felt about it. After all, she had married a devout atheist, albeit a very young one. Ruth told her that there were some initial difficulties. She had asked herself more than once, apparently, "What's a nice Jewish girl doing surrounded by all these priests and nuns?" It was a bit of an exaggeration, but Ruth had attended my baptism and confirmation and graciously hosted the party afterwards. Ruth then told our friend that she finally had welcomed the change because "it made him a better person."

There was one other important final exchange. As the cancer spread, finally attacking the spinal column, Ruth needed heavy doses of morphine to control the pain, and she was often only semi-conscious. Even before then, there was little to be said. It was strange. It was the most devastating time in our lives together, and yet, because of that, we couldn't afford to show too much emotion. Looks, even glances, sufficed. When she was more alert, we watched old musicals. But on the day before she died, she simply said to me, quietly and with almost no emotion, "You've been a good husband." That was more than enough.

Her greatest regret — and this she expressed tearfully — was that she wouldn't live to see her grandchildren. This was a regret we've all shared ever since, and I know she would have been proud of our grandsons, Alex and Ben. Terry's husband, Larry, and Bethe's fiancé (and, later, husband), Rick, became essential members of our little family overnight.

Old friends, such as Jim, became somehow even closer. George, a university professor with his own research lab at USC, was a recognized specialist in neuroscience. He was stunned by Ruth's illness and asked to see the X-rays. I had shared with him what was then my greatest fear: that the brain tumors might cause Ruth to lose her sight before she died. She was spared this. But I'll never forget George, sitting across from me at a deli, studying the X-rays, silently, the tears starting to stream down his face.

My "girls," Terry and Bethe, revealed themselves to me as strong women and, sensing my growing vulnerability, joined the hospice team. They were there night and day, and then took over for the last difficult hours. We were all with Ruth when, heavily sedated, she died peacefully in her sleep.

The girls left me alone with her. I looked out the window into our garden, streaming with morning sunlight. Though I fought it with a raging incomprehension, death was somehow being filtered with light, a light bringing with this unbearable pain a slow, rising sense of new life, and not just for me.

The funeral was, of course, at a Jewish cemetery where I had quickly secured plots for both of us. All of our friends became family, even those whom I hadn't seen for years. Jim spoke with great feeling and sensitivity, somehow controlling his emotions as he recalled Ruth's distinctive laugh. My new brother, Paul, a deeply religious Jew, spoke for me, expressing my hope that the love Ruth and I shared could somehow help heal the past, but, honestly, I remember little of the day.

Immediately afterwards, George and the girls wisely insisted that I join him in the West Indies, in Grenada, where he was teaching at a medical school. I literally walked the white beaches and looked out at the sea for several days. I will not — cannot — explain any of what happened then or later. Saint Teresa had once exclaimed, "Isn't it wonderful how God mixes sadness and joy!" I found nothing wonderful or joyful about it then. Yet, slowly, over the years, the pain and something close to peace began to mix. And even at that early moment, on the white sand, looking at the sea, speaking to Ruth, I felt some slight swell of an inexplicable reassurance.

*   *   *

The worst possible event that I could imagine, other than the deaths of my children, had occurred, and all of my prayers and newfound faith couldn't prevent it. My old life had been split apart. What would my new life possibly be like?

In one of our last conversations, Ruth managed to smile and tell me that she wasn't really worried about me (probably not altogether true, given my dependence upon her in so many ways) because "you're probably going to become a monk."

Well, not exactly. A year after Ruth's death I did explore the priesthood and visited a seminary. Although the church team was ready to facilitate my "late vocation" by reducing the number of years I would have to attend seminary, I, at that point nearly sixty, felt that this was the wrong economy of time. I still have some lingering regrets about not pursuing what I know would have been a gratifying life as a priest, but, even so, I believe I made the right decision. I decided that I could serve the church more effectively as a layman with whatever abilities and talents I had cultivated over a lifetime.

I moved out of the lovely home in which Ruth and I had lived for more than twenty years and rented a small house nearby. I am not by nature a passive person, and my disposition helped. I plunged increasingly into church activities. I couldn't have been busier if I had become a priest.

The loss of Ruth drew me closer to God, Jesus, and Mary, and, in time, perhaps to other human beings as well. I appreciated the blessing of my marriage now more than ever; but it was also true that the comfortable family life we had shared together left me with little desire or seeming need for anything other than the company of good friends. I had not known what it meant to be alone since childhood, though I certainly knew it then. I now discovered what it meant to seek out and at least try to serve others, including strangers.

The Love of Women

There was now, of course, a major change in the role of women in my life, and, in time, I would decide that, though I would not enter the priesthood, I would take a personal vow of celibacy. This has often puzzled my more secular yet sympathetic friends; I can best explain this as a highly personal decision. My love for Ruth, for one thing, has remained so strong and persistent that it might well have hindered a future relationship. But there was also an element of spiritual search involved. I was seeking another level of love or, at least, another form of intimacy.

I had been blessed and truly rescued by the love given by women, yet I was struck by their differences as much as the consistency of their devotion. This is why I've never accepted gender roles as fixed by traditional cultures, biological determinism, or political correctness.

Ruth's mother, Alma, for instance, was a remarkable woman, strong and independent, yet strikingly different from Ruth, whom I think she never quite understood. Ruth disdained many of even the most benign aspects of feminine vanity, clothes and jewelry, and expressed herself most fully in her painting. Alma, having struggled so hard to achieve independence, preferred the outward material evidence of her achievements.

Needless to say, Alma wasn't thrilled by the youthful romance between Ruth and me, and my ambitions as an actor or a revolutionary hardly promised her daughter security. Yet, once Ruth and I were married, Alma and I became good friends, and then grew even closer after the girls were born.

The range of emotional responses among women was more striking than I could have imagined. Ruth was little like her mother in temperament, and as different as Terry and Bethe. My aunt was the life-saving presence in my early life, yet her emotional life was largely closed and anxious. Later, in a Utah prison, I would encounter the polar extremes of vulnerability and aggression among the female inmates.

Men often joke about "not understanding women," and appropriately so; but, in my later years, I've come to acknowledge the Mystery of the Other as feminine in a new if not a deeper way, and ultimately to cherish it.

*   *   *

My spiritual life was, again, in time, deepened while my emotional life was being healed as well by my spiritual director, Father Ralph. At the Franciscan retreat on the cliffs above the sea at Malibu, I could look out at the Pacific and pray the Stations of the Cross, now more meaningful than ever, amid the beauty of nature. This was healing in itself, but Father Ralph's quiet and patient counsel was, I believe, life-changing.

Death, of course, changes life for all of us. I've reflected over time that it was significant that Father Ralph never offered words or insights about grieving or anything really distinct or memorable. What he conveyed, other than the Spirit that guided him, wasn't meant to be original — far from it. He quietly immersed me in the peace that comes from Christ; he "re-baptized" me, so to speak, in the Holy Spirit, and let God's presence heal me, following a schedule that neither of us had fixed.

*   *   *

Ruth's initial reluctance in accepting the implications of my growing faith had revealed a paradox. The attitudes we both shared when young had questioned religion of any kind. After all, religion hadn't brought the peace and justice we sought. What proved paradoxical for us both was that our relationship was becoming the real test of what I believed, and Ruth was too honest not to welcome the results. No debate was necessary. Conversion means a transformation put into action in concrete terms and tested by time. After Ruth's death, with the loss of her loving yet challenging presence, my honesty about myself would now be sorely tested.

*   *   *

End of the Affair

As I attempted to resume my life, I found my "Catholic Hollywood" to still be in recovery as well. The new organization CIMA, Catholics in Media

Associates, joined by another fellowship group for younger Catholics, Open Call, had grown, and there were signs among Protestants and religious Jews as well that a "new spirituality" was evident in Hollywood.

There are several reasons for this. The "local gods" of radical politics and the myriad forms of psychotherapy went the way of the great god Pan, collapsing as quasi-religions. A drug epidemic, particularly cocaine, then swept Hollywood in the eighties, and twelve-step programs flourished. Some of these, typical of Hollywood, were even "A-list" gatherings. The problem that people were then facing was "life after sobriety." Without the escape routes of drugs, sex, or suicide, people were having to face themselves. Not surprisingly, at least a few were finding their way back home to traditional ties and to faith.

Looking back at Hollywood in the last decade of the century, my farewell glimpse, I witnessed a brief period of what one might have called a "spiritual awakening," a sincere but rather unfocused attempt to find lasting meaning in something more than a career or a second marriage.

As a "usual suspect" — that is, a known Catholic — I was interviewed several times, including on a PBS special, about the meaning and authenticity of this new interest in religion. Several prominent producers and talented writers identified in some way as religious or at least "spiritual" were also interviewed, and I was struck by how everyone pulled their punches. They made it quite clear that by "religion" they meant no overt affirmation of traditional faith or creed. "Spiritual," in effect, meant a form of personal fulfillment, though with "pro-social" values. Whatever that meant, it wasn't bad. It just wasn't religion in that it lacked the test of community and continuity.

Oddly enough, PBS gave me the last word in a close-up, asking what I thought would come of Hollywood's spiritual search. I smiled, shrugged, and said, "We'll see . . . we'll see." My skepticism was justified; the spiritual mood didn't produce a sea change, only an ebb tide. This was not surprising and in no way should undermine the sincerity or value of those explorations. Indeed, who knows how many individuals might have been positively affected?

* * *

My long love affair with Hollywood had come to an end, but I didn't feel that I had jilted anybody. The old town, Jewish or otherwise, was gone, and what remained were sets and facsimiles. Jim and I would frequently walk among the crumbling remnants of movie sets and streets on the back lot at MGM. Our favorites were the New York street where Gene had sung and danced "Singing in the Rain," and the railroad platform where Fred, in the opening of *The Band Wagon,* had strutted, singing, "I'm all by myself alone."

I think it's all a parking lot now.

CHAPTER SIXTEEN

Mountains to Climb: My Utah Life

After nearly a decade of life without Ruth, I decided to move to Utah, where my aunt, now close to ninety, was living alone. There was no shortage of family members to visit her; many of them still lived in the Bear River Valley to which she had returned. But I felt a special obligation. I had always wanted to live close to nature, and so I can't pretend that it was a sacrifice. I found a mountain home just over the hill from her with a nearby stream visited regularly by deer and occasionally a moose. My Mormon neighbors were friendly and helpful, but there was also a close-knit Catholic community and a Cistercian monastery a short distance away. After the death of Father Ralph in California, I found a new spiritual director, Father Patrick, at the monastery, and his consoling friendship alone was worth the move.

*　　*　　*

Shortly after I arrived in Utah, the county opened a new correctional facility in Ogden, the nearest town to my mountain valley. It was one of the late-model, high-tech, supermax variety that I had known so well in California; it would house not only the local miscreants doing short time for drunk driving, spousal abuse, and misdemeanor possession, but a fair number of hard-core prisoners from the state penitentiary. There were also to be some federal detainees, mostly Latinos pending deportation, plus, in this day of equal opportunity, a housing unit for women.

My parish priest, Father Charles Cummins, known to all as "Father Chuck," was, as I've recounted, the first priest I'd approached at a church service more than twenty years before in California. He knew of my previous experience, and, always busy himself, was happy to turn the prison ministry over to me. I became the first and, for a while, the only chaplain, offering counseling and services in English and Spanish. I was even on the interfaith committee that approved the new chapel. My Mormon colleagues were, again, cordial and considerate. When I pointed out that the pulpit, fixed permanently where an altar would be in a Catholic chapel, prevented my placing a cross during my services, the situation was quickly corrected. A lovely wood cover was made to fit over the pulpit, and the chapel became truly ecumenical.

After some months at the jail, I started to feel at home in Ogden. I would occasionally run into familiar faces in the downtown area, men and women who were now "on the outs," at least for a while. They would greet me cautiously at first with a timid "Remember me?" If they were with someone, I'd just nod and greet them with a noncommittal smile. Most of them would assure me that they were never going back inside again, but all too often I'd spot them back in blue denim and wearing their plastic wristbands, filing into the jail chapel once again.

At the Ogden facility, like the L.A. facility, I was usually taken for a priest, and many persisted in considering me one because they wanted my special blessing and welcomed my authority. But this persona often allowed me the privilege of getting to know women in a way that permits, at least at times, a remarkable honesty. Perhaps the male-female tensions that arise from needs and fantasies, repressed or otherwise, are never entirely extinguished, but my age and my celibacy gave me access to a different kind of intimacy.

I started doing some group work in the women's unit during the last years I was in Ogden, and naturally some of the experiences were distinct from what I'd known working with the men.

*   *   *

Sandra

On the first day of a new group, about a dozen women were seated in a circle in one of the rec rooms when a girl named Sandra gave a low moan and, falling off her chair, went into a grand mal seizure. This was the second of Sandra's seizures I'd witnessed. The first occurred when she was leaving the chapel and collapsed in the hall. I knew enough to take hold of her head to keep it from banging on the concrete floor, and the guards were quick to respond.

On that first occasion, Sandra, as she came out of the seizure, screamed and fought us with ferocity. She told me later that as she slowly became conscious, she assumed that she was being gang-raped. She was in the infirmary for a couple of days but then went back into population.

When she applied to be in our new group — a recovery program for substance abusers — I had some reservations. Beyond the seizure problem, Sandra seemed too emotionally fragile for the sometimes rough and confrontational sessions. Recovering addicts can be tough on each other, particularly if they finally see the possibility of actual recovery. They won't tolerate having their hopes "drowned in bullshit," as one of them once put it.

But Sandra's written application, though even more scrawled and illiterate than most, indicated a sincere, even desperate desire on her part to find a new life. She was sensitive about her background, insisting that while she had been addicted to numerous drugs over the years, she had never turned tricks. She had been a topless dancer, she admitted, perhaps worrying about my moral judgment, but never sold her body outright. It was a line she drew that seemed important to her.

Though she wasn't much more than thirty, her prettiness was already fading. She had been physically abused by men more than once, starting with her stepfather. In fact, she attributed her seizures to head injuries from a severe beating by a drug dealer with whom she had been living.

So when Sandra tipped over during a group session and began having a severe seizure, I was somewhat ready. I grabbed her rigid, shaking head, and, shouting at one girl to pick up the phone and call for help, I instructed the others to take hold of Sandra's arms and legs. It took two girls to get a firm grip on each of the shaking limbs, and we held Sandra as well as we could. I was speaking quietly, reassuring her, and hoping that the staff would double-time it.

When I looked at the girls around Sandra, I was touched. They were hanging on gamely, but several of them were crying out of fear and sympathy, tears running down their faces. Most of them were tough, gangbanger girls from the *barrio*, but they were as frightened as children.

Soon Sandra was taken out on a stretcher to a waiting ambulance. I tried to pull the group together for at least a brief session, but we were all left emotionally exhausted.

*   *   *

Big Mama

I started a new woman's group every three or four months, and I looked forward to it, curious to see who would apply, who would show up, and who among them might finish the course.

I learned not to make judgments about the women in the group; I didn't even make much of an effort to figure out if what they were telling me was true. Over the years I discovered that it didn't make much difference how much information I had, or whether it was reliable. I had to know the people in front of me, and accept them each day as they were. I wasn't a psychotherapist; I was a chaplain, and the healing we were seeking together would come not from my smarts but from the grace of God.

Sandra, sadly, was no longer there. Another grand mal seizure prompted me to lean on the "senior," the officer in command of that unit, and, because Sandra was doing time on a federal bust, he consented to have her transferred to a federal hospital. The other girls missed her, and so did I, but we knew it was best for her.

Besides, another challenge had emerged in the form of "Big Mama."

I had been hearing about Big Mama for weeks — in fact, ever since she was booked in. She had come to our Catholic services only once, and I assumed her identity based on her size and manner. She was no sweet mama, but she was certainly big. Of course, "Big Mama" is a title rather than a name, and almost every female jail facility has at least one contender. It designates rank and dominance, usually by force, the equivalent of what the men termed "shot callers." In truth, it is these domineering, often ruthless inmates, usually backed by a gang or at least cohorts, that, in a perverse way, make the prison system work. They provide the internal discipline that only a costly squad of guards could secure.

The big mamas are usually less violent than the shot callers, but toughness defines their roles as well. Our Big Mama had apparently made her bones quickly by assaulting her only potential rival, a Chicana almost as large, for which she spent some days in solitary. Big Mama then consolidated her power and reputation by settling a violent dispute within her housing unit by fiat. Anyone wanting to fight would have to fight her first. Peace quickly reigned.

So when I realized that the name "Alicia" on the group application form was actually the given name of our Big Mama, I was taken back a bit. She would be welcome, of course, because she admitted to an addiction problem and she wanted help. But would I have to arm-wrestle her, or worse, for control of the group? In fact, I didn't initially "realize" anything. I was informed by the excited whispers of two of my regular girls that "Big Mama" was part of our new group. Their excitement worried me. Were they simply surprised at Big Mama's interest in recovery, or anticipating some kind of showdown?

There was, blessedly, no confrontation or showdown. It's true that as we assembled for our first group session, the dozen or so women placing chairs in a circle in the rec area cast some nervous glances in the big woman's direction. They were all making highly strategic decisions as to where they would sit, based on status, race, and even sexual alliances too complex for me to fathom. (I would soon, as usual, confound their games by announcing that at the following meetings no one could sit next to the same person.)

Big Mama sat where she wanted, right in the middle of the row of chairs, and it was left to the quickness of a couple of the others to grab the privileged places next to her.

I had already spotted one of her acolytes, Stacy; she was potentially the most problematic girl in this group. Younger than most, just eighteen and thus barely qualified for adult detention, Stacy was attractive, distracting, and distracted, her attention span short to non-existent.

Stacy would turn around in the middle of my chapel service to scan the hallway through the glass partition, eyeing any male inmate in sight. I didn't want to eighty-six her, but once I finally had to stop the service, turn her around, and bring her to order as a passing group of orderlies were starting to bang on the window in response to her come-on looks.

Big Mama's other self-designated deputy, sitting on the other side of her, was Brenda, who was also worrisome. Brenda's problem wasn't overt sexuality or an attention-deficit issue, but, I'm afraid, a rather conspicuously low IQ. I'm not sure whether it was due to brain-damaging drugs or inherited deficits, but Brenda had trouble tracking even the most elementary instructions. A short, stubby, pimply girl in her late twenties, she tried to make up for her lack of intelligence through belligerent stubbornness. I guess this made her a suitable sidekick for Big Mama, but there did seem to be a genuine relationship between them.

This was my first clue to a side to Big Mama that I hadn't recognized. She was an enforcer capable of brutality and, I'm sure, self-aggrandizement, but she was also genuinely compassionate. She protected Brenda, not just to secure her loyalty, but because Brenda, too slow to spot danger or even to recognize ridicule, needed protection.

I'm certain that there was the guidance from above that I always require, but whether my contribution came from the right instinct or just plain luck, I not only started out right with Big Mama — I won her over immediately.

I called her Alicia.

I didn't make a big deal out of it. After all, it was her name. She didn't write "Big Mama" on her application. At first, the other women didn't know whom I was addressing. Then, when they figured it out, some risked slight smiles, though not audible snickers. Big Mama — the reborn Alicia — responded immediately and with barely contained emotion. I don't know when she had last been addressed by her proper name.

We never had a moment of difficulty after that first introduction. Alicia truly became the big mother of the group, using her powerful, possibly even threatening influence to encourage honesty and openness in our discussions. When she started crying once — not really sobbing but crying big tears that streaked her big face — it gave everyone in the group permission to do the same, and we soon had a good, healthy sob session. Alicia had been describing the horrible abuse she had suffered as a child.

Addicted to drugs in her teens, she had become, despite her almost grotesque appearance, a prostitute in Vegas — not on the Strip but in the seedy parts of the downtown area. Unlike Sandra, Alicia had never been beaten by men since reaching her considerable maturity (who would dare?); but it is beyond my imagination to conceive the humiliations she endured.

Several of the women in the group (though not most) had also been prostitutes, or close to it, trading their bodies for drugs, at least, and Alicia's display of open remorse and grief was healing for all of them. This woman, whom they had all feared and respected for the wrong reasons, now became their model for the first step of recovery — an open display of one's wounds.

When I "graduated" that group, I gave each of them a diploma signed by me and the jail senior. The sheriff even dropped by to congratulate and encourage them. It was a nice ceremony held in the rec room. I brought in punch and cookies and even had a tape recorder playing some music. I don't think many of the women had graduated from anything since middle school, if that, and it was touching to see how pleased and proud they were.

Alicia, though still referred to as Big Mama by most of the women, received the diploma with more emotion than most, staring at her real name written across it.

Neither Stacy nor Brenda had completed the group requirements for graduation, consisting simply of regular attendance and participation. In fact, only seven of the original twelve made it. Stacy had somehow arranged a sneaky liaison with an orderly in the laundry room, and though nothing happened but some quick groping, I gather it was the final straw, the last of several violations, and she was transferred to an all-female Y.A. camp. Brenda lost it one day and hit another girl in the chow line for reasons none of us, including Alicia, could determine. It's possible that Brenda, in her belligerent confusion, didn't know the reason herself. She was put in the disciplinary lockup for a couple of weeks, and I was told she cried when she saw the other girls' diplomas.

Alicia gave a spontaneous little speech when I handed her the diploma, and, though she was choked by emotion and rambled a bit, everyone was very attentive. She concluded with a flourish of eloquence.

"I know that a lotta you girls thought I was just one tough bitch when I got here. That's okay, but what Brother Ron here helped us to see is that we're all special to God. Right?"

No one was going to differ.

"So it doesn't matter if some bitch calls you some dirty name or gets down on you. We gotta remember it's what's inside that counts. Nobody can take your dignity from you without your permission!"

There was considerable applause. She was quoting me in that last line, and I had borrowed it from Eleanor Roosevelt.

I hugged each girl as we concluded, something I did only on this parting occasion, and Alicia, teary-eyed, nearly broke my ribs.

*　　*　　*

My prison ministry ended with the century, mostly due to health reasons. My eyesight had become impaired, perhaps suggesting the need for another kind of vision.

My years, first in the *barrio*, then on the "mean streets" of a drug-ridden Hollywood, and finally in prison, constituted a hard school. Yet this experience provided no answer to the despair and desperation I confronted other than faith and relationships rooted in faith.

The often-cited underlying causes of poverty and crime, such as discrimination or unemployment, are always in need of response and re-dress, but they themselves are symptoms as much as causes. The deepest sources of poverty and crime are the broken ties and the loss, not just of love in all its nurturing forms, but the absence of an even deeper love, and thus a loss of faith in any enduring relationship.

My own faith and relationships were now also tested. In her last days, my great fear was that Ruth would lose her sight due to the brain tumors. She was spared that, but my own loss of sight, though only partial, not only prevented my continuing prison ministry, but limited my viewing of films and artwork. Ruth and I had both been visual artists, though in dif-ferent ways, and this new limitation struck at the heart of what had been not just my work but my passion. At times, an increasing loss of light and clarity seemed more of a spiritual threat than a physical one. Yet, over the years, I have found blessings in this loss. I not only value more what I do and can see, but appreciate more fully the gift I've received in knowing my limitations and recognizing my dependency on others.

Christians and religious Jews call the source of our lasting and deeper love "God." Others may express this differently, but, whatever the formu-lation, I've learned that if one has this love, one can survive the worst life can bring — even impairment or death.

ACT THREE

Two People, One Witness

CHAPTER SEVENTEEN

Two Steps Forward, One Step Back

After "two steps forward," it is sometimes prudent to take "one step back" and assess where you've been and where you're going. To do so is by no means a rejection of the path taken.

This is my assumption in offering an overview of the present state of Catholic-Jewish relationships in America. My intention in these concluding chapters is to also offer to both Christians and Jews, particularly laity, some suggestions about the central questions and issues we will face as we move forward together.

As I stated at the outset, I'm grateful for what has been accomplished since the Second Vatican Council, and the dialogue between Jews and Catholics in the wake of the Holocaust has been miraculously healing. The Vatican document *Nostra Aetate* defined a new relationship between the two communities, and Pope John Paul's subsequent visits to the synagogue in Rome and to Israel were unprecedented acts of reconciliation.

However, as I've indicated, we are now facing a growing anxiety among Jews and a generational change in attitudes among Catholics due to the loss of proximity to the Holocaust.

In addition to experiencing generational divergence, the Catholic Church is also in the process of changes of considerable magnitude. The noted Catholic journalist John Allen, based at the Vatican, has perceptively described the transformation of the church into a more truly "catholic" institution with perspectives reflecting those of the majority of its adherents, who now live in the Southern Hemisphere. The Catholics of Latin America, Asia, and Africa, the demographic future of the church, do not feel a complicity in the tragic European wars of the twentieth century or, therefore, in the Holocaust. As Allen notes, their concerns will center more on their relationship with Islam. Clearly, considering even the best intentions of all concerned, this will have implications for future Catholic-Jewish relationships.

I'm not alone in perceiving a hiatus in our relations, even a dispirited one. This may have begun with the largely negative reaction of Jewish commentators to the Vatican's 1998 document, *We Remember: A Reflection on the Shoah*, which some felt was inadequate, even evasive. Given the extraordinary role that Pope John Paul played, his death undoubtedly contributed to the lull, but there has been a sense of mutual disappointment for some time.

This setback is ironic: In the year 2000, an unprecedented declaration by over two hundred distinguished Jewish scholars, published as a full-page ad in *The New York Times*, unequivocally absolved Christianity as the cause of the Holocaust. Equally significant, Pope Benedict, in his volumes on Jesus of Nazareth, provided an important theological basis for the church's now-established teaching that Jews were not responsible for the Crucifixion. Neither of these groundbreaking declarations have been much noticed or absorbed as yet, and this firm foundation for future progress seems, at least momentarily, obscured by fears and disappointments.

*   *   *

The Changing Context of Our Dialogue

I believe that a new context for our dialogue must be recognized if it is to be reinvigorated. This context is the crisis arising from nothing less than the end of modernity as a historical period. We are now engaged, whether we like it or not, in a "postmodern" conversation.

The postmodern characteristic most relevant to our mutual concerns is the loss of moral authority on nearly all institutional levels in the West. Christians and Jews share the risks of this cultural dissolution, but we often view them differently. This is because we view the history of the modern era through different lenses.

For all of the vast literature, we still don't fully understand either the causes or the lasting effects of the devastating violence of the twentieth century. From a Catholic perspective, however, the survival of the church in the modern period is nothing less than a miracle. Jews, by and large, given their own perils and sufferings, seldom recognize the degree to which the church has been persecuted since the French Revolution.

In several major countries — France, Germany, Russia, Spain, Mexico, and China — for periods that lasted decades or longer, there were determined governmental efforts to eradicate the Catholic Church. Millions of Catholics were killed, priests and nuns among them, and venerable churches, missions, and shrines were demolished and desecrated. Even in less violent circumstances, Catholics faced political and social discrimination for generations. Without acknowledgment of this history, a Catholic sensibility will not be understood. The critics, and its own dissenters in particular, tend to exaggerate the diminished status of the church in present-day society, ignoring the fact that the number of Catholics is growing worldwide, and is now at well over a billion people, close to 20 percent of the world's population. With its current rapid growth in Africa and Asia, and the numerical dominance in Latin America, there is little likelihood that the Catholic Church will become, as many of its critics wish, "irrelevant."

Nonetheless, the moral and cultural influence of Catholic Christianity is now far less than its historic role in shaping Western civilization might suggest. The church continues to grow in the United States — Catholics now constitute about 20 percent of Americans — but this is primarily due to Hispanic and Asian immigrants. The influence of the faith on political leaders is limited, and nearly negligible on the social elites who manage the higher institutions of education and culture.

The long-term implications of this are lost, however, on those who think in media terms of political "winners" and "losers." Faithful, churchgoing Catholics are now their own countercultural force, and it is significant that they, along with comparably large Christian groups such as evangelicals, are increasingly in conflict with public mores and policies. A politicized interpretation of these sociological factors that tallies only congressional votes or Supreme Court decisions is dangerously short-sighted.

*   *   *

The cultural crisis we face, however, is not simply that religion has lost its influence but that the alternatives to religion initiated by the Enlightenment have failed. The secular ideologies that once promised a "new man" or a "new morality" provided neither. The result is, politically, a prolonged stalemate. There are no longer transcendent values that provide a foundation for public policy or moral judgment, or even an adequate basis for appeals to justice.

Contemporary Catholics and Jews no longer face the aggressive posture of a confident secular elite; now they confront the defensive condition of a secularism traumatized by history.

This is not to say that there wasn't much that was noble and courageous in the modern struggle for liberty and equality. The defeat of fascism and communism and the gains in equal rights for minorities and women were positive accomplishments, as was the growth of material well-being for at least a small portion of humanity. These achievements were accomplished through the efforts of Catholics and Jews in alliance with others, and we should continue to support the underlying principles of liberty and equality as well as reaffirm the value of rationality.

Nonetheless, this progress, however genuine, masked the gradual eroding of core values that were far more important than material or technological achievements. We are now facing the consequences of the loss of this spiritual foundation.

Catholics and Jews are living in a society that is in a state of fragmentation, and our relationship as peoples of faith cannot be isolated from this social context, particularly when religion itself is walled off from meaningful public discourse. It is no wonder that our dialogue is muted or on hold.

The end of Europe as a Christian civilization and the radical secularizing of American society signal the termination of a historical period. The unique American covenant based on the merging of the Judeo-Christian ethos with natural law has given way, at best, to pragmatic contract law. This, in sum, constitutes the "end of modernity." While we must recognize that we have entered a cultural desert with few maps to guide us, we might also view what we are witnessing as "birth pangs" — a reminder that something new is being born.

*   *   *

Being Jewish: The Question of Modern Identity

Ruth and I "became one" with every passing year. We did so, though, by affirming each other's sometimes mystifying difference. For our two peoples to move forward together, we must affirm each other's distinctiveness as valuable and worthy of respect. Like many American Jews, Ruth defined herself not through religion but through culture, history, and temperament. This sense of self can be unequivocal and deep, yet it can seem impenetrable to others. Accordingly, we must first address the often thorny and disputed question of Jewish identity.

"Catholic" and "Jew" are no longer designations offering easy recognition. A Catholic is more easily identified by his or her adherence to canonical church teachings, the Magisterium, and to its governing hierarchy, the pope and the worldwide ecclesial order. There are Catholics in public life, usually in politics or show business, who sustain their public image by challenging church teachings, but "dissident Catholic" is no more definitive of a lasting identity than is "ex-Catholic." Perhaps the simplest and best way to identify a Catholic is to look around and see who is in church every Sunday.

A Jewish identity is, if anything, harder to fully define. The terms "Jew," "Hebrew," and "Israelite," we should note, are not synonymous. Indeed, at times in history, the differences in these designations have been highly significant. Hebrews were the wandering people, among them Abraham, who in ancient times "crossed the river" from Mesopotamia into what is now Palestine or what Jews call "Eretz Israel," the more extensive homeland of the twelve tribes. "Hebrew" was originally more of a social or tribal identity than a religious one.

"Israelite," one of the "children of Israel," on the other hand, is a religious designation referring roughly to "one who strives for or with God," and indicates a member of one of the twelve tribes who descended from Jacob, renamed Israel. A "Jew" was, strictly speaking, a member of the tribe of Judah, one of the original twelve tribes that survived political dispersal. In our day, however, "Jew" can mean both an ethnic descent and a religious commitment.

It is more difficult to define a religious Jewish identity due to the lack of uniform theological norms and a central governing body to maintain them. It is common for Jews both to celebrate this diversity and self-governance and to lament its divisive consequences.

*   *   *

"Who is a Jew?" is an age-old question that I prudently do not intend to try to answer. I want to simply offer some partially defining characteristics of "Jewishness" as they relate to our dialogue.

In terms of religion, a Jew is identified by participation in the covenant made by God with the children of Israel. This is both a historical (or prehistoric) reality and a primal spiritual commitment. A covenant is not a contract. It cannot be broken without consequences. It is said that "to break a covenant with God is to self-destruct."

In modern times, many Jewish thinkers have tended to identify "Jewishness" with either ethical or even political principles. However noble the principles, this is clearly a diminution of the traditional understanding that preserved Jewish identity for centuries. It has also led some successfully assimilated Jews to graft Jewish moral ideals onto purely secular and, hence, contingent commitments.

For instance, the late Tony Judt, a distinguished critic, writes poignantly of his early days at Cambridge and then Oxford, where he witnessed the loss of the intellectual heritage of his highly demanding tutors. Judt's generation of British intellectuals had been left with only remnants of that great tradition in the wake of the disasters of war. Where did this demise leave Tony Judt or other Jewish intellectuals who so identified with this fading high culture? A similar dilemma has been faced by numerous Jewish luminaries who made notable contributions to their host cultures only to watch them decline or, worse, self-destruct. Does one need any further citations beyond Spain, Germany, and Russia?

The Jewish identity that lasts, as I see it, is primarily a form of consciousness rooted in a frequently conflicted sense of particularity. Less evident but, in my judgment, equally as definitive is a desire for a universalism that is, in essence, messianic. This is an ahistorical yearning that has frequently been distorted by a mistaken identification with time-limited historical forces.

This Jewish consciousness, however, is not fully recognizable until it takes on a religious character. As with Catholics, the religious vision exists in tension with the world. There has been a continuous Jewish interaction with the world of power and wealth, but never a fully integrated relationship. While there are parallels with the Catholic awareness of "being in the world but not of it," there is a basic difference, which was identified by Jean-Marie Lustiger. The Jew is "centripetal," while the Christian is "centriphical." This is to say that the Jewish impulse throughout history has been to protect the core identity by closing inwardly, while the Christian moves out into the world, interacting through inevitable conflict while evangelizing. The Jews preserve the heart of the covenant with the One God, while Christians emit its rays.

There is, nonetheless, a basic commonality. At the heart of Jewish religious consciousness is the demand for repentance and the search for redemption. This is immediately recognizable to Christians for the obvious reason that it constitutes our own Jewish inheritance.

Jewish consciousness is also delineated by an inescapable contradiction. While Jewish identity remains rooted in particularity, the struggles to overcome this exceptional status, or the attempts to deny it, reveal, paradoxically, the universal nature of all human consciousness: a conflicted awareness of the self and God. The Jew, in this sense, is the definitive human being. Perhaps this is what Bernard Malamud realized when he said, "Every man is a Jew, though few know it."

* * *

Facing the Hard Questions

For Christians, of course, the full revelation of our human nature came in the human form of Jesus Christ, a first-century Jew. The Christian recognition of Jesus as an utterly unique figure, as both human and divine, is, needless to say, as profound a contradiction as the paradox of Jewish identity. Both are perceptions of a radical particularity that reveals the most profound universality, and, whatever their differences, they are, philosophically speaking, equally paradoxical. Yet these similarities remain the stumbling blocks and the dividing lines between us.

We will not resolve this difference through any human effort, because both perceptions come from the inherently contradictory nature of divine revelation itself — the particular revealing the universal, the human revealing the divine.

* * *

There are some corners we must turn, and we must turn them together.

The tragic conflicts of the past, particularly the persecution of the Jews, have been recounted now for a half-century, and the retention of this memory is crucial for all of us, but there is a certain point at which the past can become inhibiting rather than liberating.

At times the exchange has seemed to Catholics excessively one-sided, with little acknowledgment of age-old Jewish antagonisms toward Christians. The continuous indictment of those who inflicted past injustices and cruelties can too easily create a comfort zone of victimhood and a temptation to remain there. Despite the progress of the last half-century, there remains, in my experience, as much or more contempt — and that's the right word — among Jews for Christians and their religion than there is residual anti-Semitism in the Catholic Church.

The divergent views about the future and status of Israel also remain a serious obstacle to reconciliation, and not just between Catholics and Jews but within each community. One of the difficulties even the most sympathetic Christians encounter in an approach to the State of Israel is the many conflicting views of Jews themselves as to its nature and purpose.

We can all strongly affirm the right of the Jewish people to a secure land of their own, and yet the nature of that territory and government has been and remains disputed by highly respected figures from Martin Buber, Albert Einstein, and Rav Kook to present-day secular and religious Jewish leaders.

For example, a highly respected figure in the early days of Israel, Asher Ginsberg, a Hasidic Talmudist known as "Ahad ha-am" ("one of the people"), saw Israel as a spiritual and cultural Jewish homeland, but felt that, as a state, it should be more pluralistic, like the United States. Other "ultra-religious" Jews have rejected the very concept of modern statehood. Because the future of Israel is not simply a difficult political issue but in many ways symbolizes the future of the Jewish people, most Christians conclude that these difficult questions must be left to Jews themselves to resolve before a mutual dialogue can deepen.

It was with great relief that many Catholics greeted the Vatican's belated recognition of the State of Israel, and this commitment must be strengthened. Yet the church's moral obligation to the persecuted Christian minority in the region will undoubtedly continue to complicate diplomatic ties. Political considerations alone will doom any possible advancement. Only a deeply shared faith and an equally firm spiritual friendship can provide the patience and understanding to preserve this relationship.

CHAPTER EIGHTEEN

Convergence

I believe that "convergence" is the concept to guide us. Its aim is not synthesis but an integrated understanding of the past. Nor does convergence imply conversion. It means being open to the insights that neither community could achieve apart from the other.

*   *   *

The convergence of Jewish and Christian thought can be seen as a new stage of revelation. Jewish history, including the sufferings and persecution as well as the repeated failures of assimilation, is in itself a form of revelation. Jews must understand that their history does not stand alone. Christians must understand that Jewish history is still shaping our own. Both groups must recognize the role of the other as an indispensable aspect of our mutual task to "redeem the world."

The present circumstances, though challenging, provide a foundation for an unprecedented convergence of Jewish and Catholic beliefs, one that is already more extraordinary than most Catholics or Jews know. Not only does the Christian faith exist as a branch of prophetic Judaism, but much of rabbinical Judaism developed, however perilously, in a Christian milieu. Rashi, the greatest Jewish sage of the Middle Ages, ignored the prohibitions of both communities and studied jointly with Christian scholars. Teresa of Ávila and John of the Cross, revered Catholic saints in the mystic tradition, are both believed to have had Jewish origins. There are many such relationships of spirit and blood, known and unknown, that have shaped our modern understanding.

*   *   *

Let's consider some of this rich legacy of convergence.

Germany and Austria, before the catastrophes of war and genocide, were essentially melting pots of national, Christian, and Jewish cultures. The thoughts of Marx and Freud, for instance, or the theories of the Frankfurt School, however secular, are incomprehensible outside this historical context.

In France, one of the most fruitful convergences was manifest in the views of Henri Bergson, the most prominent philosopher at the turn of the century, and subsequently in the interaction with his former student, Jacques Maritain, one of the pre-eminent Catholic philosophers of its middle decades.

A Jew drawn to Catholic spirituality, Bergson followed a classic Greco-Roman path that related human thought to history and nature. Maritain, a modern Thomist, a disciple of St. Thomas Aquinas, integrated philosophy with theology, incorporating the gift of God's grace into his perception of reality. For Bergson, Christ was the "breakthrough" in human history, though one requiring an interpretation "by the mystics" and not just philosophers. Maritain's view on the role of Jews, on the other hand, changed significantly over the years, moving from a stance of benign tolerance to passionate denunciations of anti-Semitism, published in London in 1939 under the title *Anti-Semitism*.

Beyond his analysis of the causes, Maritain saw the attacks on the Jews as an augury of nothing less than "an apocalyptic period of history." He mocked the attempts to use Christianity as a tool against Jews and Judaism, exposing the underlying animus against Christ. He asked scornfully whether one could look forward to a "Christian mustard gas and a Christian bombardment of open cities." He was tragically prescient. He would remain a political refugee in America for the rest of the war.

Maritain's Russian-Jewish wife, Raissa, joined him in entering the Catholic Church as an adult and was herself a philosopher, but wrote more as a poet and even a mystic. Raissa had a deep sense of her Jewish heritage, and saw Abraham as the first exemplary human being who heard the voice of God without intermediaries. In rejecting human sacrifice, Abraham then followed a "bitter road of illumination" that was nothing less than the "ascent of conscience," a revelation of the future of human beings.

*   *   *

Though increasingly challenged by secular skepticism, for a short time after the Second World War, the merging of Christian and Jewish ideas still provided the moral foundation for much of modern political thought. This religious consensus is reflected in the United Nations' Universal Declaration of Human Rights.

This important document was drafted after the war by a group of notables headed by Eleanor Roosevelt, a devout Episcopalian, Charles Malik, a Lebanese Orthodox Christian, and René Cassin, a Jewish legal scholar and advisor to the war-time French leader Charles de Gaulle, a staunch Catholic. The philosophical grounding of their work was provided by a previous assemblage of world thinkers strongly influenced by Jacques Maritain. As detailed in Mary Ann Glendon's definitive historical account, this was perhaps the last gathering of modern political leaders who so strongly affirmed religious principles, and this provided a foundation upon which we still rely.

*   *   *

The modern Jewish religious thinker with the widest influence on Catholics and other Christians was Martin Buber. This is because Buber first addressed the existential human condition and then turned to Judaism for an answer. Buber's "philosophical anthropology" anticipated an approach that later Jewish and Christian thinkers would adopt. For Buber, the Other, divine and human, constitutes a form of revelation that defines reality and the Self, an understanding that develops only out of relationship.

Buber was himself influenced by the Catholic mystic Blaise Pascal's account of sewing a paper into his cloak that bore words commemorating a mystical experience. Pascal had encountered "the God of Abraham, Isaac, and Jacob," whom he realized was clearly not "the god of the philosophers." Buber, similarly, in his book *Eclipse of God and Heaven*, argues that the rendering of God into "an idea" by Enlightenment thinkers had caused this "eclipse" of the Divine — an obscuring of the reality of God as a living relationship.

An intellectual encounter between Buber and Hans Urs von Balthasar, one of the leading Catholic thinkers of the modern age, took place in print when von Balthasar wrote *Martin Buber and Christianity* in 1958. Its subtitle

— *A Dialogue between Israel and the Church* — indicates the seriousness of the Swiss theologian's effort in engaging Buber.

What is revealed in this work is the fruitfulness of a dialogue that does not attempt or presume a full reconciliation. Von Balthasar, writing years before the Second Vatican Council, saw clearly that the covenant of the children of Israel remained unbroken. He went further, describing the Jew as "the representative man . . . at the very center of human existence," and noting, "In him man's struggles take on an exemplary level."

*   *   *

Confronting the Holocaust, the Jewish soul had been deeply wounded by what seemed the betrayal of history. Inevitable questions were raised about the possibility — or impossibility — of retaining faith in God after a tragedy that seemed inconceivable in religious terms.

Some of the younger commentators saw the Holocaust as nothing less than the decisive turning point in history and, indeed, Judaism. Most prominent at the time was Rabbi Richard Rubenstein, who, in effect, promulgated a Jewish version of the "God is dead" position assumed by some Protestants after the world wars. Beyond promoting atheism, the "death of God" premise led to the conclusion that there is no transcendent meaning in life or death.

The more prominent teachers of the older generation, such as Rabbi Leo Baeck and Martin Buber, responded by reaffirming the traditional understanding of evil, whatever its terrible scale, as a human failing, fatal error, or profound ignorance. Buber saw evil as the human loss or neglect of the "Thou," the sacred Other. Evil signaled the loss not only of faith or belief, but of primal bonds. Even Rabbi Abraham Joshua Heschel, a sage noted for his compassionate social liberalism, saw the Holocaust as a result of an overestimation of human capabilities and an excessive faith in a self-governing humanity.

The most influential response to the despairing and negative voices came from Rabbi Emil Fackenheim, who reaffirmed faith in God as a moral obligation in itself. Fackenheim offered no "explanation" for the Holocaust, just as Job's friends could not explain his woes. Fackenheim's determination was to continue Jewish life and faith as a challenge to evil. What he deemed as his "614th law" — an addition to the traditional religious legal requirements — was to give Hitler "no posthumous victory" by abandoning hope and faith in God.

178

To choose life and never despair, as always, means more than will-power or self-preservation. It is at the core of religious life, and another thread that weaves Jews and Christians together.

*   *   *

Hannah Arendt, a highly significant Jewish philosopher, was primarily an astute observer of modern history. Like many of her contemporaries, she had a keen sense of historical closure, including the loss of moral authority in modern times, and wrote of the "radical world-alienation" that was pervasive following the Second World War.

Arendt was also a prophetic figure who, in her analysis of totalitarianism, warned of its recurrent dangers and, by extension, the ever-present threat of terrorism. Arendt's insights have been clearly vindicated by recent history. She recognized that it is not the truly aggrieved or exploited but the "mass man," the anonymous person without real identity, who is swallowed up by totalitarian movements, or driven by irrational rage. This angry and socially isolated "underground man" — to use Dostoevsky's term — ultimately finds satisfaction only in the "great equalizer," death.

The "suicide bomber" is such a figure, but it is risky to narrow the definition. A need for recognition and identity, merging with a desire for revenge and equality, has produced continuous violence in our times. While it has been displayed most recently in the form of radical Islamist terrorism, the common roots lie below any religion, or, for that matter, any political stance. Given the vast numbers of uprooted young people in Europe and the United States, Arendt's diagnosis may become even more relevant in the future.

*   *   *

In Catholic thought, the development most compatible with modern Jewish sensibilities is the Personalism identified with twentieth-century philosophers such as Gabriel Marcel. From a French family with both Jewish and Protestant origins, Marcel urges us to "retrieve" a consciousness of being — that is, our very existence — before lapsing into conceptual thought. Like Buber, Marcel is kindling a gratitude for life itself.

Personalism is a philosophical orientation that emphasizes personal experience and relationships. It is related to the Catholic Church's effort to integrate the positive aspects of modernity, particularly personal liberty, while at the same time preserving the core of our beliefs rooted in faith and revelation.

Today, Personalism is perhaps most identified with Pope John Paul II, who, as a young philosopher, wrote extensively on the subject. Through his teaching and papacy — indeed, his life — John Paul further defined the approach as an understanding of what it means to be human and a rejection of any method that denies the essential dignity and mystery of the human person.

*   *   *

The Risks of Going Deeper

There has been an uneasiness among Jews about any form of convergence that suggests conversion or absorption. Because many important Jewish contributors to this convergence in the past did indeed convert, we cannot entirely allay this fear. Yet Jews and Catholics now have new opportunities as well as a more pressing necessity to come together.

Another obstacle to overcome, therefore, will be attitudes toward the most prominent converts themselves. Figures such as Edith Stein, Simone Weil, and Mortimer Adler have, unfortunately, generated as much resistance as respect.

The canonization of Edith Stein, sadly, provoked more controversy than reconciliation. A Jewish-born philosopher turned Carmelite nun, Edith Stein died as a Jew at Auschwitz. Now known as St. Teresa Benedicta of the Cross, she is growing as a highly significant figure among faithful Catholics. Given her profundity as a philosopher — a protégé of the esteemed Jewish philosopher Edmund Husserl — as well as her recognized sanctity, she might well serve as a spiritual bridge figure, yet the fact of her conversion seems to have blocked that path.

We must wait patiently to see how Edith Stein might further serve to bring us together. If we turn the corners of fear and resentment, I think her presence will be healing, as it was ultimately in her own family. After the deeply painful divisions caused by her conversion, many in Stein's Jewish family came to see her life as truly "saintly" and in their own terms. Her niece, Susanne Batzdorff, has written candidly about this, including the conflicts, in her book *Aunt Edith: The Jewish Heritage of a Catholic Saint*.

Stein's identification with the Jewish people never ceased, and she saw herself as called to play a reconciling role through prayer. She saw Hitler as a modern Haman, the biblical arch-enemy of the Jews, and described him as such, and she wrote of herself as "a very poor and powerless little Esther" ready to sacrifice herself if necessary to save her people. Whatever judgment one makes about the efficacious nature of her life and prayers, her intentions clearly grew out of love and compassion.

To fully understand Stein's mode of devotion once she emerged as the Carmelite nun Sister Teresa Benedicta, one would need to grasp the challenging nature of Carmelite spirituality. The order originated in a community of holy men and women on Mount Carmel in Palestine, and its spiritual path is one of the most rigorous in its effort to achieve self-abandonment and complete surrender to the will of God. Two of the most remarkable figures in this tradition are St. Teresa of Ávila and the mystical poet St. John of the Cross. As we have noted, both of these Spanish spiritual reformers were known to have had Jewish ancestry, and it is not difficult to hear the Psalmist's voice in John of the Cross's plaintive yet ecstatic writings.

As a figure of reconciliation, Edith Stein has already drawn a good deal of attention among Catholics, and there are now numerous books and studies, an overwhelming number written by women of different backgrounds and nationalities. If Jews and Catholics are ultimately drawn together by her, we will be among many others.

*   *   *

Simone Weil presents a different challenge, not because of her Jewish origins but because her philosophical writings often contain a Manichean strain. This is an ancient tendency of thought that reappears periodically, if not relentlessly, reflecting a life-denying dualism incompatible with Catholic beliefs. A brilliant intellectual and classical scholar, Weil lived a short but remarkable life. Born in 1909, she died in 1943 due to her refusal to take adequate nourishment, a spiritual act of solidarity with those suffering in the war which also revealed that strain of self-abnegation that may not have been wholly sound.

In the view of André Gide, Weil was "the patron saint of outsiders" who, despite her passionate devotion to the figure of Jesus, her identification with the saints, and her love of the liturgy of the church, refused to be baptized. She did so to show solidarity not just with fellow Jews, but with all poor and rejected people who did not have access to the sacraments.

She had spent an Easter with Benedictine monks and found in Christ the God who "is in the midst of affliction."

Simone Weil's intense, flame-like devotion to Christ and the Cross, while sincere and profound, has some irreducible elements of self-rejection that go beyond the humility inherent in the mystic tradition. Nonetheless, her spiritual insights into literature and history are invaluable, and her desire to serve others, particularly the poor and suffering, through self-sacrifice, whatever the defects, was ultimately ennobling.

*   *   *

The Bridge of Art and Beauty

We should add to those who have merged the traditions the many Jewish artists and writers who found inspiration in shared religious modes of expression and symbolism.

In this respect, Marc Chagall deserves a place by himself.

My life with Ruth was blessed by being a life in and with art. From our earliest days of marriage, when she dropped out of the UCLA art school to work in animation, to our last trip together, a virtual art tour of France, our shared passion was the visual arts. I had minored in art history, and so my appreciation was not untutored. I think I'm reflecting something more than a personal preference when I say that Marc Chagall was not only among the greatest painters of modern times but in many ways the most significant. Furthermore, his significance is inseparable from his Jewish identity.

Chagall (1887-1985) is an important model of convergence, including the convergence of art and faith. He molded his traditional Jewish beliefs and culture into the great artistic tradition that included Giotto, El Greco, Raphael, and Monet, as well as his contemporaries, including Cubists, Surrealists, and *les Fauves*. Yet as his recent biographer, Jackie Wullschlager, notes, Chagall's "Jewish soul" was always nurtured by images of figures from the Bible, including Abraham, Moses, and the prophets.

Perhaps more than the work of any other modern artist, Chagall's work became a testimony to the "hope that comes out of darkness," most clearly evident, as Wullschlager observes, in works such as his 1957 painting *Clowns at Night*, in which his celebratory clowns, always religious figures for Chagall (as they were for the Catholic artist Rouault), literally emerge out of a black night. Scarred by his own losses as well as by history, Chagall was never personally secure, but he was saved by the beauty of his own art.

In his series of paintings of the Crucifixion, Chagall transcends easy analysis. His earliest paintings of Vitebsk, his largely Jewish hometown in Belarus, a province of Russia, established his reputation. Yet his series of astonishing masterpieces — *The White Crucifixion* (1938), *The Yellow Crucifixion* (1943), and *The Crucifixion of the Bridge* (1951) — created a mystical fusion of the Jewish world with the figure of Christ. Chagall's images thus bridge the chasm that history created.

Perhaps my appreciation of Chagall is further enhanced by his sensitive merging of "tears and laughter." Chagall said that the contemporary artist with whom he felt the greatest affinity was none other than Charlie Chaplin. In Chaplin's little tramp he saw the "holy fool" of Hasidism, while Chagall's own sensibility resulted in his once being called a "Jewish St. Francis"!

While lionized by Parisian society between the wars, he deplored modernist France's "materialism" and "lack of soul." The growing anti-Semitism filled him with foreboding, and he found strength and inspiration not just in the figures of the prophets but also in spiritual companionship with the Maritains. (He was not the only Jewish artist to seek them out.) Jacques Maritain considered Chagall to be a "modern prophet" whose "illuminating images" lit up an otherwise darkening time. Chagall became a close friend of the Maritains, and Raissa wrote poetry about his work as well as a book, *Marc Chagall* (1943). Observing that "Jewish joy resembles no other," she found in his painting a spirit that resonated with her Christian mysticism. Yet, at the same time, in Chagall's "world of innocent beings" Raissa saw "an image of the imperishable Israel."

Chagall rejected any "religious" designation for his work, and his rejection of this label is, for me, highly meaningful. Ruth also had rejected religion. Her beloved grandfather Jacob refused, as an Orthodox Jew, to teach her, a girl, Hebrew; frustrated, she turned her back on the synagogue. However, as I related, when we visited Israel together, she wept openly at the Western Wall. Ruth was Jewish to her heart's core, just not in the synagogue. Her artwork — her modest, lovely watercolors — cannot be compared to the work of Chagall or Matisse; yet she too expressed something deeply spiritual as well as personal and not subject to theoretical analysis. The form, color, and structure of art, like those of music, reveal a different kind of harmony and coherence, which, at its height, as with Chagall or Bach, provides its own sublime theology.

*   *   *

Let me suggest two final but exemplary figures for our consideration as bridge-builders.

Abraham Isaac Kook, known as Rav Kook (1865-1935), was the Chief Rabbi of Palestine for many years before and after the establishment of a permanent Zionist settlement. A remarkable figure with the deepest possible roots in the Jewish religion, he provides a bridge for Christians as well.

Rav Kook was an extraordinary holy man, scholar, and mystic in the Kabbalist tradition. Facing the many divisions among the Jewish settlers, he was entangled in many controversies but remained a reconciling figure who attempted to unify the Jewish people while strongly affirming the value of other religions. He believed that it was human destiny to move toward the light of revelation and unity. He argued that all religions played a role in the redemption of the world, but emphasized the Jewish commitment to ethics and human concerns. He recognized the defensiveness of many Jews as inevitable, given their history, yet believed that the most fundamental Jewish desire was to "overcome separatism."

Rav Kook's remarkable openness and tolerance make him, in my judgment, particularly relevant to our own times and the challenges we face. As Rav Kook saw it, it isn't simply a matter of moral principle that Jews should welcome a harmonious relationship with Christians — it is a necessity if they are to fulfill their redemptive role in history.

*   *   *

One of the most significant modern Jewish converts to Catholicism was Aaron Lustiger, who not only converted but became a priest and ultimately Cardinal Jean-Marie Lustiger, the primate of Paris until his death in 2006. He was so widely respected within and without the church that there is speculation that if it had not been for his age, he would have been on the "short list" for consideration as pope.

Converted to the Catholic faith during the war while hidden and protected by Catholics, and while his mother perished in a death camp, Lustiger retained his formal Jewish identity, but not in a religious sense. This was, of course, a controversial stance, challenged by some, and yet he remained a cordial and respected friend of prominent Jews such as Elie Wiesel and Emil Fackenheim. This respect was undoubtedly due to

Lustiger's honest assessment of his own life. In converting to Catholicism, he felt that he had discovered, as did Pascal and Buber, not the "God of philosophy" but the "God of Abraham, Isaac, and Jacob." Clearly, he had discovered a deep and hidden unity.

Lustiger devoted his life, as a Jew and a Catholic, to reconciliation. Politically, he avoided the bitter extremes of the postwar period in France and chose the church's "third way," which rejected Marxism yet questioned liberal capitalism. He was always accessible to non-believers, many of whom he genuinely admired. He felt that some of his contemporaries, such as Aron and Albert Camus, were seeking a form of "secular salvation," which, however inadequate in religious terms, recognized ongoing personal transformation as a universal necessity. Lustiger recognized Camus's integrity in proclaiming that "human nobility came from facing one's own self-deception."

In his book *The Promise*, written shortly before his death, Cardinal Lustiger wrote that he saw Jews and Christians on a path of mutual recognition, but that we were only in the beginning stages of the journey. The establishment of a new and promising relationship must begin, he urged, with forgiving — but forgiving not just the other but oneself. Christians and Jews must forgive themselves for repeatedly putting worldly power and prestige before God. Lustiger recognized that powerlessness had been the source of the spiritual strength of Jews throughout history, and that Christian spiritual failures often relate to our desire for power.

Cardinal Lustiger remains, I suggest, a healing figure not because his Catholic faith can be fully reconciled with his Jewish origins, but because it can't be. Reconciliation, we realize, must follow a new path, unencumbered by demands on the other.

To truly love means to affirm others as they are, not as we wish them to be.

CHAPTER NINETEEN

Our Walk on Common Ground

Beyond the difficulties and obstacles to overcome, there is much common ground to be further explored. Let me stress that in none of this am I suggesting theological agreement. In fact, what is necessary for the two peoples to come closer is not only a better appreciation of what we have in common, but a better understanding of those tenets which, indeed, are not shared.

The Mysteries at the heart of Catholic faith are deeply rooted in the Jewish understanding of God. A Catholic belief as articulated in the Gospel of John — that God is Love and that His love is manifested in human history — should not be problematic for any religious Jew. We must acknowledge, however, that many Jews hold critical views of the Christian Mysteries — the Incarnation, Crucifixion, and Resurrection. ("Mystery" does not mean obfuscation but denotes faith in a truth revealed beyond human reason.)

The Incarnation is not an insurmountable problem when it is differentiated from the Christian messianic claim. That claim is a different question, and one that we are laying aside. The concept of the Incarnation, in itself, affirms the divinity residing within the human, a central Jewish belief. Similarly, the Crucifixion is not a stumbling block if the question of blame and responsibility is laid aside, as it now has been. The suffering of an innocent man on the Cross depicts the universal human condition.

The most serious difficulty, as I see it, concerns the last of these Christian beliefs. It is unfortunate that one of the most central tenets of traditional Judaism — the anticipated resurrection of the dead — should be a major stumbling block between Jews and Christians, yet it is and must be addressed. I further believe, however, that the conflicting views as to the meaning of the Resurrection, the central Christian Mystery, stem from fundamental internal conflicts within each tradition concerning the interpretation of Scripture.

There is an existential experience at the core of the Christian belief in the Resurrection: the recognition that one must suffer one's own crucifixion before the reality of eternal life can be affirmed. This existential truth evokes fear and pain, and explains the resistance we all feel to the inevitability of suffering and death as the necessary precursor to a new life. How we interpret these experiences varies widely from person to person as well as among differing religious cultures.

Nonetheless, Rabbi Pinchas Lapide's original and admittedly controversial interpretation of the resurrection of Jesus points to the common origin of this belief as well as a possible bridge of understanding.

Lapide, an Orthodox Jew, affirms the resurrection of Jesus not only as an authentic historical event but as one completely consistent with Jewish tradition. Such a miraculous event would have been understood by faithful Jews of the time, including Jesus' apostles. Numerous resurrections had been previously affirmed in the Jewish tradition, including those performed by the prophets Elijah and Elisha as recorded in the Book of Kings, as well as others cited in the post-biblical rabbinical literature.

During Jesus' time, resurrections from the dead were accepted not only as signs of God's power and presence but as the fulfillment of common expectations. The crucial distinction for Lapide is that this fulfillment of Jewish expectations did not confirm Jesus as the Messiah. The Messiah was not necessarily expected to be a resurrected figure, and, most important, his appearance was expected to bring a total transformation of the world. Because this change did not take place in the aftermath of Jesus' resurrection, he was not, according to this view, accepted as the Messiah.

Rabbi Lapide concludes, in a reconciling spirit, that Jesus' life, death, and resurrection remain a great blessing to the world. In this light, the resurrection of Jesus can still be seen as a redemptive sign for humanity and perhaps even as a forerunner of the messianic age. While this more favorable interpretation can be acknowledged by Christians in the same spirit, it cannot be reconciled with Christian belief in the radical uniqueness of Jesus. Yet, in a spirit of reconciliation, this serious doctrinal difference can still be respected.

The Catholic understanding of the Resurrection is articulated most clearly by Pope Benedict in the second volume of his magnum opus, *Jesus of Nazareth*. Benedict believes that the resurrection of Jesus reveals nothing less than a new form of existence and one unfathomable to human reason. Benedict writes, "In Jesus' Resurrection a new possibility of human existence is attained that affects everyone and that opens up a new kind of future for mankind."

The Catholic traditional belief has also been shaped by the lives of the saints and martyrs. This understanding makes the nature of the Resurrection less a matter of theological speculation and more related to the test of life and death. Those who are willing to suffer and die for others, as did Jesus, are seen as affirming life beyond our own particular existence. This not only means "dying for the faith" but demands sacrificial love in all its forms. There is a traditional Jewish belief that "terror and darkness bring the Messiah." In this respect, the Resurrection is affirmed not by tradition alone but by the most profound human experience. Those who have had this experience "believe"; those who haven't may not.

The basic reason that most Jews reject the concept of Christ's resurrection, in my experience, has less to do with the specific claims of the apostles than it does with our common reluctance to accept the human condition. The idea that eternal life lies only on the far side of death is neither reassuring nor comforting for many of us. In other words, Jews resist the Resurrection for the same reasons that we Christians do.

My glimpses of resurrection came in moments after Ruth's death, and then in my struggle with my own failing body. This and the memories of us together continue to reveal who I was, who I am, and who I will be. My later partial loss of vision and the necessity of the surrender of my will to God — these pointed to a light that I could have found only in darkness. All I can attest to is that this light endures.

*   *   *

Our Reciprocal Gifts

I believe that we have exchanged reciprocal gifts over the centuries, often without realizing it. What is it we have given and can still offer to each other?

The Jewish gifts to Christianity are innumerable because Christianity grew out of the Hebrew covenant. Asking what the Jewish faith has given to the Christian faith is like asking what gifts we receive from a mother or father. It is the gift of life itself.

The wisdom of the Psalms has been incorporated into every Mass, and praying the Psalms has been the foundation of Catholic prayer since antiquity. However, I would suggest that in the present day, the most valuable gifts that have yet to be fully received, so to speak, are the Sabbath and a deeper understanding of the Holy Spirit.

The Sabbath gift may seem superfluous because it is, of course, central to Christian practice as well. However, as Judith Shulevitz observes, there is more in this Jewish gift than is usually appreciated. The Jewish concept of *kadosh*, the "holy," has its roots in the word for "apart" and "separate." This also is a common Christian understanding, but there is a deeper dimension to be explored. The full experience of *kadosh* is that of timelessness. *Shabbat* is not simply a "day of rest," but an entrance, a partial penetration into God's time. On the Lord's Day — *Shabbat*, which is Saturday for Jews and Sunday for Christians — we are, so to speak, outside of our own time, or are meant to be.

I can't speak for Jews, but I think few of us Christians fully enter into this experience. Convergence might facilitate a greater openness and fuller observance.

Needless to say, my personal experience of a precious Jewish gift came from a Jewish woman, and was a distinctly feminine offering. I believe that this came, in part, from Ruth's heritage.

The *Shekinah*, one of the most ancient Hebrew designations of divinity, can be understood as an "indwelling" of God, but it also corresponds to a Jewish tradition that recognizes Wisdom as female. There is also a Hasidic view that renders the *Shekinah* as a "bride." Metaphorically, this recognizes a feminine aspect of the Divine. This suggests, at least, a different spiritual perspective on gender roles related to love and power as manifested in authority. This differentiation has been a challenge to contemporary Catholics and is potentially a valuable concept to be shared because it affirms the interdependence of love and power.

Applied to gender roles, this distinction has been abused and misunderstood. Women have an equal right to and capacity for authority, of course, but perhaps a more distinctive ability to find personal intimacy in divine love. This is, I believe, a special offering that men receive from women, and I think I can claim some personal experience in this.

It is worth noting in this respect that among the most respected converts to the Catholic faith have been remarkable Jewish women such as

Edith Stein, Raissa Maritain, Simone Weil, the poet Denise Levertov (whose father was a Hasid), and the late Oxford philosopher Gillian Rose. Again, if we move beyond the fear of convergence as loss, these figures reveal not a rejection but a bridge. One can now stay within either tradition and appreciate the insight that God is embodied in both.

In considering questions relating to gender, we might also remember another once-celebrated but now somewhat neglected figure, Karl Stern. A Jewish convert to Catholicism, Stern was a brilliant psychoanalyst whose work and especially his book, *Flight from Woman*, came out exactly at the wrong time, the mid-sixties, flying straight into the feminist fog of war. Stern's insights into the eternal struggle between love and power as manifested in gender relations now seem more relevant than ever.

As Stern observed, the struggle between love and power is the most fundamental key to human behavior and our personal and shared fates. The denigration or repression of the female, particularly as wife and mother, thus signals the most serious form of social fragmentation. At the time of his writings, however, Stern's recognition of the rejection of the feminine as a signal characteristic of an efficiency-driven technological society could not have been fully appreciated.

* * *

The gift of Christianity to Jews is, of course, Jesus. Initially, this may seem, as it has in the past, more a provocation than an offering. This will be the most important corner that we must turn.

If, however, one doesn't pursue or even imply conversion — our new opportunity — then Jesus' gifts will be not only welcome and acceptable but familiar to Jews. Jesus is, in many ways, a reciprocal gift, and, as it is said, you can't have too much of a good thing.

Jesus, after two thousand years of history, not only embodies a Jewish faith in God in the tradition of the Prophets, and an obedience to the Commandments to the point of death, but provides a concrete moral way of life. He is the universal symbol of all this and more. The familiar gifts will be the recognition of God as love, the necessity of suffering for transformation, and finding peace through forgiveness. However expressed, these are shared core beliefs and provide invaluable building material.

* * *

Perhaps an even more challenging gift, at least initially, is that of Mary, the mother of Jesus. Jesus is at least recognizable as a great prophet in the Jewish line. Mary, *Miriam* in Hebrew, though as Jewish as her son, isn't always perceived as such.

For Catholics, Mary as a woman, the Woman, is the archetype and paradigm for all humanity, and, as such, she is undoubtedly the most universally recognized female figure in history. As a figure of convergence, Mary has united Catholics from diverse races and nationalities for centuries. As a mother, the Mother, she calls all humanity to be children of God.

As with the Jewish perception of Wisdom as female, Mary is at the core of a Catholic feminine spirituality that is experiential, corporeal, compassionate, and deeply human. Mary has always been embraced, even possessively, by the poor as well as those assimilating into new cultures and trying to preserve their identity. The growing Hispanic Catholic presence in the United States will enhance this figure through their unique gift of finding sanctity and beauty in ordinary daily life — the way most mothers do.

In the Scriptures, from Genesis to the Apocalypse, the female figure is a pivotal intercessory figure that, in the end, overcomes power with love. In the Early Middle Ages, the vast collection of "Mary stories" related miracles based on a single theme: her love. Sometimes her love alone can redeem a sinner. This was the basis of the Faust story in its many versions over the centuries. Significantly, Mary is represented as a bride as well as a mother. As Karl Stern observed, "All Being is nuptial" — that is to say, all creation is a love affair.

I myself have experienced Mary as a mother and a Jewish woman. Rachel was an archetype and biblical model for Mary, a mother who weeps for her children. To this day, pregnant women come to Rachel's tomb outside Jerusalem, preparing themselves to suffer to bring new life.

Rachel was also Ruth's Hebrew name.

*   *   *

A "Wedding Present"

My final suggested Catholic "gift" may also seem more like another provocation. Let's view it then as simply an offering or, better, a kind of wedding present.

The gift may be discomforting because it touches on unavoidable political and "culture war" issues. I recognize that the highly divisive public issues of divorce, abortion, and homosexuality may seem to be insurmountable barriers between Catholics and secularized American Jews, but I believe that we can find some common ground beyond the minefield. However, if this present isn't suitable, then just put it on a high shelf out of sight.

The challenge we share, I suggest, is how to find a basis for marriage and family life that transcends present attitudes. How can we find a firmer foundation than simply mutual satisfactions?

The form of marriage and family life that has emerged in American society in my lifetime wasn't actually proposed by anyone but evolved, seemingly with inevitability, out of the social transformations of industrialization, the suburbs, and the impact of war and technology. The rhetoric of individualism and self-fulfillment facilitated these changes, but, on the other hand, few predicted and even fewer welcomed the results.

However, the reality of "marriage" in America today is that it has become what is called "serial monogamy." This assumes probably more than one intimate relationship before marriage and probably more than one marriage. In fact, first marriages are now called "starter marriages" by some. A further result of this trend has been the disregarding of marriage altogether. A large and increasing number of children in America are now born outside of any formal committed relationship.

Many Americans still insist on viewing marriage as a covenant, a lifetime pledge, rather than as a contract with mutually convenient "breaker" clauses. Many others would not want to replace a contract with a binding covenant, nor consider this even feasible; but a surprising number still prefer to vow "until death do us part" even though they might not fully grasp what they're saying, much less vowing.

In view of these conflicting desires, a dialogue between faithful Catholics and religious Jews might be a worthwhile exploration of alternatives to the status quo, at least for those who seek them. Some exploration of the religious roots of Catholic marriage may also be salubrious for Jewish couples seeking to discover the similar spiritual roots within their own religion.

As a starting point for some reconsiderations, we might begin with the concept of love.

Far beyond merely mutual attraction, the Catholic understanding of love is deeply religious, and, in fact, based on an imitation of Christ. This form of love can be defined as a "total act of self-giving which is indifferent to being received." One can see immediately that this is in tension with the modern, psychologically oriented emphasis on mutual gratification. The underlying premise is theological: The love of God is an action, not a sentiment, and an act of giving, a gift that has no conditions.

Catholics recognize marriage as a "natural relation" based on biology and human nature, but they understand love as a gift from God that cannot be grasped other than as a sacrament — that is, a sign that reveals the sacred. Furthermore, the sacrament of marriage is meant to be a healing process that overcomes the human condition of fear and loneliness. Again, it is clear that this meaning of marriage lies far beyond psychology or social utility — or an arrangement that simply facilitates friendships, however deep and sincere.

This religious concept of marriage is fundamental in defining gender roles because it considers the distinctions indispensable. The separation of male and female is the fundamental division that must be healed — the mysterious process of creating a "unity of opposites." Marriage, in this sense, offers us the very meaning of being "man and woman." It is our most fundamental nature and identity that must be healed and unified by God. For Catholics, Jesus and Mary are the models and the means by which all men and women are to be redeemed. In this relationship, there can be no sameness, but also no question of inequality.

Mary's role is to heal and rescue the archetypal "Eve," who, reflecting the fallen human condition, has been condemned to servitude. Eve's subsidiary position is in no way desirable or to be imitated. It is a condition from which she is now liberated through Jesus and his mother, and she and Adam, equally fallen, are to be healed together, restoring the primal unity designed by God.

This theological and existential understanding of the roles of men and women gives the vow "until death do us part" its true meaning for us as Catholics. It is a vow based on mutual dependence but also on freedom and equality. It is a vow that seals our relationship not just with each other but with God.

I recognize that Jewish and Catholic concepts of marriage are not the same. I suggest that there are, nonetheless, common origins worth exploring. Our shared roots are too often neglected. Even what is distinctive about the contemporary Jewish wedding is sometimes misunderstood because the religious meaning has become obscured. For example, the breaking of a glass at the end of the ceremony is not a "good luck sign." It is a "mourning" symbol commemorating the loss of the temple. It is also meant as a symbolic reminder of the perpetual fragility of marriage without holiness.

Catholics and Jews might learn from each other in exploring the roots of their traditional understandings of marriage. At the very least we may be helpful to each other in the recovery of memory.

*   *   *

It was only after Ruth's death that I was able in time to witness to my own love in a sacramental sense, and I finally understood how, more than anything else, it was her abiding love that had brought me to the transcendent love revealed by Jesus Christ. Ruth would have been astonished to consider our relationship in this way, and perhaps not entirely comfortable with the idea, but I know she would never have rejected the love.

Ruth and I never had a religious ceremony, nor was our union at first a sacramental one — grace and nature added that later. Because there is a "baptism of desire" that the church recognizes, an entering into the divine life by seeking it, then I have to believe that our life together was, in itself, a kind of redemption for both of us. This grace became clear to me only after Ruth's death. I had always feared her death more than my own, and, once it happened, she took my fear with her. This is a gift, a blessing that is hard to describe, and I don't want to strain words to do so. There are some truths you come to know before you have words to describe them, if you ever do.

All her life Ruth remained deeply Jewish in her self-identification and consciousness, and I had become, as I remain, what might be called a "committed Catholic." (I'm also "practicing," but that always sounds more like a musician.) Yet in all that time I never considered for a moment that she should be anyone but who she was. Conversion was never even a passing thought on my part. For some Catholics, this may be discomforting, but our mutual acceptance and her eventual recognition of the strength and peace that my faith brought to our marriage provide the heart of my conviction that this is the relationship that God wants for us.

When love is strengthened and sustained, something is going right.

CHAPTER TWENTY

Conclusion

The death of the new is nothing new. Contingency always wears disguises of permanence.

We are living in prophetic times, and who should understand this better than the Jews and their Christian siblings? We will continue to have our differing interpretations of history, just as we have within our own spiritual families. But together we know some things out of long experience. We know that even great civilizations are not eternal and that they can blaze like stars in their terminal stages. We know that power is even more contingent than biological life. We are coming to recognize that while human reason remains one of God's invaluable gifts, it can also lapse into a futile defense against the terrors of life and history.

As Cardinal Newman once observed, "Reason, while God's gift, can be as guilty as passion."

Our convergence will move us not beyond paradox but further into the ultimate paradox. The children of Israel and Jesus of Nazareth are the bearers of revelation within historical time, yet beyond it, timeless — the invisible made visible in human form, an eternal people and a son born of woman, a divine son of man.

*   *   *

The Two Next Steps

Two major and precarious steps remain to be taken for our journey together to resume.

The first step, already begun, is the affirmation by the Roman Catholic Church that God's covenant with the Jewish people is unbroken — now an official teaching promulgated by John Paul and theologically validated by Pope Benedict, perhaps the leading theologian of our era.

This Catholic step must be completed through concrete actions and commitments. This will happen over time as the teaching is disseminated and absorbed.

The Jewish step will be just as momentous, and perhaps even more difficult.

It is not a prerequisite for Jews to accept the Catholic concept of the Trinity, One God as manifested in Three Persons. There is a shared recognition of the Father, the Creator we both worship, and a *de facto* recognition of the power of the Holy Spirit. Franz Rosenzweig and other Jewish thinkers viewed this aspect of the Divine as a symbol of an emerging new age.

The Second Person of the Trinity, Jesus Christ, remains the "alpha and omega" stumbling block for Jews. This is not because of a Jewish lack of respect or even admiration for the figure of Jesus. The epithets of the past rooted in perceptions of heresy are now as obsolete as the blood libel against Jews. The lasting obstacle is the Catholic belief in Jesus' divinity; this claim cannot be overcome, and, again, it may be that it is not meant to be resolved in any way we can understand.

There is, however, a possible next step that, in itself, need not entail an alteration in any fundamental Jewish conviction or a Catholic lessening of belief. What is needed is the recognition that Jesus is, historically and anthropologically, in a "category of one." To some, this may seem an arduous or unreasonable demand, and yet it is a step anticipated by Martin Buber, who, in his important book *Two Types of Faith*, describes Jesus as beyond "any of the usual categories."

In other words, Jesus is as singular in human history as are the children of Israel.

The evidence of Jesus' unique presence for two thousand years should suffice. If Christianity is not seen as simply a misguided two-millennia-old "error," then Jesus cannot be dismissed as a mere anomaly. Nor does his pivotal role in history allow him to be categorized as merely a sage or a great prophet. Without attempting to resolve the question of the nature of the Messiah, I believe a recognition that Jesus is beyond these categories is enough to constitute the next Jewish step toward a mutually rewarding convergence.

*   *   *

Jews were "chosen" by God to bring redemption not to themselves alone but to the whole human race. So was Jesus, whose followers assume the same responsibilities as their "elder brothers." Together we testify that God is love found in human form, time, and space. God is found in each other's suffering, and this discovery in our own tragic times has opened the way to the next stage of our convergence as a mysterious unity, one witness in two peoples.

Let us now, once again, step forward.

*   *   *

Curtain Call

In proposing "convergence" as the key to our future as peoples of faith, it is fair to ask what this might mean in concrete terms and not just as wish fulfillments. My response comes, again, primarily out of my lifetime with Ruth.

As our lives intertwined and we matured, we had to face our fundamental differences, first as a man and a woman and then as a Christian and a Jew. We had to ask, simultaneously, "Who am I?" and "Who are you?" on a deeper level than we had anticipated.

I'm sure this relates to the postmodern philosophical concepts of "Otherness" and "difference," but our context was life, not theories. Our "Other" was physically intimate and yet remained mysterious. The love would prove indestructible, but there was always fear, however irrational, of a difference that implied separation.

For Jews and Christians, it will be necessary to recognize this irreducible otherness, even "strangeness," if our relationship is to survive the present cultural meltdown and social dissolution. As long as Jews remain fearful, not so much of a failed assimilation but of its ultimate costs, they will be uneasy in confronting any "difference," and perhaps especially the "difference" of someone eager to embrace them.

Ruth and I never analyzed — much less debated — our differences in intellectual terms. She was uneasy about the sacrificial aspects of the few masses she attended, the "flesh and blood" symbolism, but then she had never really encountered the sacrificial aspects of her own religion. The Jewish predilection toward intellectualism to which I was drawn — and with which I often competed — was never a trap for her. Her deep honesty, profound morality, and orientation toward the visual and concrete kept her from abstracting life or people.

Our shared sense of the visual arts provided a language for us, whether it was the beauty of nature or the faces, eyes, and gestures in good movies. She was more open to innovation in art and often frustrated by my sometimes close-minded views, while I felt that she was perhaps too susceptible to the lure of changing fashions. We never felt the necessity to fully agree.

In any case, I came to appreciate and learn from her ability to simply "see," whether it was art, nature, or people. I offer this as an antidote to endless analysis and reconsiderations. Can we simply learn to "see" each other? Can we acquire eyes unclouded by fear and rivalry? All of my speculations as well as the critiques of others will mean nothing if we can't.

*   *   *

In looking not just back but deeper, have I idealized Ruth?

We had, as they say, our "ups and downs," and the down times were painful. The conflicts were common enough to most marriages, sometimes about money or about my misplaced priorities. At times I put my career ahead of Ruth and the girls without thinking that there was any inherent conflict, but, of course, there was. But none of these conflicts lasted long enough to fester and, in time, were healed. Ruth and I didn't always "talk things through," though we tried. In fact, our communication was often, at its best, non-verbal. I was too verbose for her to ever win an argument other than by throwing something at me.

If I've idealized Ruth as a person, it wasn't hard to do. I wouldn't want to idealize our marriage, however, because I'd like others, especially those anticipating that stage of life, to know that the obstacles to a good marriage are very real and that some differences are never wholly overcome. Nonetheless, a marriage not only can last but can become life's greatest blessing.

Conclusion

*   *   *

I have often been asked by caring and sensitive friends if I believe that Ruth and I will be together again in a future life. While I fully accept the Catholic Church's teachings about eternal life with God as the fulfillment of our Christian journey, I think that for most of us to even try to answer this question is less a test of faith than of our imaginations.

Visions of heaven, especially those embellished by pearly gates, green fields, and choirs of angels, may be beautiful poetic images, but we should cherish them only as metaphors. Otherwise, we run the risk of trivializing the mystery we are engaging. Visions of heaven should evoke a sense of the whole of God's creation, including the living and the dead. God's eternal life is an ultimate reality that can be accessed only through prayer, grace, and revelation.

To convey what we experience or even mean by an "afterlife" is dependent upon metaphorical language as well. God is outside of time, and so "before" or "after" must also inevitably run into the wall of our time-limited imaginations. I am particularly drawn to Dante's astonishing vision of *Purgatorio* and *Paradiso* as perhaps the best the human mind can do in the face of this mystery, and I treasure his words and images. What I believe, however, is more what I feel and sense rather than what I can imagine.

Ruth has always been with me, and we will continue to be part of each other, perhaps in as mysterious a way as we are part of God and God's creation. This is what I meant at the outset by suggesting that this was a love story that began before time. Our love, however splendid as we experienced it together, is part of something even more worthy of the word "Love."

Accordingly, my confidence in our "being together" isn't speculation or merely a projection of a profound hope, but an integral part of what I've experienced in our love itself. It is something so deep and defining of who we are as human beings that while I can neither fully describe nor fully define the experience, it is more real in a sense than I am. I "believe" because I love, more than the other way around.

Again, I'm sorry that these words are so inadequate. I'd recommend Dante or Donne, Wordsworth or Eliot for a better rendition. When Wordsworth writes "the props of my affection were removed and yet the building stood," I know what he's saying. When Eliot writes of his vision when the "Rose and the Fire are One," an ultimate fusion of beauty and redemptive pain, his words make sense out of sense. All these fellow creatures speak for me, and music says it even better.

*   *   *

By the end of the century I had more or less retired to Mexico, first to Mexico City, and then, after the death of my good friend "Moishe," Murray Goodman, a longtime resident who introduced me to much of the heart of Mexico, I left for San Miguel de Allende, a lovely colonial town. I spent a few years there writing my book *Peregrino*, about Mexican Catholic culture. The title means "pilgrim," and that's what I have finally become wherever I reside.

Old friends, Gil Bailie and the novelist Ron Hansen, led to my meeting new friends when I was inducted into the College of Fellows at the Dominican School of Philosophy and Theology at Berkeley. Beyond the honor — including an honorary doctorate, no less — Father Michael Sweeney, our president, challenged me, and probably the audience, by asking me to give the commencement address at their graduation.

I was glad to do so. I introduced myself, as usual, not as a philosopher or a scholar but as a "survivor," a "refugee from a strange and mythic land called Hollywood."

I think that's about right.

*   *   *

Needless to say, there's no end to this story.

I've borrowed — or, as a true Hollywood hack, tried to steal — the words of others to describe my life with Ruth.

My own vision, being from Hollywood, is in movie terms.

Ruth and I looked at each other for a lifetime and, in the end, silence and glances were all that remained. But they were enough.

If I've learned one hard lesson, however, it is that life is not a movie. There are no easy cuts around what doesn't work, and no one waiting with a quick, convenient rewrite. Even if there's good background music, it still can't save the scene unless there's truth in it.

But our eyes met. This is a cliché, but I'm not afraid of clichés anymore. They met and still meet.

As you can see, this is still a love story.

Photo Gallery

Mother and son
With the mother I never knew, Hollywood, 1935.

Ruth at age six, 1939
Ruth, the girl from Brooklyn, a little before we met.

Ron at the Young Actors Company, 1948
At fourteen, I played "Han, the War Lord," in Viola Spolin's production of *The
Emperor's New Clothes*, complete with horns, whip, and floppy moustache.

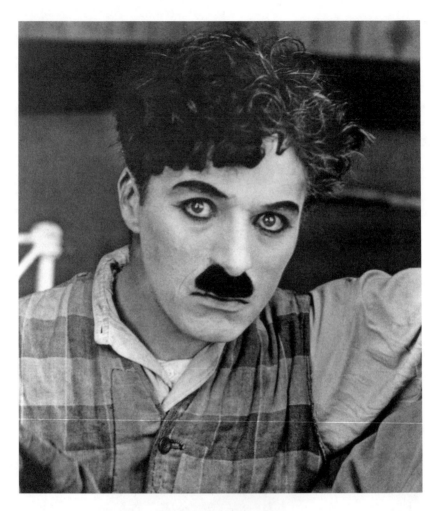

A true star
Charlie Chaplin as the beloved tramp.
Photo credit: ScreenScene Agency

Charlie Chaplin at the Circle Theater, Hollywood, circa 1950
My hero Chaplin attended many performances and often
directed our dress rehearsals.   *Photo credit: PhotoFest*

Ron and Ruth, 1950
At age sixteen, we were too young to drink or vote.
But in just over a year we would become a married couple.

Ruth Austin, 1952
Ruth at 18, a married woman and a hard-working artist.

Ron and Ruth Austin, 1992
Forty years later, still married, still in love.

Astaire and Kelly
Two great stars of the "Golden Age" of Hollywood, Mr. Astaire and
Mr. Kelly, and I had the good fortune to work with both of them.
Photo credit: ScreenScene Agency

Farrah Fawcett and Ron Austin, 1979
Farrah Fawcett on location for *Charlie's Angels.*
My Mephistopheles t-shirt celebrates an opera, not temptation.

Jim Buchanan and Ron Austin, 2009
Always called "the boys," Jim and I were a
writing team for over two decades.

Chiara Lubich and Ron Austin, Rome, 2003
I greet the founder of the Focolare Movement and stand
as close to a saint as I'll probably manage in this life.

Ron at Bar Mitzvah, 2008
A proud grandfather at my grandson Alex's bar mitzvah.

Dominican School of Philosophy and Theology, 2010
"Doctor" Austin is inducted into the College Fellows by
Father Michael Sweeney, O.P. — a long, winding road from Hollywood!

Bibliography

This highly selective bibliography, just over fifty books, does not include many fine scholarly and historical works that I consulted. The literature concerning the Holocaust and Jewish history alone is too extensive to even easily catalogue. There are also numerous books of thoughtful dialogue between Jews and Catholics, and I have suggested only a couple. Nor have I included the classics of Catholic and Jewish spirituality that would be essential for a full understanding of our faith traditions. A serious student of any of these subjects will need to carefully review the further works most relevant to their specific interests.

My short list cites books that I recommend as the most accessible and helpful to non-specialists such as myself. They offer varied but basic insights and interpretations of Catholic and Jewish beliefs and history, and several point in the direction of a renewed relationship. I also include works and authors that were most frequently referenced in this book and which relate directly to the central questions that I explore, even though their conclusions may differ from my own.

Given the vast literature, this should be considered at best as just a sampling of many and varied riches.

*   *   *

John L. Allen. *The Future Church*.
Hannah Arendt. *The Origins of Totalitarianism*.
Raymond Aron. *The Opium of the Intellectuals*.
Hans Urs von Balthasar. *Martin Buber and Christianity*.

Julien Benda. *The Treason of the Intellectuals.*

Benedict XVI. *Jesus of Nazareth* (2 vols.).

Isaiah Berlin. *The Proper Study of Mankind* (essays).

Eugene B. Borowitz. *Choices in Modern Jewish Thought.*

Martin Buber. *I and Thou.*

Martin Buber. *Two Types of Faith.*

Olivier Clement. *Being Human: Spiritual Anthropology.*

Yves Congar. *The Meaning of Tradition.*

Avery Dulles and Leon Klenicki. *The Holocaust: Never to Be Forgotten.*

Louis Dupré. *Christian Spirituality and the Culture of Modernity: Conversations with Louis Dupré.*

Albert Einstein. *Out of My Later Years.*

Emil Fackenheim. *The Jewish Writings of Emil Fackenheim: A Reader.*

Neil Gabler. *An Empire of Their Own.*

René Girard. *The Girard Reader.*

Irving Greenberg. *The Jewish Way.*

Romano Guardini. *The End of the Modern World.*

David Bentley Hart. *The Doors of the Sea: Where Was God in the Tsunami?*

Abraham Joshua Heschel. *God in Search of Man.*

John Paul II. *Theology of the Human Body.*

Abraham Isaac Kook. *Collected Writings* (Classics of Western Spirituality).

Elias Kopciowski (editor). *Praying with the Jewish Tradition.*

Pinchas Lapide. *The Resurrection of Jesus.*

Christopher Lasch. *The Culture of Narcissism.*

C. S. Lewis. *The Abolition of Man.*

Henri de Lubac. *Catholicism.*

Henri de Lubac. *The Drama of Atheist Humanism.*

Chiara Lubich. *The Cry.*

Jean-Marie Lustiger. *The Promise.*

Alasdair MacIntyre. *After Virtue.*

Gabriel Marcel. *A Marcel Reader* (edited by Brendan Sweetman).

Jacques Maritain. *Integral Humanism.*

Paul Mendez-Flohr and Yehuda Reniharz (editors). *The Jew in the Modern World.*

Jerry Muller. *Capitalism and the Jews.*

David Novak. *Jewish Catholic Dialogue.*

Gerald O'Collins, S.J. *Believing in the Resurrection.*

Walker Percy. *Lost in the Cosmos: The Last Self-Help Book.*

Pheme Perkins. *The Resurrection.*

William Pfaff. *The Bullet's Song.*
Philip Rieff. *The Triumph of the Therapeutic.*
Anne Roiphe. *Generation without Memory.*
Gershom Scholem. *The Messianic Idea in Judaism.*
Judith Shulevitz. *The Sabbath World.*
Yuri Slezkine. *The Jewish Century.*
George Steiner. *Real Presence.*
Karl Stern. *The Flight from Woman.*
Paul Tillich. *The Courage to Be.*
Simon Tugwell, O.P. *Reflections on the Beatitudes.*
Simone Weil. *A Simone Weil Reader.*
Elie Wiesel. *Soul on Fire.*
Robert Wistrich. *Revolutionary Jews.*

I would like to offer a special thanks, once again, to Gabriel Meyer for his invaluable help in my research, and for his recommendation of several of these books.

Index of Names